本研究为：

临沂大学校级特色课程《跨文化交际》

临沂大学认知科学与语言学能研究基地

全国高校外语教学科研项目

重点课题子课题阶段性研究成果

临沂大学学术专著
LINYIDAXUE XUESHU ZHUANZHU

 Study of Classroom Nonverbal X-Factor
from Intercultural Communicative Perspective

跨文化交际课堂中
无声语言的研究

·刘乃美 著

前 言

　　随着信息和交通技术的高度发展,人们之间的空间距离大大缩短,文化交流日益频繁。但空间距离的缩小并不意味着文化距离或心理距离的缩短,交际中的失误、矛盾和冲突加大了人们之间的心理距离。矛盾和分歧的背后不只是利益的分歧,更多的是文化差异所滋生的巨大隔阂,正是这些隔阂使得"地球村"的人们虽然近在咫尺,却如隔天涯。如何消除这些隔阂成为世界各国人们关注的焦点。随着"一带一路"、"亚投行"等国家战略政策的实施,我国与其他国家的交流更加广泛,实现《国家中长期教育改革与发展规划纲要》(2010-2020)提出的培养大批具有国际视野、通晓国际规则、能够参与国际事务和竞争的国际化人才目标,进行有效的跨文化交际成为我国语言学界一项重大研究课题。

　　跨文化交际涉及两个层面:语言交际和非语言交际。非语言交际也称作无声语言交际。研究表明,交际中信息传播的总效果=7%的语言+38%的语调语速+55%的表情和动作,由此可见非语言行为的重要性。非语言交际行为在很大程度上体现的是一个文化群体的意识形态,如宗教思想、哲学伦理、道德观念、处世方法、行为准则、风土民俗、语言规范等;折射出的是一个民族的文化体系和价值取向;是保持跨文化交际畅通的重要前提和渠道,也是跨文化交际研究的重要内容之一。

　　与国外的研究相比,我国在该领域的研究多集中在社会学、人类学、心理学和精神病理学等方面,针对教育领域中非语言行为的研究相对匮乏。本书对国内外该领域研究成果进行了较为全面地剖析,建构了符合我国跨文化交际国情的交际能力新模型。采取定量和定性研究相结合的方法,从跨文化交际的角度分别对我国高校教师和学生的非语言行为的现状、在课堂教和学中产生的效果等进行了实证研究。为充分发挥非语言交际在教学中的作用,提高教师和学生的非语言交际意识和跨文化交际能力提供了有价值的借鉴。

　　本书分为四部分,每部分各包括两章。

　　第一部分为导论。第一章论述了跨文化非语言交际研究的背景、必要性、本研究的目的、意义等。第二章对前人在该领域研究的成果进行了较为详实的剖析;对非语言交际的定义、特征、分类、功能等进行了梳理;阐述了语言和非语言交际的差异；论述了非语言交际在教学中的重要性。

第二部分为理论研究。第三章分析了非语言行为在文化中的作用；对比了东西方在体态语、身势语、副语言、时间语和环境语等方面的文化差异；探讨了文化因素对非语言交际行为的影响，揭示了跨文化交际中因非语言行为引起交际失误和冲突的根源。第四章对跨文化交际研究的进程进行了分析；论证了非语言交际能力、交际能力、文化能力、跨文化交际能力与第二语言习得的关系；剖析了非语言交际在交际能力模型中的地位。根据前人的研究成果，构建了符合我国国情的跨文化交际能力新模型，阐释了非语言交际在跨文化交际能力中的地位和作用。

第三部分为实践研究。该部分通过大量的实例分析了不同文化背景下教师和学生在课堂教学中各种非语言行为的体现、作用、内涵以及其对教和学的影响。为了了解中国高等教育领域中外语教师和学生在课堂中非语言行为的实际情况，该研究借助于问卷调查、访谈、课堂观察、学生日志等手段，分别从教师和学生的角度开展了针对课堂教学中教师和学生非语言行为的实证研究。第五章从学生的角度对教师在课堂中的非语言行为进行探讨，结果发现：（1）学生认为穿着得体的教师具有较强的交际能力，表现出对工作的热情和对学生的关爱，具有良好的专业发展前景；（2）教师的身势语、面部表情、眼神交流等能够带给学生大量的信息，教师得体的肢体语言能够起到引起学生关注和活跃课堂气氛的作用，而且对学生的学习成绩有积极的影响。同时还发现，与女生相比，男生对教师的非语言行为的敏感程度较弱。第六章从教师的角度对学生在课堂中非语言行为研究，结果发现：（1）教师认为举止得体的学生具有较高的信誉度，他们能力强，有良好的发展前途。学生的亲和行为能够激发教师的职业荣誉感，使教师更加自豪、热爱教师职业；（2）学生在课堂中的沉默行为受到客观和主观因素的影响。客观因素包括传统的教育观念、班级人数过多等；主观因素涉及面子问题、学生个人性格等。

第四部分为总结。第七章针对研究中发现的问题，就如何提高教师和学生的非语言交际能力提出了相应的策略。第八章总结了本书的研究成果，并就未来该领域的研究方向提出了个人的见解。

本书基于作者多年教学经验的反思和总结。该书的出版得到临沂大学学术部的资助；审稿人提出了有价值的修改意见，在此一并感谢！

Contents

前言 / i

Part Ⅰ Research Background / 1

Chapter One General Introduction / 3
1.1 Background Information / 3
1.2 The Significance of the Study / 7
1.3 The Purpose of Present Study / 11
1.4 The Organization of the Book / 12

Chapter Two Literature Review / 14
2.1 Introduction / 14
2.2 An Outline of Nonverbal Communication Research / 14
2.3 The Definition of Nonverbal Communication / 23
2.4 The Classification of Nonverbal Communication / 25
2.5 Characteristics of Nonverbal Communication / 29
2.6 Differences between Nonverbal Communication and Verbal Communication / 31
2.7 Functions of Nonverbal Communication / 33
2.8 The Importance of Nonverbal Behavior in Communication / 37
2.9 Conclusion / 39

Part Ⅱ Nonverbal Communication and Intercultural Communication / 41

Chapter Three Cultural Impact on Nonverbal X-Factor / 43
3.1 Introduction / 43
3.2 Background Information / 43
3.3 Nonverbal Communication and Culture / 44
3.4 Cultural Differences in Nonverbal Communication / 49
3.5 Conclusion / 77

Chapter Four Nonverbal Communication and Intercultural Communication Competence / 78

4.1 Introduction / 78
4.2 Development of Intercultural Communication / 78
4.3 Basic Concept / 88
4.4 Nonverbal Communication in the Models of Language Proficiency / 98
4.5 Nonverbal Communication and FL Teaching and Learning / 107
4.6 Conclusion / 111

Part III Research on Classroom Nonverbal X-Factor / 113

Chapter Five Chinese Teachers' Classroom Nonverbal X-Factor / 115

5.1 Introduction / 115
5.2 Background Information / 115
5.3 The Functions of Teachers' Nonverbal Behavior / 122
5.4 Teachers' Nonverbal Communication in Classroom / 125
5.5 Investigations on Chinese Teachers' Nonverbal Behavior / 147
5.6 Conclusion / 159

Chapter Six Chinese Learners' Classroom Nonverbal X-Factor / 161

6.1 Introduction / 161
6.2 Background Information / 161
6.3 The Functions of Students' Nonverbal Behavior / 173
6.4 Students' Nonverbal Behavior in Classroom / 174
6.5 Investigations of Students' Nonverbal Behavior in Classroom / 185
6.6 Conclusion / 196

Part IV Strategy for Improving Classroom Nonverbal X-Factor / 197

Chapter Seven Approaches to Developing Nonverbal Communicative Competence / 199

7.1 Introduction / 199
7.2 Pedagogical Implications / 199
7.3 Summary of Good and Bad Classroom Nonverbal X-Factor / 213
7.4 Developing Intercultural Communication Competence / 214
7.5 Conclusion / 217

Chapter Eight Conclusion / 218

8.1 Introduction / 218
8.2 Major Findings and Implications / 218

8.3 Suggestions for Future Research / 220
8.4 Conclusion / 221

Appendix A / 223
Appendix B / 224
Appendix C / 225
Appendix D / 227

References / 229

Part I

Research Background

Chapter One

General Introduction

1.1 Background Information

Communication is the basis of all human contact and integrated part of our lives. We communicate in different ways to express our thoughts, feelings, knowledge, skills, and ideas. It is normally assumed that communication is identified with speech and sounds, but communication is, in fact, the combination of verbal and nonverbal transmission of knowledge, in other words, effective human communication falls into two types: verbal communication and nonverbal communication.

Verbal communication is commonly considered to be the most important, efficient, powerful means of communication, and is regarded as the main and most important way of transmitting information about our daily business, knowledge, tradition, culture, teaching and learning. Scholars in various research fields through the recorded history relating to the study of human communication had focused on verbal messages. They believed language was the only way to deliver and grasp information. As a result, a great number of books published before about verbal communication, while the study on nonverbal communication has been neglected to a large extent and is comparatively lagging behind. For a long time, only the verbal communication occurred to us immediately when we discuss human communication.

However, communication is much more than just expressing ideas and feelings through words. A simple gaze can reveal either a sensation of pleasure or disgust. Nonverbal signs, as part of the process of human communication, show different types of communicative meanings. What a person does while conversing might strongly sign his/her personal feelings much more than when it is verbally expressed. The fact that nonverbal communication is woven inextricably into our daily interactions was confirmed by Abercrombie (1968, cited in Lörscher, 2003) who believes that "we speak with our vocal organs, but we converse with our entire bodies. Conversation consists of much more than a simple interchange of spoken words." (55) The process of communicating through sending and receiving wordless messages is known as nonverbal communication (Kendon, 2004; Pike, 1967).

Nonverbal communication is of interest to a number of fields, including anthropology, communication, psychology, sociology, and child development. Anthropologists believe that our ancestors communicated with one another by using their bodies. For example, they gritted their teeth to show anger; they smiled and touched one another to indicate affection. Although we have come a long way since those primitive times, we still use nonverbal cues to express superiority, dependence, dislike, respect, love, and other feelings. It can be expressed through body language, or even through clothing and hairstyle and by voice quality, emotion and speaking style; or prosodic features, such as rhythm, intonation and stress. Likewise, written texts may also include nonverbal elements that surface in the handwriting, layout or the use of images. Thus, nonverbal communication acts as an indispensible component to communication. It can account for a large portion of information in communication. Many researchers provide different statistics to explain the amount of information which nonverbal communication conveys.

Mehrabian, as a pioneer researcher of body language in 1950s, found that as much as 93 percent of the emotional meaning is transmitted nonverbally. His research (1971) indicated that in face-to-face interaction only 7% of the emotional meaning is expressed verbally, 38% is vocal expression and 55% is facial expression (Mehrabian, 1971). Birdwhistell made some similar estimates of the amount of nonverbal communication that takes place between humans: "that the average person actually speaks words for a total of about ten or eleven minutes a day and that the average sentence takes only 2.5 seconds" (cited from A. Pease & B. Pease, 2004, p.9) and "we can make and recognize around 250,000 facial expressions" (ibid, 32). Samovar and Porter (1981, 4), also pointed out that in a normal two-person conversation the verbal components make up less than 35% of the total social meaning of the situation and that over 65% is expressed nonverbally. Miller (1988) found only 7% a message is sent through words with the remaining 93% sent through facial expressions (55%) and vocal intonation (38%), which means that, as the receiver of a message, people can rely largely on the nonverbal cues of the sender since his/her nonverbal behavior is a better indicator of the meaning behind the message than his/her words (5-6). We are not clear that whether or not these figures are accurate and scientific enough, at least they inform us that in person-to-person communications nonverbal messages deliver a large amount of information.

Then how important is nonverbal behavior in human communication?

A very simple example can illustrate this. The way a person portrays himself/herself on the first encounter with others can become a last long impression. Although the first impression which may take only one-tenth of a second to judge, it can become a lasting nonverbal communicator and can be positive and negative interpreted through the way a person presents himself/herself, such as clothing, tattoos, and other visible attributes. Although sometimes misleading, first impression can in many situations be an accurate depiction of a person. In verbal communication, when we listen to a speaker's words, no matter whether we realize it or not, we are also influenced by the way the speaker talks as well as by the speaker's actions. Whether we are aware of the nonverbal messages or not when we speak, we may communicate when we don't speak, so it is impossible not to communicate. Even when we are silent, we are communicating. Before we begin to speak, for example, when we pause, or when we leave the speaker's stand, we are still sending information to the audience. We communicate nonverbally by the way we dress, the way we position our hands, the way we touch things and the way we listen. Therefore, communication doesn't use words. Our smiles, frowns, where to sit at a meeting—all communicate pleasure or anger, friendliness or distance, power and status. But most of the time we are no more conscious of interpreting nonverbal signals than we are conscious of breathing.

Bovee, Thill, and Barbara (2003, 48) further confirmed, "People's actions often do speak louder than their words." Sometimes some people can deceive others much more easily with words than they can with their nonverbal behaviors since words are relatively easy to control and nonverbal behaviors are not. By paying attention to these nonverbal cues, people can detect deception or affirm a speaker's honesty. Because nonverbal communication is so reliable, people generally have more faith in nonverbal cues than they do in verbal messages. If a person says one thing but transmits a conflicting message nonverbally, listeners almost invariably believe the nonverbal signal. Chances are, if we can read other people's nonverbal messages correctly, we can interpret their underlying attitudes and intentions and respond appropriately.

Then why human beings use nonverbal communication? We can get the answer from Miller's (1988, 5) explanations:

(1) Words have limitations. It is easier to explain the shape of something or give directions using hand gestures or head nods.

(2) Nonverbal signals are powerful. They primarily express inner feelings and evoke immediate action or response.

(3) Nonverbal messages are likely to be more genuine. Nonverbal behaviors are

not as easily controlled as spoken words with the exception of some facial expressions and tone of voice.

(4) Nonverbal signals can express feelings too disturbing to state. Social rules limit what can be said, but nonverbal cues can communicate thoughts. They can show the feelings of superiority or dislike that etiquette may prevent from being stated verbally in interpersonal communication. Conveniently, if people have not verbalized their feelings, they can change their minds freely without having committed themselves.

Then why are we not all aware of nonverbal communication although it is so important?

Turk (2003, 145) explained, "The main reason is that we are heavily word-oriented, that we tend to undervalue other ways of communication. Because of our cultures, and our schools that emphasize verbal ability so heavily, we tend to overlook the expressive possibilities of the nonverbal." Turk further pointed out that nonverbal signals appear before language. Even animals manage to negotiate their social lives by nonverbal signals. They make friends, find mates, rear children, work out their political hierarchies, and work together in groups, by means of nonverbal signals. The same is probably true of human beings.

Locker (2004, 300) provided another explanation why people undervalue the way of nonverbal communication, "Nonverbal signal can be misinterpreted just as easily as verbal symbols do. And the misunderstandings can be harder to clear up because people may not be aware of the nonverbal messages that led them to assume that they aren't liked, respected, or approved." For example, an Arab student assumed that his American roommate disliked him intensely because the student sat around the room with his feet up on the furniture, soles towards the Arab roommate. The miscommunication resulted from that Arab culture sees the foot in general and the sole in particular as unclean; showing the sole of the foot is an insult. Since nonverbal actions are not easily controlled consciously, they can precisely betray one's true feeling without distortion and deception. For example, it is difficult to control a blushing face when we are embarrassed or a clenched jaw when we are angry. Researches indicate that we will believe nonverbal messages instead of verbal ones when the two contradict each other. Accordingly, the significance of nonverbal communication has grown to such an extent that it is how we say the words counts instead of what we say.

From above discussion, we can conclude that nonverbal signs play an important role in communication. It can help us project the image we want to present and make us more aware of the signals we are sending and interpreting. In order to reduce misunderstanding in communication, it is necessary to extend the research of nonverbal communication. Especially with the rapid development of mass media, the wide spread of knowledge and the frequent communication among people in the new century, nonverbal communication is important in the study of intercultural communication because some of nonverbal behavior can speak a universal language. Behaviors such as smiling, frowning, laughing and crying tend to have similar meanings, whether in China, America or any countries in Europe.

However, compared with the study of verbal communication, nonverbal communication is often neglected. One reason is that nonverbal message is less structured, so it's more difficult to study. It also differs in terms of intent and spontaneity. We generally plan our words when we say something, we have a conscious purpose. But when we communicate nonverbally, we sometimes do so unconsciously. For example, we don't mean to raise an eyebrow or blush. Those actions come naturally without our consent. Another reason is that nonverbal communication is somewhat ambiguous, subconscious and spontaneous. Therefore, in order to help people be fully aware of their nonverbal signs in communication, research in this field becomes necessary and indispensable.

1.2 The Significance of the Study

1.2.1 The Limitation of Precious Research in Education

The importance of nonverbal communication has made many researches conducted in the field of anthropology, sociology, psychology and psychiatry in the past decades. While in educational area, it has been neglected for a long time as White and Gardner (2012, 6) point out that "it is surprising that given the potency of nonverbal communication and its value to our daily forms of communication it is given scant attention by the education world."

One reason is that the cumbersome and costly nature of undertaking research on nonverbal communication, such as the videotaping. And this nature of nonverbal communication is unique to each individual and it is often picked up within seconds with no "text" record and usually no video record, we have little tangible record of its use. Its impact may be clear and sometimes individuals will remember "the way he speaks", but because it is often spontaneous, subtle and fleeting, it leaves little tangible evidence (White & Gardner, 2012, 6).

Another reason is that in education environment, both teachers and students tend to ignore the important role of nonverbal behaviors in classroom on the one hand they take them for granted, on the other hand, curriculums and textbooks seldom mention or discuss the use of nonverbal communication, and most teachers are normally unaware of the nonverbal signals they send out in class, which are the main causes of the study of nonverbal communication being relatively short in the past decades.

Lastly, the importance of nonverbal behavior has been acknowledged in elementary and secondary settings but largely ignored by college classroom, this is due to the assumption that college students learn what they need to regardless of teaching competence, or from a university norm that teaching is secondary to research and university service, or assuming that college professors automatically have adequate teaching skills. Content competence and instructional competence are presumed to be one and the same capacity. For whatever reason, few college professors are aware of how to use their nonverbal behaviors to enhance instructional effectiveness.

1.2.2 Classroom Nonverbal X-Factor: The Silent Language

Everyone has this experience: at get-togethers, we talk of funny stories, school plays, and we also inevitably talk about our favorite teachers and classmates. The lesson some teacher taught may not be our best subject but we still remember how the teacher sparked our enthusiasm. Remember the teacher who never seemed to have problems getting students' attention or captivating students' every interest. We look forward to his/her class, hang on his/her every word, watch his/her every move. So how did he/she do so? Why did some teachers have such an ability to engage and enthuse us? The teachers' faces, voices, the classrooms, and the teaching methods all interwoven gave us impressions. The more we thought about it, the more we realized there was something else. In this book, the author borrows White and Gardner's (2012) metaphor "X-Factor" to stand for the quality of a teacher who uses nonverbal signs in the teaching to enthuse the students and of students who try to become effective learners in classroom, that is, the silent language in classroom.

Originally, the term relates to the TV show in UK entitled *The X-Factor*." It is a UK musical talent contest which auditions thousands of contestants and ultimately whittles them down through successive performances and public voting to one single individual who has the X-Factor (White & Gardner, 2012, 4). The term is defined by the *Cambridge Advanced Learner's Dictionary* as "a quality that you can't describe which makes someone very special." This book tries to unravel the indescribable quality which can make teachers and students "very special."

It is apparent that the subject knowledge and teaching ability are not the exclusive requirement of the classroom X-Factor. The inspiring teacher has much more than subject knowledge, teaching ability and clear voice. Their magnetic quality comes in many subtle ways of which we are often unaware: the way we "carry ourselves" in the classroom, our body language, whether we smile or grimace, how we dress, how we gesture, etc. Academically, this collection of X-Factor attributes is known as "nonverbal communication." Calling it X-Factor can reminds us that there are "forces" at play in our classroom practice which are mysterious and tangible to us (White & Gardner, 2012, 7).

1.2.3 The Urgency of the Study

Study on classroom nonverbal communication is urgent in China. On the one hand, one key recent policy launched by Chinese government— "The Belt and Road" strategy aims to re-establish ancient land and maritime trade routes across the Eurasian continent. This will deepen the regional economic cooperation in the process of infrastructure development and trade across the region. In order to cooperate with other countries well, many talented graduates are urgent needed who are required not only having professional knowledge but also commanding intercultural communicative competence (ICC) in various walks of life. Thus, how to improve students' ICC has become an urgent task for language teachers. Accordingly, as an important component of ICC, nonverbal communication should be incorporated in language teaching and learning. What is more, in the wake of globalization, many teachers and students come from different cultural backgrounds and nationalities and their communicative patterns are unique, especially their nonverbal symbols and cues. Not only should teachers be equipped with knowledge of nonverbal communication, but also the students should be encouraged to improve their nonverbal communicative competence. Therefore, the study of nonverbal communication has been necessitated by the diversity of student and teacher population in higher education and has accelerated with increasing globalization.

On the other hand, the teaching and learning in college classroom is a social interaction between teachers and students which is conducted through verbal and nonverbal means. Bi Jiwan (1993) has stated that the role of nonverbal communication in classroom teaching is greater than that of formal teaching for students' learning. It is obvious that both teachers and students use nonverbal and verbal means to communicate consciously or unconsciously. So it is necessary to explore the importance of nonverbal communication in actual classroom settings and to investigate the impact of the skill on teaching-learning process. To be specific, several reasons can account for the importance of this study.

Firstly, teachers' nonverbal behaviors in classroom have great impact on students. Compared with didactic verbal language of teachers, nonverbal behaviors convey many messages and are invaluable for teachers in helping the message across. They are used to transmit the empathy and understanding and responding with warmth (Grant & Hennings, 1997, 84-85). References argue that the systematic introduction of nonverbal communication in education, facilitates the teacher to make more effective teaching and make the lesson more vivid, thus, more attractive, more pleasant and easier to be understood. Nonverbal communication is especially important in Chinese classroom since Chinese students are usually stereotyped as being silent, shy, taciturn, introverted, sensitive and conservative. They are more observant to teachers' nonverbal behavior rather than their drab speech. What is more, teachers' nonverbal messages can influence the learning and response outcomes as Miller (1988, 7) stated, "Teachers express enthusiasm, warmth, assertiveness, confidence, or displeasure through their facial expression, vocal intonation, gestures, and use of space. When teachers exhibit verbal messages that conflict with nonverbal messages, students become confused, and this confusion often affects their attitudes and learning." Feldman (1990, 5) asserted that nonverbal research in education demonstrates that educators often send messages regarding their expectations via nonverbal cues. These nonverbal cues can have a notable impact on outcomes of student response and behavior. With the realization that nonverbal communication can play such an important role in the process of education, there is a direct impetus to further examine this issue.

Secondly, students' nonverbal behaviors also offer teachers continuous feedback information if the teacher can perceive them and decode them properly. Communication is a process of reciprocity. Students' positive nonverbal cues can also influence the teacher's state of mind and the classroom atmosphere, and further improve the effect of classroom instruction. Understanding students' nonverbal behaviors in the classroom can help to facilitate the teaching. Therefore, both teachers and students should understand and learn how to use nonverbal behaviors in classroom so that they can have a better understanding with each other.

Thirdly, foreign language teaching in China has focused largely on the verbal aspects of communication for some time so that some linguistic scholars admit that nonverbal behavior is largely out of awareness. Many of the nonverbal events and behaviors are interpreted through verbal symbols and it is impossible for us to study nonverbal communication in isolation from verbal communication. Both verbal and nonverbal communication make up the whole communication activity. The interaction of culture and communication is so pervasive that separating the verbal and nonverbal communications is virtually impossible.

In addition, the study is likely to promote awareness of both teachers and students in nonverbal communication. It would also pave way for introducing new trends in the teaching-learning process for promoting better learning of the students. The recommendations of the study might be useful for educators and curriculum planners at the time of designing syllabi by using the outcomes of the study.

1.3 The Purpose of Present Study

The field of nonverbal communication has grown rapidly over the last few decades, and it has applications in business, media, international relations, education, and indeed any field which significantly involves interpersonal and group dynamics. Research in the educational field, especially in the field of foreign language (FL) learning should be further enhanced as the importance of nonverbal communication has accelerated with increasing globalization and diversity within today's classroom.

This book intends to help both teachers and students become aware of the nonverbal communication X-Factor, recognize its importance in classroom and to help them develop their own X-Factor. Specifically, it attempts to bring into limelight use of nonverbal communication both by the Chinese teachers and students in actual classroom settings during teaching and learning process, and assesses how both of them utilize this mechanism for better teaching and learning. And also help them improve outcomes when conflict arises in class. This was done through experimental approach in the subject of English learning at the college level. The following objectives were formulated for the study:

(1) To identify and comprehend the major theoretical perspectives of nonverbal communication that help to explain and understand the cultural differences in nonverbal communication.

(2) To become aware of socio-cultural influence on nonverbal cues and use

theoretical knowledge to predict how teachers' and students' nonverbal behaviors could affect each other in classroom.

(3) To find out how the mechanism of nonverbal communication contributes to better learning outcomes of students.

(4) To make recommendations for the use of nonverbal communication strategies to improve classroom effectiveness.

1.4 The Organization of the Book

The book is organized into four parts.

Part One constructs the research background which contains two chapters. Chapter One is the general introduction for the present research, including the significance, the purpose of the study and the reason why the author carried out the present research and why the metaphor X-Factor was used to illustrate the quality nonverbal communication in classroom. Following the introductory chapter, Chapter Two provides a broad overview of historical research on nonverbal communication. It looks at relevant theories and examines nonverbal communication in general and intends to help the reader understand the specific "mechanics" of the various types of nonverbal cues in communication. To be specific, it discusses the previous researches in the field including the definition, classification, characteristics, functions of nonverbal communication, and the differences between verbal and nonverbal communication, and the final section accounts for the importance of nonverbal behavior in communication.

Part Two mainly focuses on the discussion of cultural impact on nonverbal communication. It begins with the discussion of the relationship between culture and nonverbal communication followed by the analysis of isolated nonverbal dimensions from the cultural perspective. In order to understand the role of nonverbal behavior in intercultural communication, Chapter Four initiates the discussion of the relationship between nonverbal communication and intercultural communication, including the exploration of intercultural communication development, the role of nonverbal communication in some well-known models of communicative competence. Based on the previous researches, a new model of intercultural communicative competence was established by the author. The importance of nonverbal communication in SLA (second language acquisition) is also presented, and the last section is about the previous researches in education and the implications for language teaching.

Based on the theoretical discussion, Part Three carried out the experimental investigations from the teacher's and student's perspectives respectively with the main purpose of examining the impact of nonverbal behavior on teaching and learning. Chapter Five firstly discusses the role, function, and research method of teachers' nonverbal behaviors, and then illustrates how teachers use specific nonverbal behaviors in classroom. Following these, it presents two experimental researches: (1) Chinese students' attitudes to teachers' appearance; (2) Chinese students' perceptions of teachers' eye contact, facial expression and gestures in classroom. Chapter Six starts with the analysis of ignorance of previous researches on students' nonverbal behavior in classroom, and then specifically emphasizes the reasons of this ignorance, the effectiveness of communication, the reciprocal relationship between teachers' and students' nonverbal behaviors, and the analysis of isolated nonverbal behavior of students in classroom, etc. The last section presents two experimental researches on teachers' perception of students' immediacy and silence in classroom. The experimental research instruments include questionnaire, interview, student self-repot, case study and classroom observation, etc.

Part Four intends to present some approaches to improve classroom nonverbal X-Factor. Chapter Seven illustrates the pedagogical implications, conclusion of good and bad nonverbal behaviors, and strategy to improve intercultural communicative competence. Chapter Eight summarizes the major findings of the study, provides recommendations for the future research and ends with concluding statements.

Chapter Two

Literature Review

2.1 Introduction

This chapter provides a historical review of nonverbal communication study. It particularly focuses on some basic concepts related to nonverbal communication, including its definition, classification, characteristics, the differences between verbal and nonverbal communication, and its functions and importance. The review will provide a conceptual framework to the present research and highlight the different dimensions of nonverbal communication on the basis of relevant literature both in local and global perspectives.

2.2 An Outline of Nonverbal Communication Research

Previous researches on nonverbal communication are rich in records. The original description of nonverbal communication abroad could trace back to the ancient Greece when Aristotle had attempted to analyze the way people conveyed their meanings. In China, people had begun to give an alarm with the beacon fire early in Zhou and Qin Dynasties and hit drums in wars to mean the command of marching forward and beat the gongs withdrawing the army. But the study of nonverbal communication is a young subject since it only has a history of sixty years as a discipline. It is believed that the scientific study of it began after World War Ⅱ.

2.2.1 Research Abroad

It is agreed that at first human beings communicate with each other through body language rather than verbal means. But the study of verbal communication is much earlier than nonverbal communication. Darwin's book *Expression of the Emotion in Man and Animals* (1872) is considered as one of the most influential pre-twentieth century works in which he made a systematic research on human's and animal's psychology and expressing ways and argued that some gestures and facial expressions of human beings have the same functions as language because they are demonstrations of people's inner motions. In other words, human utilize facial expressions as external evidence of their internal state. Darwin has spawned the modern study of facial expressions, and his initial ideas started the abundance of research on the types, effects, and expressions of nonverbal communication and behaviors. Many of his observations and ideas have been validated by other researchers (Ekman, 1973) from all kinds of perspectives, such as linguistics, sociolinguistics, pragmatics, semantics, etc.

2.2.1.1 The First Half of 20th Century—A Burgeoning Period

Despite the introduction of nonverbal communication in the 1800s, the emergence of behaviorism in the 1920s paused further research on nonverbal communication. The behaviorist such as B. F. Skinner trained pigeons to engage in various behaviors to demonstrate how animals engage in behaviors with rewards. Generally speaking, in the first half of the 20th century, unsystematic and isolated studies were made on the voice, facial expression, physical appearance and dress while the other fields of nonverbal communication were paid less attention. The publications during this period suggest that studies of proxemics, the environment, and body movement received even less attention, and the least attention was given to the investigation of eye behavior and touching. For many years, the early study in nonverbal communication remained one of the few scholarly books on the subject. Only in the mid-twentieth century did scholars truly begin taking body language seriously as a subject of study. Nonverbal communication has since been analyzed by experts in many fields, including zoologists, psychologists, and anthropologists.

The most influential work is Kretschmer's *Physique and Character* in 1925 which is supposed as the first book on nonverbal communication and shows that people are capable of knowing others' characters through their appearance. This was followed by Sheldon's book *The Variations of Human Physique* in 1940 which mainly focuses on the study of human physique. And a three dimensional scheme for describing human physique is formulated. Sheldon's belief that certain characteristics are associated with certain body types—the thin ectomorph, the muscular mesomorph, and the fatty endomorph—is still debated. The publication of Efron's book in 1941—

Gesture and Environment has become a classic due to its important contributions. It is a tentative study of the "spatio-temporal" and "linguistic" aspects of the general behaviors of eastern Jews and southern Italians in New York City. Efron's innovative and detailed methods of studying gestures and body language, along with his framework for classifying nonverbal behavior, influenced future generations of scholars. Efron's work documented the important role of culture in forming people's gestures and body movement, which was contrary to the belief at that time when most thought that people's behavior was not subject to much modification by changing contexts and environments.

2.2.1.2 The 1950s— A Breakthrough Period

In the 1950s, nonverbal communication made a breakthrough development. The research of this decade covers almost all areas of nonverbal communication, such as the body movement, space, paralanguage, tactile communication and the environment language.

A group of psychiatrists began the research of nonverbal communication in 1955. For example, Adam Kendon, Albert Scheflen, and Ray Birdwhistell, analyzed a film using an analytic method called context analysis (Hecht & Ambady, 1999). This method was later used in studying the sequence and structure of human greetings, social behavior at parties, and the function of posture during interpersonal interaction (Hecht & Ambady, 1999).

Among the most important pioneers in the study of body language was anthropologist Ray L. Birdwhistell who pioneered the original study of body movements and their meanings, a field he called kinesics. His influential book— *Introduction of Kinesics* published in 1952 which was a system of annotation for analysis of body motions and gestures and considered as a classic book on nonverbal communication. Birdwhistell (1952) pointed out that "human's gestures differ from those of other animals in that they are polysemic, that they can be interpreted to have many different meanings depending on the communicative context in which they are produced"(213). He argued that every body movement must be interpreted broadly and in conjunction with every other element in communication (Birdwhistell, 156). At that time, Birdwhistell had noticed that body language should be combined with environment language. During the 1950s, Birdwhistell was the only person studying the method of communication. His efforts have contributed greatly to our present knowledge and understanding of nonverbal communication. The first time the phrase "nonverbal communication" was used in 1955 by G. W. Hewes when he wrote *World*

Distribution of Certain Postural Habits.

Another famous book was written by an American leading anthropologist, Edward Hall— *The Silent Language* in 1959, which marked the beginning of the study of nonverbal behavior in intercultural communication. During the 1950s, Hall worked at the Foreign Service Institute of the US Department of States teaching intercultural communication skills to foreign service personnel. In this book, he analyzed many aspects of nonverbal communication and considered the concepts of space and time as tools for the transmission of messages. He stated the importance of nonverbal communication in the following way:

> I am convinced that much of our difficulty with people in other culture stems from the fact that so little is known about cross-communication…formal training in the language, history, government, and customs of another nation is only first step in a comprehensive program. Of equal importance is an introduction to the nonverbal language which exists in every country of the world and among the various groups within each country. Most Americans are only dimly aware of this silent language even though they use it every day… In addition to what we say with our verbal language we are constantly communicating our real feelings in our silent language— the language of behavior.(Hall, 1959, 10)

Together with Birdwhistell's *Introduction to Kinesics,* the two books are seen as the influential works during this period and the foundation stone. They are considered as the remarkable symbol of the birth of nonverbal communication as a discipline and are responsible for taking some of principles of linguistics and applying them to nonverbal phenomena. The two books provide new labels for the study of body movement and space, and launch a program of research in each area.

In this period, other works are also considered as the milestones presented by Knapp, Hall and Horgan (2012, 22) as follows:

(1) Trager's 1958 delineation of the components of "paralanguage" greatly enhanced the precision with the later study.

(2) Another book published by psychiatrist Jurgen Ruesch and photographer Weldon Kees in 1956 is titled *Nonverbal Communication: Notes on the Visual Perceptions of Human Relations*. The book provides additional theoretical insights into the origins, usage, and coding of nonverbal behavior; it also provides extensive visual documentation for the communicative role of environment.

(3) An oft-cited study in this time is Maslow and Mintz's article titled "Effects of Esthetic Surroundings: I. Initial Effects of Three Esthetic Conditions upon Perceiving

'Energy' and 'Well-Being' in Faces" which was published in 1956 in the *Journal of Psychology*. It studied the environmental effects of a "beautiful" room and an "ugly" room and is considered as a highlight in the history of environment forces impinging on human communication.

4) Frank's comprehensive article "Tactile Communication" appeared in 1957 and suggested a number of testable hypotheses about touching in human interaction.

2.2.1.3 From the 1960s to 1970s— A Flourishing Period

If the 1950s produced an increase in the number of nonverbal studies, the 1960s must be classified as a nuclear explosion of the topic. The study was developed into a new stage in which the movement of each part of human body was researched by a number of psychologists and researchers. Knapp et al. (2012, 23) presented some researches of this period: Exline's work on eye behavior; Davitz's work on vocal expressions of emotion which culminated in *The Communication of Emotional Meaning* in 1964; Hess's work on pupil dilation; Sommer's continued exploration of personal space and design; Goldman-Eisler's study of pause and hesitation in spontaneous speech; and the study of a wide range of body activities by Dittmann, Argyle, Kendon, Scheflen, and Mehrabian. During this time, psychologist Robert Rosenthal and his colleagues brought vividly the potential impact of nonverbal subtleties when they showed how experimenters can affect the outcome of experiments—and teachers can affect the intellectual growth of their students—through their nonverbal behavior.

During this period, Ekman conducted and published researches on various topics in the area of nonverbal communication. His works on lying, for example, are not limited to the face, but also to the observation of the rest of the body. Together with Friesen, they made a series of publications. Their classic theoretical piece in the 1960s is the article on the origins, usage, and coding of nonverbal behavior in which they (1969, 1967) divided nonverbal communication into five categories: emblems, illustrators, affect displays, regulators, and adaptors that served as a guide for their own research and ultimately that of many other researchers. In the 1970s, a technique for the measurement of nonverbal movement was made by Ekman and Friesen (1976, 1978a, 1978b). They developed the Facial Action Coding System, also called FACS. It is a system of analyzing and interpreting even the smallest facial movement. Today, it is used by psychiatrists to diagnose patients who have trouble in communicating and by law enforcement officers to get a read on suspects. It is also studied by filmmakers of animated movies who want to make their characters' expressions look as real as possible. Several other works studying on one specific aspect of nonverbal communication in the 1960s were provided by Hetch and Ambady (1999). For example, Bridwhistell's book—*Kinesics, Inter- and Intra-channel Communication Research and Communication without Words* focuses on the study of kinesics. Exline's book—*Gaze Behavior in Infants and Children: A Tool for the Study of the Emotions* specifies the study of looking patterns while speaking and looking while listening. Davitz's book—*The Communication of Emotional Meaning* studies on vocal expressions of emotion, and Sommer's book— *Personal Space: The Behavioral Basis of Design* explores the relationship between personal space and environment. Argyle and Dean examined the relationship between eye contact and conversational distance (cited from Hetch & Ambady, 1999, 1-12).

1970s was a period of a huge amount of publications of works and articles and was characterized by further exploration of nonverbal study from the perspective of various researchers. Most of them are just the recap and synthesis of previous studies. The representative work was Fast's *Body Language* (1971) which introduced the common expression "body language" and the principles of kinesics. The study states that common gestures can reveal people's hidden feelings and thoughts, so people can learn to know how to read them. This book provides a theoretical base for the following linguistics. Following that a number of scholarly volumes in psychology summarized the growing body of research that attempted to make nonverbal findings understandable and usable to the American public were published, such as, Weitz's (1974) *Nonverbal Communication* and LaFrance and Mayo's (1978) *Moving Bodies*. Besides, two books: *Body Language* (1970) which focuses on how to use nonverbal communication to attract people and *How to Read a Person Like a Book* (1971) which examines nonverbal behavior in negotiation situations, were also considered as two popular books (Hetch and Ambady, 1999, 1-12). Knapp et al. (2012, 24) argued that these books not only aroused the public interest in nonverbal communication, but also incurred some anticipated fallout. They pointed out that readers were often left with the idea that reading nonverbal cues was the key to success in communication. Some books implied that single cue had single meaning. Not only is it important to look at nonverbal clusters of behavior but also should recognize that nonverbal cues rarely have a single denotative meaning. And some didn't sufficiently remind readers that the meaning of a particular behavior is often understood by looking at the context in which communication occurs. Another reaction to these books was the concern that once the nonverbal code was broken, people would be completely transparent and know everything about the communicators since people can't control the nonverbal signals to some degree.

The importance of culture in nonverbal communication was also further explored in the 1970s. In his second book, *The Hidden Dimension* (1969), Hall describes the culturally specific temporal and spatial dimensions that surround each of us, such as the physical distances people maintain in different contexts. In 1976, he progressed further towards an integral vision of culture and released his third book—*Beyond Culture,* which is based on his personal, firsthand experiences. In the book, Hall introduced the highly important concepts of man's extensions and identified the misconception of extension transference as a major source of erroneous thinking in all facets of culture. The theme of this book is the path to improvement in intercultural communication. In Hall's view, resolution of problems that arises in the contemporary society, where different cultures have more and more contact with each other, can only be achieved if each side is able to transcend the ingrained stereotypes present in its own culture. Throughout his career, Hall introduced a number of new concepts, including polychronic and monochronic time, proxemics, high and low context culture, etc. He is considered a founding father of intercultural communication as an academic area of study (Rogers, Hart, & Yoshitaka, 2002; Leeds-Hurwitz, 1990).

The 1970s was also a time of summarizing and synthesizing. In 1972, three books appeared: Ekman's *Emotion in the Human Face* which explores the field of the human face; Mehrabian's *Nonverbal Communication* focusing on the research on the meaning of nonverbal cues of immediacy, status, and responsiveness; Scheflen's *Body Language and Social Order* which studies kinesics in the framework of general system theory. In 1975, Hess's *The Tell-Tale Eye* which studies the pupil size; Argyle's *Bodily Communication* focusing on the body movement and eye behavior were also published. All attempt to bring together the growing literature, or a particular research program, in a single volume. Knapp's *Nonverbal Communication in Human Interaction* (1972) which summarizes the research on nonverbal behavior became the highly readable fashion. In 1978, the *Journal of Environmental Psychology* and *Nonverbal Behavior* were also founded.

2.2.1.4 From the 1980s to the Present— A Diversified Period

1980s was the further development period of nonverbal communication and a haphazard bundle of different researches appeared in archaeology, biology, culture, linguistics, etc. Some researchers continued to specialize, while others focused on identifying the ways in which various nonverbal signals work together to accomplish certain communicative goals.

After the fever of the 1970s and 1980s, some scholars became aware that people couldn't fully understand the role of nonverbal behavior in accomplishing the communicative goals if they don't look at the role of co-occurring verbal behavior and tried to develop theories about how various verbal and nonverbal behavior interact in the process. The research perspective has widely changed from the micro-angle to the macro-angle. Researchers began to learn how to put the pieces back together after several decades of separating them to examine them microscopically. This trend is a manifestation of a larger movement to bring the research efforts more in line with the way of human communication. For example, Streek and Knapp's *The Interactions of Visual and Verbal Features in Human Communication* (1992), Stanley, Jones and LeBaron's *Research on the Relationship between Verbal and Nonverbal Communication: Emerging Integrations* (2002) all argued that an integrated approach in which verbal and nonverbal messages should be studied as inseparable phenomena when they occur together so that more holistic understanding of social interaction may emerge.

From the above discussion of historical research on nonverbal communication in Western countries, we can see that the research of the field of nonverbal communication has grown swiftly over the last few decades, and it has functions in business, media, international relations, education, and indeed any field which notably involves interpersonal and group dynamics. Knapp et al. (2012, 24) summarized the change of nonverbal communication research in past decades in the following ways:

From studying noninteractive situations to studying interactive ones;

From studying one person to studying both interactants;

From studying a single point in time to studying changes over time;

From studying single behavior to studying multiple behaviors;

From the view that we perceive everything that occurs to acknowledging that we need to know more about how people perceive signals during interactions;

From single-meaning and single-intent perspectives to acknowledging that often multiple meanings occur and multiple goals exist;

From a measurement perspective focused almost exclusively on frequency and duration to on that also includes issues related to when and how a behavior occurs;

From attempting to control context by eliminating important and influential elements to attempting to account for such effects;

From studying only face-to-face interaction to examining the role of nonverbal messages in mediated communication settings;

From an overemphasis on studying how strangers interact to one equally concerns about how intimates interact;

From studying only culture or only biology as possible explanation of behavior to examining the roles both play.

2.2.2 Research in China

The study of nonverbal communication in China actually happened in ancient times even though people didn't realize that. In Confucius' book *The Analects of Confucius*, he paid much attention to the nonverbal signals. In the tenth chapter, Zi Lu said, "A superior man did not use deep purple or any puce color in the ornaments of his dress." The rules of dressing showed that Confucius at that time had noticed the importance of nonverbal messages. However, the scientific study on it began in the 1980s. With more and more attention on nonverbal communication, many works were published and translated since the late 1980s.

The first book on nonverbal communication is Geng Erling's *An Introduction to Body Language* in 1988. The author mainly discussed the characteristics, functions and skills of using body language. At the same year, Meng Xiaoping translated *Body Language* by J. Fast and in 1991, *Nonverbal Communication* by Malandro, Barker & Barker. was translated by Meng Xiaoping et al.

The most profound work introduced into China is the one written by American professor Leger Brosnahan—*Chinese and English Gestures: Contrastive Communication* in 1991 and was translated by Bi Jiwan. This book compared systematically the differences between China and English-speaking countries in fifteen aspects of communication. It is still perceived as a reference book in language learning and teaching. Following that, Hu Wenzhong edited a series of books on intercultural communication, such as *Intercultural Communication and English Study* in 1988, *Culture and Communication* in 1994, *Crossing Cultural Barriers* in 2002. In these books, he systematically introduced the latest finding on nonverbal communication. In 1999, Bi Jiwan published his famous work *Intercultural Nonverbal Communication* which has a profound influence on the study of nonverbal communication in China. Other Chinese scholars have published academic books such as Deng Yanchang and Liu Runqing's *Language and Culture* in 1989, Wang Fuxiang and Wu Hanying's *Culture and Language* in 1994, Li Jiequn's *The introduction to Nonverbal Communication* in 2002. Recently, more researches focusing on nonverbal communication also have been carried out, such as Wang Jian (2007), Liu Naimei(2005, 2007), Xu Mingyang (2015), they all have contributed a lot to the study of nonverbal communication in China.

From the above description, we can see that nonverbal communication research witnesses a fast development in China since 1980s. In the new century, recent discoveries in neuroscience founded from the 1990s to 2000s have proved a clearer picture of what the unspoken signs in this corpus mean. However, the study of nonverbal communication in education is still far from enough (Liu Naimei, 2013), particularly research on teachers' and students' nonverbal behavior in classroom. Accordingly, this book attempts to make an exploration in this aspect.

2.3 The Definition of Nonverbal Communication

The word "communication" comes from the Latin word "communicare," which means to share, impart or make common. Anderson (1986) stated that "communication is a process that occurs whenever one person stimulates meaning in the mind of a receiver or changes the behavior of a receiver." Canale (1983a, 4) defined communication as "the exchange and negotiation of information between at least two individuals through the use of verbal and nonverbal symbols" (4).

Communication is not necessarily an intentional process, nor is it a conscious one. It is inseparable with behavior since any behavior has communicative potential which is realized when meaning is attached to the behavior by a receiver. Nonverbal means communicative messages which are nonlinguistic, analogic, and processed primarily by the brain's right hemisphere. As for the definition of nonverbal communication, there are a variety of versions given by different scholars, some of which are very simple, while the others are more specific.

In the early time, Hall (1959) has referred nonverbal communication to the metacommunication, paralinguistics, second-order messages, the silent language, and the hidden dimension of communication. Later, Stanton (2009, 39) confirmed, "All the nonverbal elements of communication like facial expressions, gestures, body postures, eye contact, proximity, head-nods, are sometimes called 'meta communication,' from Greek word meta meaning 'beyond' or 'in addition to.' Metacommunication is therefore something 'in addition to communication' and we must always be aware of its existence."

Miller (2005b) provided a rather simplistic view of nonverbal communication as communication without words. Zoric, Smid, and Pandzic (2007, 161) considered that it refers to "all aspects of message exchange without the use of words" and "it includes all expressive signs, signals and cues (audio, visual, etc.)" (161).

In Knapp's (1980) viewpoint, nonverbal communication is the signals to which meaning will be attributed—not the process of attributing meaning (18). Simply, it can be used to describe all human communication events that transcend the use of words spoken or written. Burgoon and Saine (cited from Malandro, Barker, & Barker, 1989, 7) held the same point that nonverbal communication is communication without the use of words. They stated that nonverbal communication is the qualities or behaviors known to all in a community without the use of words and such qualities or behaviors are intentionally given by the speakers and consciously received and responded by the listeners. That is, nonverbal communication is the process of one person stimulating meaning in the mind of another person nonverbally.

Wood (1976, 184-185) claimed, "Body language can be defined as any reflexive or nonreflexive movement or position used to communicate an emotional, attitudinal, or informational message to someone else." In the author's view, body movements, such as waving, winking and positions, such as hunched shoulders and wide open eyes are the basic categories of body language. Although any movement or position during communication is capable of message value, not all the motions necessarily communicate.

Ellyson and Dovidio (1985) defined nonverbal communication as the "behavior that is not part of formal, verbal language" (1). This definition encompasses a wide variety of messages the receiver may receive within a context. It would include aspects such as context temperature, time of day, etc. Henley (1977, 2) claimed that nonverbal communication is related to "how we say things with our body postures and movements, facial expressions, gestures, touching, eye contact, use of space, and so on" (2).

Malandro, et al. (1989, 5) defined nonverbal communication as "the process by which nonverbal behaviors are used, either singly or in combination with verbal behaviors, in the exchange and interpretation of messages within a given situation or context." This definition centers on the combination with verbal and nonverbal behavior and a fixed environment.

Samovar, Porter and Stefani (2006, 149) made a great effort to interpret the term. They proposed that "nonverbal communication involves all those nonverbal stimuli in a communication setting that are generated by both the source and his/her use of the environment and that have potential message value of the source or receiver." This definition is a bit lengthy, but it discloses the multi-channeled nature of nonverbal communication and is more comprehensive. They argued that the definition would not only mark the boundaries of nonverbal communication, but also reflect how the process actually works. Here the role of the environment, the message value of nonverbal stimuli and the communicative setting are emphasized as the three important factors in nonverbal communication and also reflect how the process actually works. It also includes unintentional as well as intentional behavior in the total communication event. That is to say, sometimes nonverbal communication is intentional, as with the use of gestures such as the thumbs-up sign to indicate approving. Sometimes it is unintentional and embarrassing when the speaker blushes.

Now we can conclude that the definition of nonverbal communication is so diverse and complex that it is impossible to give a perfect definition. It covers a wide range from apparent behaviors to less obvious messages. In this book, we would define nonverbal communication as that which happens wherever a person receives any message transmitted by another without using any words.

2.4 The Classification of Nonverbal Communication

Nonverbal behavior is a multifaceted phenomenon. There is no consensus on its components and the appropriate framework for the classification of these components. This complexity is partly due to the difficulty of defining the concept of nonverbal communication. Researchers have identified and categorized literally hundreds of objects, behaviors, and events as forms of nonverbal communication. The term "nonverbal" can be used to refer to both visible phenomena, i.e., gestures and facial expressions, and the audible phenomena, such as tone, pitch and accent. Literature review reveals the following entries as the main components of nonverbal communication.

2.4.1 Classification by Western Researchers

The earliest one is raised by Ruesch and Kees (1956) who presented their classification based on foundational components of nonverbal communication: sign language, action language and object language (cited from Bi Jiwan, 1998, 5). Sign language includes the signs and gestures to express the meaning of words, numbers and punctuations. Action language consists of all actions that not purely refer to an action but some other meanings as well. Object language includes all objects used intentionally or unintentionally, such as tools, machines, clothing, etc. This classification is so rough and general that it is difficult to apply it into practice. And also it does not include environmental factors, some culturally framed concepts of time, space, personal distance, etc. Thus, it is too narrow.

Conden and Yousef (1975) thought cross-cultural communication is an interdisciplinary study in which many things are not included and the amount of the excluded is larger than the included. Then they sorted the most common nonverbal communication means into 24 kinds and proposed that it was unnecessary to study the whole region of nonverbal behaviors since its range was very wide and the amount of study increased rapidly.

In his book *Nonverbal Communication*, Mehrabian (1977) focused on the discussion of five categories of nonverbal communication developed by Ekman and Friesen in 1969 and widely used by sociologists since. The first category, emblem, refers to the small class of nonverbal acts that can be accurately translated into words (for example, a handshake, shaking a fist at someone, a smile). Emblems often carry intrinsic meaning and are easy to understand to someone who has experience with them. The second category, illustrator, is very much a part of speech and serves the function of emphasis. For example, head and hand movements that occur more frequently with primary-stressed words. The third category is affect display. These are actions that are paired with emotions. These body movements may indicate whether a person is open and receptive, angry, distracted, or other emotions. Regulator movements are the fourth category. It refers to acts that help to initiate and terminate the speech of participants in a social situation. Regulator actions are made by the listener to help the speaker improve communication. The last category is adaptor, refers to acts that are related to the satisfaction of bodily needs. Adaptor actions are often unconscious movements made for reasons of comfort or clarity.

According to Argyle (1986, 2), nonverbal communication, or bodily communication, takes place whenever one person influences another by means of facial expressions, gaze, gestures and other aspects of appearance and nonverbal vocalizations. Feyereisen and de Lannoy (1991) classified nonverbal communication according to modality, such as face, gaze, voice, bodily expression and function, such as emotional expression, intimacy regulation, etc. Based on the analysis of previous studies and works, Knapp (1997, 12-20) proposed seven categories of nonverbal communication: body motion and kinesics behavior, physical characteristics, touching behavior, paralanguage, proxemics, artifacts, and environmental factors.

Malandro et al. (1989) identified the specific classes of nonverbal communication including: (1) body types, shapes and sizes; (2) clothing and personal artifacts;

(3) body movements and gestures; (4) facial expression and eye behavior; (5) environment; (6) personal space, territory and crowding; (7) voice characteristics and qualities; (8) taste and smell; (9) culture and time.

With a quite different perspective, Anderson (2007a, 239-240) divided nonverbal signs into eight categories, including (1) physical appearance, the most obvious code of nonverbal behavior playing an important role at the beginning of communication; (2) proxemics, the most fundamental code of nonverbal behavior concerning a communication via interpersonal space and distance; (3) chronemics, the study of meaning, usage, and communication of time; (4) kinesics, the aspects of facial expressions, body movements, gestures, and conversational regulators; (5) haptics, the study of the tactile communication; (6) oculesics, the study of messages sent by the eyes, including eye contact, blinks, eye movements, and pupil dilation; (7) vocalics, or paralanguage, the study of voice, including the almost completely ignored areas in music and singing, universal forms of aesthetic communication; (8) olfactics, the study of interpersonal communication via smell.

Based on literature review, Birjandi and Nushi (2010) pointed out that there are seven entries considered as the main components of nonverbal communication: kinesics, proxemics, haptics, eye contact to eye gaze (oculesics), chronemics, paralanguage and posture. Besides, other ways of nonverbal communication such as sound symbols (grunting, mmm, er, ah, uh-huh, and mumbling), silence (pause, wait, secrecy), adornment (clothing, jewellery, hairstyle), olfactics (smell) and locomotion (walking, running, staggering, limping) are also included in nonverbal categories.

2.4.2 Classification by Chinese Researchers

Chinese researchers also make surveys on the category of nonverbal behaviors. In 1988, He Daokuan divided nonverbal communication into five groups: time language including punctuality, promptness, time orientation; space language consisting of body touch and personal distance; body language such as posture, stance, gesture, facial expression, eye behavior and any other movement of any part of the body and appearance; voice modulation including speed, pitch, volume, pause, etc.; and environment which refers to the location, decoration, temperature, light, etc.

Bi Jiwan (1999, 6) divided nonverbal communication into four kinds: (1) body language, including basic postures, gestures, basic manners and movements of any part of the body; (2) paralanguage, referring to these elements such as pitch, speed, volume, tone, rhyme, silence and pause; (3) object language, consisting of smell, complexion, clothing, cosmetics, furniture, etc; (4) environment language, including time, space, color, city planning and any human effect on nature. And according to him, the former two can be called "nonverbal behavior" and the latter two "nonverbal means".

Yang Ping (1994) developed the concepts of nonverbal communication into three aspects: (1) proxemics, which studies man's use and perception of his social and personal space; (2) kinesics, the main part of nonverbal communication, which studies the meaning conveyed through movements of any part of the body; (3) paralanguage, which deals with how things are talked about.

From the above discussion we can see that nonverbal communication covers a wide range of areas, so it is impossible to include every aspect in classifying it.

2.4.3 Classification Examined in the Present Study

In this book, the author intends to examine the nonverbal communication used in classroom by teachers and students. Considering the teaching and learning environment, the author divides the nonverbal behaviors into four major categories: kinesics, paralanguage, proxemics, and chronemics.

1. Kinesics, or body language, refers to gestures, facial expressions, eye contact, body positions, body movements used by teachers and students in classroom. Certain kinds of body movements are physiological, such as yawning, stretching, relaxing and so on. Other kinesics patterns—such as staring, walking slumped over, raising a clenched fist, showing a victory sign, and the like—are personally and culturally conditioned.

In this research, five kinds of kinesics have been examined: (1) general appearance, such as the dress or attire; (2) gestures, or hand and arm movements; (3) postures, the ways that teachers and students hold their bodies when they sit stand or walk, and it can send positive or negative nonverbal messages; (4) facial expressions, including basic human emotions, such as surprise, fear, anger, disgust, happiness and sadness; (5) eye contact, including direct eye contact and indirect eye contact.

2. Paralanguage is everything in voice besides the words. It refers to the communicators' tone of voice, pitch, rhythm, tempo, intensity (loudness), emotional content and vocal segregates such as an "uh-huh." Paralanguage plays an important role in classroom teaching and learning. Silence is usually included in paralanguage.

3. Proxemics refers to the study of the use of space in nonverbal communication. The space used by teachers and students can have different communication meanings.

4. Chronemics refers to the study of how teachers and students use and interpret and understand time. In English teaching and learning, teachers' and students' view of time can influence their temporal concepts, such as appointment, schedule, punctuality, etc.

2.5 Characteristics of Nonverbal Communication

2.5.1 Common Characteristics

Nonverbal communication is universal to all human beings, but it is modified by such things as culture, age, rank and gender, etc. Thus, it has all the characteristics of communication and shares some features with verbal communication.

Firstly, nonverbal communication is symbolic. Words or behaviors are all symbols that people employ as a way of representing the shared meaning people communicate. A symbol can be a word, action or object that stands for a unit of meaning. People's behaviors are frequently interpreted symbolically, as an external representation of feelings, emotions, and internal states. For example, flags can symbolize a country, and most of the world's religions have symbols that are associated with their beliefs. The ability to produce and use symbols enables human beings to share their feelings, which distinguishes from other animals.

Secondly, nonverbal communication is an interactive process between two persons or within a group or groups. Both verbal and nonverbal communications involve three basic elements: the context of communication, the participants, the messages being communicated. These elements work simultaneously and interlocking. In other words, nonverbal communication must take place between senders and receivers. Usually this implies two or more people. In this situation, communication is characterized by the fact that both parties bring to a communication event with their own unique backgrounds and experiences, which serve as a backdrop for communication interaction. Interaction also implies a situation in which each party attempts to influence the other. That is, we are constantly affected by others' messages and as a consequence, we are always changing.

Thirdly, like verbal communication, nonverbal communication is contextual. This means that communication takes place in both physical and social contexts. Communication can not take place in a vacuum. When we interact with someone it is not in isolation but within a specific physical surrounding. Setting and environment help to determine how we communicate since we have to adapt the messages to our communicators and surroundings. Our dress, language, topic selection and the like have to adapt to the context. For example, we dress formally in an employment interview, and casually in playing game. We talk differently to our friends than to a stranger. The surrounding includes specific physical objects such as furniture, window coverings, floor coverings, lighting, noise levels, etc. Many aspects of the physical environment can and do affect communication, such as, the comfort of a chair, the color of walls, or total atmosphere of a room, etc.

2.5.2 Specific Characteristics

Verbal and nonverbal means form the whole process of human communication, and it is indispensable to separate nonverbal means from verbal means in discussing the characteristics of nonverbal communication. Compared with verbal communication, nonverbal communication has its unique features.

Firstly, nonverbal communication is a kind of communication without words. As its definition displays that nonverbal communication conveys information by no words but with eye contact, facial expression, posture, etc.

Secondly, nonverbal behaviors are unconscious and its potential implications will be more likely to be adopted by the receivers. However, the sender tends to be unaware that he/she is sending a nonverbal message but he/she can notice the impact that the message may have. When contradiction occurs, people usually choose to believe the meanings behind the nonverbal signals rather than relying on their ears.

Thirdly, nonverbal communication is irrevocable. As the saying goes, "what is done can not be undone," the same is true with nonverbal communication. Once the nonverbal behaviors are made or the signals are transmitted, the sender can not take it back. Even if the sender makes effort to modify, it can not change the truth that his/her previous behavior or signal has made sense.

Fourthly, nonverbal communication is culture-bound. Nonverbal behaviors vary from one culture to another. Many of them are unique to the culture or subculture to which people belong. In the course of communication, culture plays a very important role. Different cultures have different nonverbal behaviors to the same situations, such as the table manner in East and West. Even the same nonverbal behavior will have the different meanings in different cultures, such as the interpretation of eye contact in China and America.

2.6 Differences between Nonverbal Communication and Verbal Communication

We can find the relationship between verbal and nonverbal communication from Weare's (2004, 114) statement: "Communication doesn't of course have to be verbal, indeed the evidence is that more of it is not, and that we gather about 90 percent of what others tell us about what they think and feel through nonverbal communication." Although verbal communication and nonverbal communication form the process of communication, there are some differences between them. Malandro, et al. (1989, 7-10) has proposed the following differences:

Firstly, structured versus less structured or nonstructured. Verbal communication is a highly structured form of communication with a set of grammar, which helps people understand and make sense of what others are saying. For example, it is a hard time for Chinese learners to use the correct verb forms at the beginning. Instead of saying "I went to see a film last night," they may say "I go to see a film last night." Thus verbal communication can be oral or written language which is structurally to communicate. On the contrary, nonverbal communication has no formal structure when it comes to communication, that is, it is performed by means of nonverbal signals, which have no structure. Nonverbal behaviors occur without even thinking. Since there is no pattern to nonverbal communication, the same behavior can mean different things, such as crying because we are sad or crying because we are happy.

Secondly, linguistic versus non-linguistic. Verbal communication has a system of symbols that have specific meanings to them and depends on language, while nonverbal messages have few assigned symbols in the system of nonverbal communication and do not necessarily depend on the presence of any language. For example, nodding head is one symbol that indicates agreement in some cultures but in others it means disagreement. Many have tried to assign specific meanings to other nonverbal communications but the only exception to this is the universal sign language of the deaf. The deaf has other nonverbal communications that do not have specific meanings. This is not the same for verbal communication. The non-linguistic features of nonverbal communication lead some people to suggest that nonverbal communication is simple "communication without words." Many nonverbal behaviors exist in the presence of spoken words, but this distinction oversimplifies the matter.

Thirdly, discontinuous versus continuous. Continuous and discontinuous go hand in hand with linguistic and non-linguistic. Verbal communication is based on discontinuous units whereas nonverbal communication is continuous. That verbal messages are discontinuous means that we say some words and then we stop saying words. Then we say some more and so on. Nonverbal messages are continuous. That means nonverbal behaviors never stop. Communicating nonverbally cannot be stopped unless we would leave the room but even then our intrapersonal processes still take place (communicating with ourselves). Without the presence of someone else our body still manages to undergo nonverbal communication. For example, after a heated debate there are no other words being said but there are still angry faces and cold stares being distributed. This is a form of how nonverbal communication is continuous. However, we can consider nonverbal signals as a whole, a "package" of simultaneous messages rather than the discrete messages of gesture, voice, touch, etc.

Fourthly, learned versus innate. Verbal communication is learned in daily life after people acquire language, while nonverbal communication is innate. The innate nonverbal behaviors are "built-in" characteristic of human communication. These innate cues are universally prevalent and regardless of culture. For example, smiling, crying, and laughing do not require teaching. Similarly, the body positions, such as the fetal position, are universally associated with weakness. Due to the universality, the ability to comprehend these cues is not limited to individual cultures. For the learned nonverbal behaviors, they require a community or culture for their reinforcement. For instance, table manners are not innate capabilities upon birth. Dress code is a nonverbal sign that must be established by society. Hand symbols, whose interpretation can vary from culture to culture, are not innate nonverbal cues. Learned cues must be gradually reinforced by positive feedback.

Fifthly, left versus right-hemispheric processing. This type of processing involves the neurophysiological approach to nonverbal communication. Early research in the United States provided strong evidence that the right hemisphere processes nonverbal stimuli such as those involving spatial, pictorial, and gestural tasks while the left hemisphere involves the verbal stimuli involving analytical and reasoning tasks. This suggests that verbal and nonverbal communications are really two separate and distinct communication systems. It is important to know the implications in processing the differences between verbal and nonverbal communication messages. Subsequent research, however, has cast considerable doubts on this distinction. Humans do not all seem to be alike. It is possible that individuals may not use the correct hemisphere at appropriate times when it comes to interpreting a message or meaning (Malandro et al., 1989, 9). For example, people in some cultures such as those in Japan and Finland have been found to process information in the opposite sides of the brain from people in the United States.

Although we have illustrated the differences between verbal and nonverbal communications, in fact, the two aspects can not be separated as Givens (2000) stated that the effectiveness of communication is a function of attending to both verbal and nonverbal aspects of the message: when we speak (or listen), our attention is focused on words rather than body language. But our judgment includes both. An audience is simultaneously processing both verbal and nonverbal cues. Body movements are not usually positive or negative in and of themselves; rather, the situation and the message will determine the appraisal (Given, 2000, 4).

2.7 Functions of Nonverbal Communication

Samovar, Porter and Stefani (2006, 150) stated that nonverbal communication encompasses more than one activity, and it is not limited to one set of messages. Therefore, this multidimensional aspect carries over to the many uses and functions of the form of communication. That is to say, nonverbal message has its own unique functions in human interaction. And many of the same behaviors can serve two or more functions, sometimes simultaneously.

Based on different research situations, researchers have categorized the functions of nonverbal communication differently. Argyle (1988) categorized four types including (1) expressing emotion; (2) conveying interpersonal attitudes (like/dislike, dominance/submission); (3) representing one's personality to others; (4) accompanying and supporting speech. M. O. Wiemann, and J. M. Wiemann (1975, 4) listed six functions of nonverbal behavior: (1) repeating what has been said verbally; (2) contradicting what has been said verbally; (3) substituting a verbal message; (4) complementing what has been said verbally; (5) accenting the verbal message; and (6) regulating the flow of verbal messages. Argyle (1986, 5) proposed five categories: (1) expressing emotions by face, body and voice; (2) communicating interpersonal attitudes to maintain friendships, and other relationships; (3) accompanying and supporting speech by head-nods, glances, and nonverbal vocalizations; (4) self-presentation by appearance or voice; (5) playing roles in rituals, such as in greetings and other rituals.

Generally speaking, six primary universal functions of nonverbal communication are widely agreed in literature: repeating, substituting, complementing, reinforcing, contradicting and regulating.

2.7.1 Repetition

Nonverbal communication can repeat, clarify what people say orally. By repeating the verbal message nonverbally, such as through a gesture, there is a better chance for the receiver to understand the message. For instance, when someone agrees with somebody, he/she says "yes" or "no" while nodding or shaking his/ her head to repeat the same meaning as verbal utterance. Another example, we might hold up hand in the gesture that signifies a person to stop at the same time we actually use the word "stop," or we point to the chest to indicate "me" at the same time we use the word "me."

2.7.2 Contradiction

Nonverbal behavior often betrays the speaker by sending contradictory messages to the verbal codes. In this sense, nonverbal actions send signals opposite from the literal meaning contained in verbal messages. People do this sometimes deliberately, sometimes unintentionally. Since a speaker often sends his/her nonverbal cues beyond his/her conscious control, the unspoken message is regarded as speaking louder than the spoken words. For instance, tears in our eyes and a quiver in our voices might involuntarily contradict a verbal message telling others that we're doing all right. A wink and a nod might deliberately send the nonverbal message that what we're saying just isn't so.

Zwozdiak-Myers and Capel (2005, 110) claimed that much communication is nonverbal, and nonverbal signals match each other. For example, if you are praising someone and smiling and looking pleased or if you are telling them off and looking stern and sounding firm, you are sending a consistent message and are perceived as sincere. On the other hand, if you are smiling when telling someone off or are looking bored when praising someone you are sending conflicting messages that cause confusion and misunderstanding.

We should be aware that when verbal and nonverbal messages contradict, people tend—for a number of reasons—to believe the nonverbal. In this way, it's simply much easier to lie than to control a range of nonverbal reactions: such as the facial expressions, pupil dilation in eyes, and tension in vocal cords, pulse rate, muscle tone, etc. The control of such things is well beyond our voluntary reach. Accordingly, nonverbal information is often found to be more reliable than the verbal one since people rely mostly on nonverbal messages when they receive conflicting information, so it should be noticed the dangers inherent in sending opposing message. As the German psychiatrist Freud noted, "Though we may lie with our lips, betrayal oozes out of us at every pore." In sum, nonverbal actions are not easily controlled consciously, they can precisely betray one's true feeling without distortion and deception.

2.7.3 Replacement

Nonverbal behavior can be used to replace verbal behavior to convey certain meanings, particularly if they are simple or monosyllabic. It may indicate more permanent characteristics, such as sex or age, moderately long-lasting features, such as personality, attitude, and relatively short-term states of a person. In the later case, we may see a downtrodden worker walk into his office with a facial expression that substitutes for the statement, "I've had a rotten day." With a little practice, we soon learn to identify a wide range of these substitute nonverbal displays—all the way from "It's been a fantastic day!" to "Oh, God, I am miserable!" We often giving a sympathetic hug for a weeping friend can produce a better effect than saying any soothing words. When meeting a very special friend, we are prone to enlarge the size of smile and throw open the arms to greet him or her, which is a substitute for all the words to convey the same feeling.

Sometimes, when substituting nonverbal behavior doesn't get the desired response, the communicator tries to verbally clarify the message. For example, when a woman wants her date to stop trying to be physically intimate with her, she may stiffen, stare straight ahead. If the suitor doesn't stop, she might say something like "Look, John, please don't ruin a nice friendship."

2.7.4 Accentuation

Nonverbal messages can accent or moderate parts of the verbal messages, such as the feelings or emotions conveyed by verbal messages by adding more information to the expressions. Accenting is much like underlining or italicizing written words to emphasize them. A forceful gesture, raised voice, exaggerated facial expression all give "accent" to the intended message. In some instances, one set of nonverbal cues can accent or moderate other nonverbal cues. In addition, accentuation is considered as a type of complement because it provides a complementary message to verbal code. For example, in some countries, you can tell your friend that you are pleased with his/her performance, and pat him/her on the shoulder at the same time, that will complement what you said.

2.7.5 Complementing

Complementing is closely related to repeating. Although messages that repeat can stand alone, nonverbal behavior can modify or elaborate on verbal messages, and add more information to messages. When the verbal and nonverbal channels are complementary, messages are usually decoded more accurately. Some evidence suggests that complementary nonverbal signals may be helpful when attempting to recall the verbal message and can reinforce the general tone or attitude of verbal communication. A downcast expression and slumping posture might accompany words of discouragement or depression; upright posture, a smile, and animated movement might reinforce a verbal expression about winning a recent promotion. Accordingly, when clarity is of utmost importance, as in a job interview or when making up with a loved one after a fight, we should be especially concerned with making the meanings of verbal and nonverbal behavior complement each other.

2.7.6 Regulation

People use nonverbal messages to tell someone to do or not to do something. That is to say, nonverbal messages can be used to control the person's behaviors. For example, the pause in a conversation is used as a signal for turn-taking. Silence for a moment sends the message that speakers are ready to begin their speech. Direct eye contact with someone means that the channels of communication are open. Nodding the head in agreement indicates that the speaker should continue talking. Accordingly, certain nonverbal movements and gestures are used to regulate the flow, the pace, and the back-and-forth nature of verbal communication. Communicators usually do this by two ways: one is that they coordinate their own verbal and nonverbal behaviors in the production of messages, and the other is that they coordinate behaviors with their interaction partners.

Firstly, people regulate their own production of messages in various ways. Sometimes they use nonverbal signs to segment units of interaction. For example, posture changes may display a topic change; a gesture may forecast the verbalization of a particular idea; pause may help organize spoken information into units.

Secondly, people regulate the flow of verbal and nonverbal behavior between themselves and interactants. The way one person stops talking and the other starts in a smooth, synchronized manner may be as important to a satisfactory interaction as the content. There are rules for regulating conversations, but they are generally implicit. When the other person frequently interrupts or is inattentive, we may feel this person is making a statement about the relationship, perhaps one of disrespect.

Conversational regulators involve several kinds of nonverbal cues. When we want to show that we finish the speaking and the other person can start, we may increase our eye contact with ending declarative or interrogative statement. If the other person still doesn't figuratively pick up the conversational ball, we might extend silence or interject a "filler" such as "you know" or "so, ah." To keep the other person from speaking in a conversation, we have to keep long pauses from occurring, decrease eye contact, and perhaps raise the volume of our voice.

Conversational beginnings and endings also act as regulatory points. When we greet others, eye contact and a slight head movement may be present. The hands are also used in greetings for salutes, waves, handshakes, handclaps, etc. Research has shown that saying good-bye can elicit many nonverbal behaviors. The most common includes the breaking eye contact more often, positioning one's body towards an exit, and leaning forward and nodding, etc.

We should notice that none of these functions of nonverbal behaviors operate alone. We convey our emotions with our face, body and other nonverbal cues. We use hand gestures while talking to help express our ideas. We use eye contact to tell the conversational partner when it is time to switch speaking turns. We can sign to express emotions and attitudes, and we can present ourselves and arrange the interaction by using nonverbal cues too. Therefore, in most communication settings both verbal and nonverbal communications are working together rather than in isolation. This tendency indicates that a holistic study encompassing both verbal and nonverbal systems is necessary to fully understand the process of human communication.

2.8 The Importance of Nonverbal Behavior in Communication

Despite the fundamental role that nonverbal communication plays in communication, second language teachers often neglect the teaching of nonverbal communication, which can result in learners' failure in grasping the true nature of communication in the target language. This failure is due to the fact that nonverbal behavior reveals basic cultural traits by which people are able to gather clues about the underlying attitudes and values of the members of the target community. It can be concluded that the study of nonverbal communication is part of the study of a bigger paradigm known as intercultural communication (Gudykunst, 2003; Wiseman, 2003).

Barnlund's (1968, 536-537) statement can show us the importance of nonverbal communication: most of the critical meanings generated in human encounters are elicited by nonverbal behaviors with or without the aid of words. "From the moment of recognition until the moment of separation, people observe each other with all their senses, hearing, pause and intonation, attending to dress and carriage, observing glance and facial tension, as well as noting word choice and syntax. Every harmony or disharmony of signals guides the interpretation of passing mood or enduring attribute. Out of the evaluation of kinetic, vocal and verbal cues, decisions are made to argue or agree, to laugh or blush, to relax or resist, to continue or to cut off conversation."

To be specifically, we can summarize the importance as follows.

First, nonverbal behavior accounts for most of the meanings we get from conversations. As discussed in Chapter One, 93% of a message is transmitted by the speaker's tone of voice and facial expressions, in which 38% through the voice and 55% through the face. This estimation at least tells us that nonverbal behaviors are so important that they deserve much of our attention. By developing the awareness of the signs and signals of nonverbal communication, we can gather clues about underlying attitudes and values of other cultures and more easily understand other people, and more effectively communicate with them.

Second, nonverbal behavior is significant because it spontaneously reflects the speakers' subconsciousness. So we can use others' actions to learn about their affective or emotional states and to form impressions of them. For example, if someone looks annoyed and says "I'm glad you come," the mixed message is difficult to interpret, but we tend to choose the nonverbal messages because we reason that the person has less control over that aspect of communication. The accomplished communicators are fully aware of the messages sent nonverbally so they consciously attempt to control the kind of impression they are making. Such impressions are made not only through smiles, frowns, eye contact and body movements but also through the furnishing and arrangement of offices, the house lived in, the clothes worn and the accent cultivated.

The third reason is that we cannot avoid communicating. Even if we choose silence, the nonverbal dimension of our communication is always present. And even if we move ourselves bodily from the scene of interaction, our absence may speak loudly. Thus, verbal communication and nonverbal communication are integrated in human communication. The latter isn't the rest of human interaction with the absence of verbal communication, nor is the additional complementary one, but an indispensable action which plays a functional role in human communication. On the one hand, a single verbal communication without any nonverbal communication can't be easily understood by people; on the other hand, it is companied by words that nonverbal communication can express explicit meanings, and there is no isolated nonverbal communication. It is the cooperation of verbal communication and nonverbal communication that forms the whole process of effective human communication. That is to say, we might see better that verbal messages are more appropriate for some exchanges and nonverbal messages for others, and that both have their natural and complementary roles to play in human society.

Therefore, a successful communication involves both the understanding of language and the nonverbal aspects of communication that are part of any speech community.

2.9 Conclusion

This chapter has made a historical review of previous research on nonverbal communication and some issues related to it. It particularly focuses on the discussion of some basic concepts related to nonverbal communication, including its definition, classification, characteristics, the differences between verbal and nonverbal communications, and its functions and importance. The purpose is to provide a broad overview of nonverbal communication in general and help to understand this specific "mechanics" in communication. It also gives the researchers an insight and theoretical base and facilitates them to know what others feel about this problem in similar or identical situations.

Part II

Nonverbal Communication and Intercultural Communication

Chapter Three

Cultural Impact on Nonverbal X-Factor

3.1 Introduction

This chapter will explore the cultural influence on nonverbal X-Factor in intercultural communication. It begins with the discussion of culture and its relationship with nonverbal communication, and then focuses on the cultural differences of isolated nonverbal behaviors and the misunderstandings resulting from cultural differences. The main purpose is to provide a wide view of nonverbal behaviors from the intercultural communicative perspectives.

3.2 Background Information

From the previous discussion, we have already known that nonverbal behavior is culturally determined. A simple gesture can have several meanings depending on the cultural context. So the use of nonverbal behavior when dealing with people from different cultures is sometimes problematic and the possibility for misunderstanding and disagreement regarding nonverbal communication is great because people tend to look for nonverbal cues when verbal messages are unclear or ambiguous.

Adjusting to another culture can prove to be a challenge. Culture shapes the way people think, the way people act and the way people interact and communicate with each other and it does so from the moment we were born. We seldom are aware of our own cultural biases since cultural imprinting begins at a very early age. Some cultural values are taught explicitly and most are absorbed subconsciously. Thus, our lack of awareness and subconscious biases creates problems when we try to translate our body language across cultures. Moreover, each cultural world operates according to its own internal dynamic, its own principle and its own laws—written and unwritten. As

LeBaron (2003) stated, "Since nonverbal behavior arises from our cultural common sense (our ideas about what is appropriate, normal, and effective as communication in relationships), we use different systems of understanding gestures, posture, silence, emotional expression, touch, physical appearance, and other nonverbal cues."Nonverbal behavior has tremendous impact on the whole communication process, so it is vital to know and accept these differences in a multicultural environment. This is increasingly important, especially in the context of globalization. Whether we are talking about business meetings, tourism, international programs or other forms of cultural interaction, knowing how the other cultures communicate is essential for establishing a solid relationship and it is a form of showing respect to cultural diversity.

Therefore, learning the cultural do's and don'ts can avoid miscommunication and help generate respect and understanding in intercultural communication. On the basis of the discussion of the relationship between nonverbal communication and culture, this chapter will explore the cultural differences of dimensions in nonverbal communication.

3.3 Nonverbal Communication and Culture

The interaction of culture and communication is so pervasive that separating the two is virtually impossible. In contrast to verbal communication, nonverbal messages are less systematized but are more ambiguous and almost entirely culturally construed. Successful interaction in intercultural setting requires the communicators from differing cultures to navigate both the verbal and nonverbal messages so that complete and shared meaning is created.

3.3.1 Definition and Functions of Culture

To fully appreciate how cultures can influence nonverbal behavior, we must first have a working conception of culture.

An early definition was provided by Tylor (1967), who considered culture as a complex whole of the social traditions and a prerequisite for people to be a member of the society. Hartley and Karinch (2007) treated culture as "nothing more than accepted social norms for a group" (38). According to Samovar, Porter, and McDaniel (1999), culture refers to "the rules for living and functioning in society" (10). And the shared rules are absorbed through social conditioning and the communicative and interactive experiences that children have as they develop. In this sense, culture is learned and is transmitted from generation to generation (Samovar et al., 11). Chen and Starosta (2007, 25) defined culture as "a negotiated set of shared symbolic systems that guide individuals' behaviors and incline them to function as a group."

Thus the word "culture" has tremendous meanings. It can be a set of fundamental ideas, practices, and experiences of a group of people; it can refer to beliefs, norms, and attitudes that are used to guide our behaviors and to solve problems. Moreover, we can view it as a system of expression practices and mutual meaning connected to our behaviors.

The function of culture is to provide a common framework for people to participate in daily activities. Basically, it has two main functions. First, culture provides a context in which three aspects of human society are embedded: linguistic, physical and psychological. Second, it can provide structure, stability and security that are pursued by the group members to keep themselves as a healthy system (Chen & Starosta, 2007, 26).

Therefore, culture enables people to deal with their survival activities such as the securing of basic needs through work. Because human beings are primarily social animals, their culture provides them with a basis for their identity as well as their social functioning. The human sense of self is thus interdependent and intertwined with the human sense of social belonging and culture (Samovar et al., 1999, 11).

3.3.2 Features of Culture

Many of the ways that culture is transmitted are symbolic, and make culture highly symbolic. For example, language, images and nonverbal communicative modalities such as gestures are all symbolic ways that human beings communicate culture with each other and define their own rules of living. Culture is dynamic, so it is continuously changing by the new individual influences and the interaction with others. Cultural is also ethnocentric since it provides a strong sense of group identity which enables them to identify themselves with other cultural groups. Culture is therefore a source of boundaries between people, making it centered on its own ethnic origins (Samovar et al., 1999, 12).

The features of culture lead to perceive nonverbal communication from two distinct perspectives: that of the modes of nonverbal communication that are universal to all human cultural groups and those that are culture specific. The universal types of nonverbal communication often make it possible for people from different parts of the world to understand each other better. Studies show that people from different cultures have similar physiological reactions to universal facial expressions. Smiling is universally recognized as an expression of happiness while frowning the brows and tensing and hardening the facial muscles are recognized as anger. Sadness is also universally understood by wider eyes and elongating of the face.

However, we should not be over-optimistic about this. All cultures do not recognize universal facial expressions at the same rates. The meaning of nonverbal behavior varies across cultures, and what is acceptable in one culture may be taboo in another. Sometimes the simple mistakes we may make in dealing with different cultures can ruin a relationship or make communication breakdown. Like verbal behavior, nonverbal language is learned and rule-governed behavior. That is, a social and cultural environment, rather than our genetic heritage, determines our nonverbal communication system. We are not born with the knowledge of nonverbal symbols and acquire such knowledge from people around us. For example, we all laugh, but our culture teaches us when, to whom, how much and under what circumstances we may laugh.

Therefore, nonverbal behavior is culturally patterned and governed by cultural rules, and the same nonverbal code may be interpreted differently by people from different cultures. The study of nonverbal communication is directly linked to the study of culture. It is thus significant to learn about the relationship between nonverbal communication and culture.

3.3.3 Relationship between Nonverbal Communication and Culture

3.3.3.1 Nonverbal Communication is a Part of Culture

That nonverbal behavior is a part of the culture and should be taught is supported in the literature. He Daokuan argued that nonverbal communication is a part of the culture that is covert, implicit and hidden (cited in Hu Wenzhong, 1988, 162). Brown (1987) pointed out, "The expression of culture is so bound up in nonverbal communication that the barriers to culture learning are more nonverbal than verbal" (209). Kirch (1979) considered that culturally inappropriate body language manifests a foreign accent as much as inadequate phonological knowledge. Raffler-Engel (1980) stated since the goal of FL teaching is to make students bilingualism, then they should be taught truly bilingual, which implies that the students should become bikinesic. Lafayette (1988, 49) also stated that one goal of language teaching is to help students be able to use appropriate common gestures.

Most theorists maintain that nonverbal behavior is highly culture-dependent. As Fiksdal (1990, 47) claimed, "Nonverbal behavior is inherently ambiguous because it is highly dependent on context for its interpretation…difficulty of agreeing on universal meanings for any gesture since gestures are culturally and individually grounded." Wardaugh (1985) remarked, "We tend to assume that nonverbal behavior, so much of which is unconscious, is universal, and we do not realize that most of it is in fact learned and therefore specific to the cultural group in which it is found" (79). Brown (1987) also commented that nonverbal behavior is subtle and subconscious in a native speaker, comparatively, verbal language seems quite mechanical and systematic. As for its unconscious nature, Thomas and Tchudi (1999) asserted that "people's ability to control their body language is grossly exaggerated…Body language is real, complex, extremely precise, and inextricably bound to our use of spoken languages as a way of accentuating, highlighting, and amplifying what we mean" (133).

We can find many illustrations about the culture-determined nonverbal behaviors. Most discussion on nonverbal communication in FL teaching relates to emblems which are symbolic actions where movement has a very specific verbal meaning, known to most members of a culture, and typically are employed with the intention of sending a message. These emblems are used to replace a word, phrase, or expression, or to repeat or qualify the verbal message. Emblems usually involve the hands and/or the arms, sometimes the head movements, facial movements, posture and leg movements. For example, the common North American emblems include the hitchhiker's thumb, the time-out "T," and the peace sign. The common French emblems include sweeping the hand over the head to indicate "*J'en ai ras le bol*," pulling an imaginary hair out of the palm of the hand to indicate "*Il a un poil dans le main*," and pulling the skin down under the eye to indicate "*Je ne crois pas un seul mot*." Therefore, the use and meaning of specific emblems can vary among different cultures, misunderstanding or failure to communication may occur when nonmembers of a culture try to use or interpret emblems according to the meaning assigned to the emblems in their own culture.

3.3.3.2 The Same Features of Nonverbal Communication and Culture

Nonverbal behavior and culture have some common features. Firstly, both of them are all-pervasive, multidimensional and boundless; they are everywhere and in everything. Hall (1959) used three metaphors to describe the invisible aspect of culture and nonverbal communication: the silent language, the hidden dimension, the dance of life. Samovar and Porter (1995, 186) sated that "culture was invisible, omnipresent and learned," nonverbal communication has the same qualities.

Secondly, both of them need to be learned. Many nonverbal behaviors are learnt after birth, not born with us. We begin to learn our culture in early life consciously and unconsciously through the process of socialization. Culture is a shared system within a relatively large group of people, so the only way for group members to reinforce this shared symbolic system is through a learning process. Culture can be learned through proverb, folklore, art, mass media and other channels. We learn our culture and the way of communication in our culture from those people with whom we interact in our process of socialization: our parents, teachers, friends and even strangers. Through learning, a baby can become a resident in a community. Therefore, in this process of learning, we should try to avoid the tendency to interpret nonverbal behaviors as we do for our own cultural groups. The more we know about others' cultures, the easier it is to understand them. Moreover, we should try to avoid the risk of ignoring nonverbal codes with meaning.

Thirdly, nonverbal behaviors, like culture, are largely beyond our consciousness. People use nonverbal signals spontaneously, without thinking about what gesture, what posture, or what interpersonal distance is appropriate to the situation. For instance, American people will automatically use direct eye contact when they are talking to people. When an American puts his feet up on his desk, his behavior signifies a relaxed, informal attitude. These actions are habitual in their culture. Words are relatively easy to control and nonverbal behaviors are not. Because nonverbal communication is so reliable, people generally have more faith in nonverbal cues than they do in verbal messages. For example, if a person says one thing but transmits a conflicting message nonverbally, listeners almost invariably believe the nonverbal signal. Chances are, if we can read other people's nonverbal messages correctly, we can interpret their underlying attitudes and intentions and respond appropriately (Allen, 1999).

We should point out that culture does not always determine the message of nonverbal communication. The individual's personality, the context, and the relationship also influence its meaning. Like verbal language, nonverbal language is linked to person's cultural background. When one person's nonverbal language matches that of another, there will be increased comfort. Accordingly, the study of nonverbal behavior and culture is meaningful and necessary if we are to appreciate all aspects of intercultural interaction. With the knowledge of important cultural differences in nonverbal behaviors, we will be able to gather clues about underlying attitudes and values. We will find some basic cultural traits by nonverbal behaviors.

3.3.3.3 Nonverbal Communication is Integrated in Instructional Models

Nonverbal communication is involved in several instructional models in language teaching. Allen (1999) summarized these models including nonverbal communication. For example, in the audio-motor unit and the series method developed by Gouin in 1880 (Brown, 1987, 34-35), gestures play an important role. The underlying concept is that simple actions associated with language will facilitate retention. Savignon's (1983, 207) Theater Arts component involves pantomime. The comprehension approach (Winitz, 1981, xiii) makes liberal use of gestures. New vocabulary in the direct method (Hadley, 1993, 92) is presented by paraphrases, miming the action, or manipulating objects. In the early stages of the silent way (Stevick, 1996, 220), hand gestures are used to indicate where further work is needed and to elicit desired responses. Lozanov's suggestology (Asher, 1981, 189) is largely dependent upon the teachers' nonverbal behaviors. Total Physical Response (TPR) synchronizes the language with body movements (Asher, Kusudo & Torre, 1974). Teachers' nonverbal behaviors are important in the natural approach (Terrell, 1986). The Capretz Method (Capretz, Abetti & Marie-Odile, 1987) emphasizes the fact that communication involves more than words and attempts to initiate learners of French in the nonverbal communication in which people engage every day.

From the abovementioned language teaching instructional models, we can see that nonverbal communication plays an important role in teaching and learning, and it is also an inevitable way to learn English.

3.4 Cultural Differences in Nonverbal Communication

In this part, we will discuss the cultural impact on isolated nonverbal behaviors from five aspects: appearance, kinesics, paralanguage, proxemics and chronemics.

3.4.1 Appearance

In all cultures people decorate and display their bodies. Clothes are the main channel which can indicate occupational roles, for example, there are special uniforms for some occupational groups, such as the policeman, the costumes for hiking and for striking. Clothing habits can show sex, cultural background, attitudes and particular culturally related values. That is, clothes have symbolic meanings. For instance, the Scottish tartans reveal the local symbolic systems. The Ethiopian toga can be worn to indicate gaiety, sadness, pride, abasement, going to church, mourning, etc. In some areas of Arab, Arab women stay at home most of time and are subject to powerful conventions about modesty. When they appear in public, they keep themselves covered very well and veiled, only eye showing. In modern times, women adorn themselves with cosmetics and ear-rings, corsets and padding, trying to make an impressive appearance to others. Bodily decoration includes: body-painting, tattooing, nose-rings, etc., which may purposefully or unintentionally convey culturally determined messages to others.

Hairstyle is another channel to show the physical characteristic, which can give positive or negative impressions and has considerable cultural implications. Within a particular culture, particular hairstyle fashions may be the result of peer group pressure or attempts to conform to be acceptable among the own group. Hair is often styled to be socially acceptable in a particular cultural group. In other cultures, individuals could be expected to style their hair in culturally acceptable ways. These are often taught from infancy within family situations. Therefore, a hairstyle can send subtle messages within a particular cultural group, but it can also be a determining factor in varying degrees from one culture to the next.

3.4.2 Kinesics

Kinesics, or body language, signifies any small movement of any part of the body. It can be defined as any reflexive or non-reflexive movement or position used to communicate an emotional, attitudinal, or informational message to someone else (Wood, 1976). Kinesics includes various kinds of gestures, postures, facial expressions, eye contact, movements of the head, feet, and legs, forms of greeting and their relation to communication. Certain kinds of body movements are physiological, such as yawning, stretching, relaxing and so on. Other kinesics patterns—such as staring, walking slumped over, raising a clenched fist, showing a victory sign, and the like—are personally and culturally conditioned.

White and Gardner (2012) divided the body movements into two types: the close body language and the open body language, which involve looking at how we use the hands, the arms, the trunk and the head. For example, if someone sits down, folds his/her arms, cross his/her legs, he/she can be described as closed body language. Lyle (1990) argued that when people use their bodies in this way, they are erecting a barrier, and such action may have a physiological basis. The author calls it a form of self-preservation since people may experience nervousness or chronic anxiety. On the other hand, when people expose their bodies, they use open body language since there is a distinct "lack of barriers of any sort" (cited from Borg, 2008, 26). Compared with the close body language, the limbs are not brought in close to the body. So the most appealing posture to adopt when talking to people is one which shows an open personality (Lyle, 1990). The common open body language in talking is like this: legs are side by side, but not tightly clamped together, with hands resting in the lap or being used from time to time, to underline what is being said.

3.4.2.1 Gesture

Gestures, or hand and arm movements, are one way we send nonword messages through our body parts. They are physical movements of arms, legs, hands, torsos and heads. As Feyereisen and de Lannoy (1991) hypothesized that "gestures would be triggered during speech production because meaning embodied in motor schemata would be activated" (73). Through the movement of each of the body parts, we can accent and reinforce our verbal messages. And we can observe how others punctuate their verbal effects with gestures. Gestures can occur with or without speech. Some gestures are spontaneous, some are highly ritualized and have very special meanings. Observing the hand movements of one person while he/she is talking, we can get a good picture of the internal emotional state of the person.

Gestures are so common in daily life that attract special attention of many experts. Generally speaking, a speaker uses gestures for two purposes: to reinforce an idea or to help describe something. Through gestures we can express our attitudes towards others.

1. Category of Gestures

Although gestural typologies abound in the literature, there is little agreement among researches about the sorts of distinctions. Based on the often-adopted category of McNeill (1992), we can classify gestures into the following categories:

(1) Iconic gestures. Iconic gestures may be kinetographic, representing some bodily actions, like sweeping the floor, or pictographic, representing the actual form of an object, like outlining the shape of a box. They are closely related to the semantic content of speech. As Schegloff (1984) put it, "Shape links them to lexical

components of the talk" (275). For example, we usually press the fingers against the lips as a signal to others to be quiet.

(2) Metaphoric gestures. They may be pictographic or kinetographic like iconics, but they represent an abstract idea rather than a concrete object or action. They give an image of the invisible. An example is circling the finger at the temple to signify the "wheels of thought" in America.

(3) Deictic gestures. They have a pointing function, either actual or metaphoric. They are used to indicate objects, events and are context-dependent. For example, we may point behind us to represent past time.

(4) Beat gestures. They have the same form regardless of the content to which they are linked. In a beat gesture, the hand moves with a rhythmical pulse that lines up with the stress peaks of speech. A typical beat gesture is a simple flick of the hand or fingers up and down, or back and forth, the movement is short and fast. Although beat gestures may serve a referential function, their primary use is to regulate the flow of speech. An example can be better illustrated by Bill Clinton's statements during the Monica Lewinsky trial. While giving the testimony, he made his protestations with quite a number of beats. Take the quote: "I did not have sexual relations with that woman." While saying the four words "not have sexual relations," he made four sharp and rapid downwards movements of his pointed index finger for each of these words.

(5) Emblems. They involve the use of gestures to communicate a message typically recognized by the community. The meanings of emblems are learned along the way in a culture, and are often used consciously by members of that culture when they wish to present specific ideas to others. The emblems can be a great source of misunderstanding in intercultural communication since the shared meanings for an emblem in one culture may be quite different in another. For example, in Turkey, to say "no" nonverbally, one would nod his/her head up and back, raising his/her eyebrows at the same time. By contrast, wagging one's head from side to side doesn't mean "no" in Turkish, it means "I don't understand."

2. The Communicative Power of Gestures

The communicative power of gestures can be shown in a number of ways. According to Hostetter (2011), there are three potential mechanisms of gestures in communication. First, gestures could improve communication since they are particularly adept at conveying information about spatial ideas, spatial relations, and motor events. When describing spatial information speakers gesture more than when describing nonspatial information and listeners may benefit primarily when the imagistic referent is important to the content of the message. Second, gestures are communicative because they frequently convey information that is not present in the accompanying verbal description. Gestures appear to help speakers produce verbal descriptions that are informative and fluent. They do alter the content and quality of speakers' verbal descriptions. Third, gestures are communicative because they provide additional cues when speech comprehension is difficult. Under this view, gestures may be more helpful to listeners with weak verbal skills than to listeners with strong verbal skills because the gestures can provide a nonverbal means of acquiring the same information. The three potential mechanisms presume that gestures have a direct influence on communication. Listeners benefit from gestures because they process the spatial information conveyed by the gestures.

Besides the above three mechanisms, gestures may also contribute to comprehension by capturing and maintaining listeners' attention. Listeners who can see a speaker's gestures may be more engaged and thus pay more attention to the speaker's messages than listeners who cannot see a speaker's gestures. In addition to any benefits for immediate comprehension, gestures may also have long-term mnemonic or educational benefits. Listeners who hear a message and see accompanying gestures may not only better understand the message in the moment, but they may also have an easier time remembering the message later on than a listener who only hears the message. Similar to the mnemonic benefits of imagery more generally (Paivio, 1991), gestures may provide an additional cue that can aid information retrieval. Furthermore, the additional cues provided by gestures may actually promote learning. Listeners who see a lesson with gestures may have better comprehension and memory of the material.

Several researchers have testified that gestures can promote a positive rapport between speakers and listeners. For example, listeners rate speakers who gesture as more competent and composed than speakers who do not gesture (Maricchiolo, Gnisci, Bonaiuto, & Ficca, 2009). Listeners also report liking speakers who gesture more than speakers who do not gesture (Kelly & Goldsmith, 2004).

In educational environment, gesture is one area that has received some empirical attention among applied-linguistic researchers. They argue that speaking and gestures appear to be linked. In general, the louder someone speaks, the more emphatic gestures are used, and vice versa. Studies show that gestures function as an indicator of language development. For example, Mayberry and Nicoladis (2000) found iconic and beat gestures have a strong correlation with children's language development. At the pre-speaking stage, children mainly use deictic gesture, such as waving and clapping. However, as their speaking ability develops, they start to use iconic gestures and beat gestures. Accordingly, understanding or interpreting nonverbal messages accurately is especially important for second language learners whose comprehension skill is more limited. Compared with the native-English-speaking children, the ESL children comprehend much less gestural information than the native speakers, which Mohan and Helmer (1988) attributed to their lower language proficiency.

Some researches show that gestures can facilitate teaching and learning. For example, Lazaraton (2004) conducted a survey on the speech and gesture used by FL teacher of English from a micro-analytic perspective. The results show that gestures and other nonverbal behaviors are forms of input to L2 learners that must be considered a salient factor in classroom-based second language acquisition research. Sueyoshi and Hardison (2005) found that the presence of gestures improves the comprehension of bilinguals who are of low proficiency in their second language but don't improve the comprehension of bilinguals who are of high proficiency.

3. Cultural Difference

Gestures vary according to cultures. The type of culture we live in has an impact on our degree of gesturing. "Gestural" language therefore often contributes more to misunderstanding than to effective communication. In many cases, nonverbal actions can support what a person is saying while other times, it can be contradictory. Thus, it is important to know how to read nonverbal communication in order to have productive personal and professional relationships with others. When traveling to another country, foreign visitors soon learn that not all gestures are universal. The West and the East differ substantially in their gesturing. They have very different gestures which have the same meanings. Also, they have gestures which have no equivalent for.

Since gestures are culturally determined, the interpretation often results in misunderstanding during intercultural encounters. People learn the gestures and movements of their respective cultures and express their thinking or feeling through them. For example, sticking out the tongue may be a form of mockery in the West, but in Polynesia it serves as a greeting and a sign of reverence. Clapping is a North American way of applauding, but in Spain and the Orient it is a means of summoning the waiter. Some Latinos, Middle Easterners and southern Europeans use considerable arm waving when they communicate, whilst this is interpreted as too emotional in Anglo-European contexts. In most Asian cultures, dignified and controlled communication involves a minimum of bodily gestures. A misinterpretation of gesture can lead to negative feelings and quite unexpected reactions. Some universal gestures which can arouse misinterpretation are presented here.

"OK" Sign

The "OK" sign has totally different meanings in different cultures. How the "OK" emblem can be interpreted depends on the culture. This emblem could create a number of communication misunderstandings across cultures. For example, the OK sign means zero or worthless in France. It is a symbol for money in Japan. So if you're doing business in Japan and you make this sign for "OK" a Japanese may think you're asking them for a bribe. While it is a derogatory statement and/or obscenity in Mediterranean countries and often used to infer that a man is homosexual. Show a Greek man this sign and he may think you are inferring you or he is gay, while a Turk might think you are calling him an "arsehole" (A. Pease & B. Pease, 2004, 119). In the 1950s, Richard Nixon, before he became the American president, visited Latin America on a goodwill tour to try to patch up strained relations with the locals. As he stepped out of his plane he showed the waiting crowds the American "OK" signal and was stunned as they began booing and hissing at him. Being unaware of local body language customs, Nixon's OK signal had been read as "You're all a bunch of arseholes" (A. Pease & B. Pease, 2004, 120).

Hand Motions

Hand motions alone can convey many meanings: "Come here," "Go away," "It's okay," and "That's expensive!" are just a few examples. The gestures for these phrases often differ across cultures. For example, beckoning people to come with the palm up is common in the United States. This same gesture in Philippines, Korea, and parts of Latin America as well as other countries is considered rude. In some countries, only animals would be beckoned with the palm up.

Head Nodding

Another gesture that can be taken completely differently depending upon where you live is nodding the head. In most parts of the world, it is a positive or "yes" gesture. Northern Europeans usually indicate agreement by nodding their heads up and down, and shaking the head from side to side to indicate disagreement. The Greeks have for at least three thousand years used the upward nod for disagreement and the downward nod for agreement. In the Middle East and the part of Africa a person nods his/her head when in disagreement. In Japan, the head nod may only mean continually paying attention to, not necessarily agreement. You might find that a Japanese totally disagrees with you but will nod out of respect until you have finished speaking.

Waving Goodbye

There are many manners of waving goodbye: Americans face the palm outward and move the hand side to side; Italians face the palm inward and move the fingers facing the other person; French and Germans face the hand horizontal and move the fingers towards the person leaving.

Warning

When expressing the idea of warning not to do something or indicating that what the other person is doing is wrong, an American wags his/her fingers with forefinger of one hand raised while other fingers clasped. The raised forefinger is wagged from side to side. This gesture does not exist in Chinese culture though some Chinese understand the meaning of it.

Using Thumbs

The gesture with thumbs is also frequent used nonverbal behavior. The "thumbs up," has three meanings in America, Singapore, New Zealand: it's commonly used by hitch-hikers who are thumbing a lift; used as an OK singnal; and when the thumb is jerked sharply upwards it becomes an insult, meaning "up yours" or "sit on this." In some countries, such as Greece, the thumb is thrust forward and its main meaning is "get stuffed!" In Nigeria, this gesture is a rude insult. In Australia, it is an obscene insult. Another funny example is spinning one's finger around his/her ear. This is known as the "you're crazy" sign in America and in some other nations, but in Argentina, it means "you have a phone call!"

When Europeans count from one to five, they use the Thumb-Up to mean "one", the index finger becomes "two", whereas most English-speaking people count "one" on the index finger and "two" on the middle finger. In this case the Thumb-Up will represent the number "five." Being the most powerful digit on the hand it is used as a sign of power in combination with other gestures, as a power and superiority signal or in situations where people try to get us "under their thumbs" (A. Pease & B. Pease, 2004, 121).

3.4.2.2 Posture

Posture is the way people hold their bodies when they sit, stand or walk, and it can send positive or negative nonverbal messages. Scholars have found at least 10000 significant different body attitudes capable of being maintained steadily. An individual posture in a specific culture can send off a strong message. Posture cues constitute very effective signs of a person's inner state as well as his/her behavior expectations of others. Although many people can describe posture when asked, it is not by any means universal since posture differs on culture, personality, religion, occupation, social class, gender, age, health and status.

Body movement can be used to detect the beginning and end of conversation. People usually give some clues when they want to change topics, to speak, or to end the conversation, such as, leaning forward 40 degrees, breaking eye contact, smiling, and tapping the floor. These cues can effectively alter communication. Considering the person who stands with arms crossed, looks constantly at a clock, taps the foot repeatedly, and breaks eye contact frequently, these signals usually mean it is time to end the conversation and leave.

The popularity of one posture over another and the emotion conveyed by a given posture seem to be largely determined by culture. For example, sitting on one's heels with knees resting on the floor is a formal sitting position in Japan, and is one position of prayer for the Moslem. Posture offers insight into a culture's deep structure. The bowing of Japanese with a lower status must be deeper than a superior. It is the superior who determines when the bowing is to end. People of equal ranks bow in the same manner and end at the same time.

Cultural Difference

Posture is also a constant source of cultural misunderstanding. The same posture may cause serious conflicts when it is transferred to another cultural setting. For example, standing with one's hands on one's hips can be viewed as extremely hostile in some Asian cultures, whilst it is taken as natural in European ones. Americans feel very relaxed at home and in their offices. They may sometimes sit on the carpeted floor, lean far back in their chair and even put feet on the desks. Some American business executives enjoy relaxing with their feet up on their desks. But showing a person from Saudi Arabia or Thailand the sole of one's foot is extremely insulting, because the foot is considered the dirtiest part of the body. We can imagine the reaction in Thailand when a foreign shoe company distributed an advertisement showing a pair of shoes next to a sacred sculpture of Buda. Another example, the squatting posture can betray one's cultural background. Chinese peasants in the northwestern regions have a strong habit of squatting. They have to learn to rest in a squatting position. Most Westerners look on this as a rather improper primitive and childish position.

3.4.2.3 Facial Expression and Eye Contact

Facial expression and eye contact are the most readily observed gestures. We focus our eyes on the face more often than on any other part of the body. Lesikar and Flatley (2005, 425-427) stated that the face and eyes are by far the most important features of body language. Facial expression results from one or more motions or positions of the muscles of the face. We look at the face and eyes to determine much of the meaning behind body language and nonverbal communication.

1. Facial Expression

The face is sometimes regarded as one of the most predominant channels of expressing attitudes or behavior or conveying particular emotions. It carries meaning that is determined by situations and relationships. Six basic human emotions can be easily reflected on our face: surprise, fear, anger, disgust, happiness and sadness. The Chinese people have always said that a person's character is clearly written on his/her face. This belief is reflected in Chinese operas in which face paintings are used to indicate the personalities and dispositions of the character. In communication, we constantly observe and interpret the meanings of expressions from the others' face. For example, sometimes a facial expression is used as a signal, such as winking an eye as a gesture of approval, or sticking out the tongue to signify playful distaste. Facial expression can express shock or great surprise. In these emotional states, a person's mouth is wide open because the jaw's muscles are relaxed due to shock and the chin drops. There is, however, a time when the mouth unconsciously opens and it is not due to shock or surprise. This happens when a person concentrates on one thing so intently, for example, when attempting to fit together delicate parts of a mechanism.

Facial expression itself is a "thing" that must be interpreted by the communicative partner as a sign of an emotional reaction. The translation of facial expression to emotional feeling in one's communicative partner is not a direct cause and effect situation but is rather the result of the interpretation of the expression. For example, the autistic people have difficulty in understanding the relationship between facial expressions and human feelings which in turn leads to a sense of social disconnection from others because the autistic person does not have the ability to understand the abstract symbolism of the facial expressions. Therefore, most facial expressions are blends of several feelings, so they are by far the most difficult of nonverbal messages to understand clearly (Calero, 2005).

The ability to interpret facial expressions is determined by the degree to which a person is acquainted with another person or a particular situation's emotional or social context, which is usually culturally influenced. Ekman, Friesen and Ellsworth (1972) found that people are able to identify correctly the primary emotions of sadness, happiness, anger, surprise, disgust and fear. Most people are fairly good encoders and decoders of the basic facial expressions. However, this does not mean that facial expressions are pan-cultural. While many cultures recognize the primary facial expressions, they do not recognize universal facial expressions at the same rate; every culture exhibits "culture-specific differences" (Ekman & Friesen, 1969) based on the context.

Cultural Difference

Studies have analyzed the relation between cultural values and norms and recognition of universal facial expressions. It has been found that individualistic cultures such as American culture were positively correlated with emotional recognition in facial expressions. Individualistic cultures have this heightened sensitivity over collectivist cultures such as Arab countries because individualistic cultures encourage and promote the open expression of emotions and thus are more motivated to interpret those individual expressions as well (Manusov & Patterson, 2006, 227). In other words, the more individualistic a culture is, the more likely the people will show emotions that are disengaged or emphasize what the self is feeling (anger, disgust, and joy). For example, showing fear is less likely to occur in collectivistic societies because it shows social withdrawal. Joy is more likely to be expressed in individualistic cultures because it is an expression of one's uniqueness and individuality, whereas in collectivistic cultures, it may disrupt the group with values of interdependence.

Although faces reveal emotions and attitudes, we should not attempt to "read" people from another culture as we would "read" someone from our own culture. The degree of facial expressiveness one exhibits varies among individuals and cultures. Across cultures, the same facial expression may say different meanings. For example, smile and laugh convey friendliness, approval, satisfaction, pleasure, merriment. However, the Japanese smiling and laughing does not necessarily mean happiness or friendship, and many people in Russia consider smiling at strangers in public to be unusual and even suspicious behavior. In Southeast Asian cultures, a smile is frequently used to cover emotional pain or embarrassment. Vietnamese may tell the sad story of how they had to leave their country but end the story with a smile. It is common for Americans and Japanese that facial expression is associated with disgust, sadness, fear, and anger, but Japanese individuals believe that it is unacceptable to display such negative emotions in public. So in public and formal situations many Japanese do not show their emotions as freely as Americans do. More privately and with friends, Japanese and Americans seem to show their emotions similarly. Many teachers in the United States have a difficult time knowing whether their Japanese students understand and enjoy their lessons or not since most of the time they keep silent in classroom. They are looking for more facial responsiveness than what the

Japanese students are comfortable with in the classroom situation. Americans are more open in their expression of positive emotions than many other cultures.

Smile

Smile is the very common facial expression which originates from the primate's grimace or fear grin to sign self-defense manners (de Araújo Nóbrega, 2012). With its evolvement in human communication, smile turns out to be related to joy, happiness and pleasure. In literature, there are several different classifications of smile.

Freitas-Magalhães (2006) argued that the smile can be defined under five categories: the primitive smile, the reflex smile, the exogenous smile, the instrumental smile and the coordinated smile. The primitive smile shows the neurobiological excitements and does not represent a relation to the outside world. The reflex or endogenous smile can be regarded as instinctive (cited from de Araújo Nóbrega, 2012).

Based on the research in the psychiatry clinic, Duchenne de Boulogne (1990) categorized smile into two groups: involuntary and voluntary. The involuntary smile involves the movement of the zygomatic muscle near the mouth and the orbicularis muscle near the eyes. This smile reveals a true smile as "it is only brought into play by a true feeling, by an agreeable emotion" (Ekman, 2003, 205-206). Because of his definition, Ekman called the true smile of enjoyment a Duchenne smile. The voluntary smile is known as the polite smile, yellow smile or masked smile. This type of smile is voluntary since it often appears "when people do not feel enjoyment of any kind …" (Ekman, 2003, 204) or, in Duchenne's words, "unmasks a false friend" (Ekman, 2003, 206). That is why the voluntary smile does not show a real meaning as it represents a mask to hide any unfavorable feeling, emotion or to avoid worry and sadness to others. The Japanese, for example, tend to smile even when a relative dies. For them, smiling is not a matter of affective insensibility but a way to prevent their sadness to others (cited from de Araújo Nóbrega, 2012).

On the basis of Duchenne de Boulogne's (1990) study, White and Gardner (2012, 41-42) made a similar division of smile, that is the real smile and false smile. In a real smile, the "zygomatic" muscles in the face are mobilized causing a movement of the lips and a crinkling at the corner of the eyes. The false smile does not reach the eyes. "The muscle around the eye does not obey the will; it is only brought into play by a true feeling, by an agreeable emotion. It is inertia in smiling unmasks a false friend"(Duchenne de Boulogne, 1990). White and Gardner (2012, 42) pointed out that the key to spotting the real from the fake smile lies in deciphering whether there is movement around the corner of eyes.

Although the smile is considered as the affective and social positive reaction to external stimuli, it has many different meanings and functions based on cultural, social patterns and experiences of social interactions. A smile presents distinguished communicative effects. For example, the exogenous smile is regarded as a response to affection and it favors affective proximity. The instrumental smile can be managed in interactive moments for intentional purposes. For instance, when a man flirts with a woman for the first time, he uses such smile in order to show interest towards her. The coordinated or organizational smile appears when the social smile has been already established, which reflects the individual's attitudinal mechanism when corresponding to someone else, for instance, the smile with a happy tone of voice (Freitas-Magalhães, 2006, cited from de Araújo Nóbrega, 2012). According to de Araújo Nóbrega (2012), the smile presents three functions: (1) the expression of emotions and interpersonal attitudes; (2) the sending of specific meaningful signs in social interactions; (3) the indication of typical aspects of the individual personality. For example, sometimes, a smile may indicate that a student is nervous or timid when he/she does not know what and how to speak in front of the classroom.

Due to the difficulty in generalizing facial expressiveness in different cultures, the key is to try not to judge people whose ways of showing emotions are the same as ours. If we judge according to our own cultural norms, we may make the mistake of "reading" the other person incorrectly. As J. Lindon and L. Lindon (2007, 39) stated in their book *Mastering Counseling Skills*:

> The muscles in the face are used, more or less consciously, to produce smiles, frowns, or puzzled or doubtful expressions. Your face can look more or less welcoming, open or closed. A smile is a typical welcome. An immoveable, fixed expression seems uninviting and lacking emotion. On the other hand, marked frequent changes in facial expression can be distracting for the receiver who focuses on the messages passing across your face than on telling you what they wish to say. You need to aim for a claim and alert expression that is not wooden and adjusts appropriately to what the clients say to you.

2. Eye Contact

Of all the elements we use to communicate with other people, eye contact is the most important and the most human. Animals are disturbed by eye contact. To them, it carries a subtext of threat. Humans are pleased with it. To them, the subtexts are the attention and interest. The real communication between two persons begins when two of the persons establish eye contact; eye contact has an important role and meaning in communication. If a person builds eye contact with you, it can be interpreted as that the person cares for you or is interested in you. However, a person who avoids eye contact might be hiding something which is a sign for lack of confidence.

Shakespeare's "your lips tell me no, but there is yes, yes in your eyes" can also describe the function of eye contact in communication. The way we use eye contact not only transmits messages to others and reflects our personality but also indicates what we are thinking. According to some scholars, when we move our eyes up and to the left we are recalling something we have seen before, and when we move our eyes up and to the right, we try to envision something we have never seen before. People in the Middle East, especially Arabs, think one can see a person's soul from the person's eyes. This is why political leaders from that area often wear sun eyeglasses when they are interviewed by reporters. It is difficult to hide information if the reporters can see their eyes directly.

Cultural Difference

Every culture has its unique social rules governing eye contact which follows some unstated rules and takes many forms across cultures. In the North American culture, eye contact is a significant part of courtship dance. Eye to body is the first step, and eye to eye is the second step. If the female does not hold the male's eye contact, she has essentially said "bug off." If the male cannot take the lack of eye contact as the cue, she will tell him verbally in the third step to "get lost." In the Japanese culture, the male and the female engaging in courtship rarely look at one another in the eye. The Japanese male will look elsewhere while they say romantic phrases. In American culture a lot of values are placed on direct eye contact. If someone does not look at them in the eye they feel he/she disliking them, is being unattractive to what they are saying, or are trying to deceive them. However, it is not customary in Japan to look at others in the eye. It makes the Japanese uneasy and uncomfortable to have a lot of eye contact.

Eye contact may give an indication of the audience's receptiveness or a lack of attention in Western European and Anglican cultures, while avoidance of eye contact can be an indication of respect for the speaker in other cultural contexts. Thus, insufficient or excessive eye contact can create communication barriers. In American cultures, trustworthiness, sincerity and directedness are communicated through eye contact, and too little eye contact may also be viewed negatively, because it may convey a lack of interest, inattention, or even mistrust. The relationship between the lack of eye contact and mistrust in American culture is stated directly in the expression, "Never trust a person who doesn't look at you in the eyes." According to some researches, the White Americans make eye contact 80% of the time while listening to another speaker. While speaking, they only make eye contact 50% of the time. Conversely, African-Americans make more eye contact while speaking and less eye contact while listening. Some scholars have claimed that one of the main sources of racial misunderstanding in America is the differences in the use of eye contact. White Americans tend to look at their communication partner more when they are listening than when they are talking, but African-Americans use more eye contact when they are talking than when they are listening.

In contrast, in many other parts of the world (especially in Asian countries), a person's lack of eye contact towards an authority figure signifies respect and deference. While in many other cultures, including Hispanic, Asian, Middle Eastern, eye contact is thought to be disrespectful or rude, and lack of eye contact does not mean that a person is not paying attention. Women may especially avoid eye contact with men because it can be taken as a sign of sexual interest.

The nonverbal process of looking directly at an individual—gazing—is also a cultural variable. In North America, it is impolite for a man to gaze at women, but Italian men may gaze at women all the time and the women don't feel offended. Across many cultures, a gaze is associated with dominance, power, or aggression (Matsumoto, 2006). Direct eye contact is a taboo or an insult in many Asian countries in which it is considered rude to make even brief eye contact with a person of higher social status. While in Arab cultures individuals tend to gaze more directly and for longer periods than other cultures (Matsumoto, 2006). Cambodians consider direct eye contact as an invasion of one's privacy. Direct eye contact is also related to age and rank in cultures such as Spain, Latin America and sub-Saharan Africa.

To sum up, facial expressions and eye contact communicate various meanings across cultures. The interpretation of them should depend on the communicative context.

3.4.2.4 Touch

Touch is also included in nonverbal communication. Humans are in constant physical contact with the outside world through the tactile sensations of their skin. As Calero (2005, 5) stated, "A human's skin is the envelope that contains the human organism." According to some researches, humans have almost 20 square feet of skin on the body and millions of touch sensors connected to a brain that record pleasure, pain, temperature, pressure and a variety of other sensations. The skin is critical to human perceptual ability. It is the external brain and nervous system. It derives from exactly the same embryological layer as the internal brain and spinal cord, both of which are very closely interrelated. The messages which the skin receives must go to the internal brain, the brain then sends the messages back to the skin and to any other organ of the body which leads directly to touching behavior. It is not easy to understand that touch can make all the differences to another human being (Stamatis, 2012). Some researchers have even demonstrated that children who have had little physical contact during infancy tend to walk and talk later in their development, and may result in depression, anxiety, violence, substance abuse, inability to adequately parent a child, inability to adequately engage in healthy adult relationship (ibid).

Therefore, touch is the most important of all senses, and our basic social sense. Unlike sight, hearing, smell, and taste, which can generally be autonomous, touch typically implies an interaction with another person. It "turns on" sight, hearing, smell, and taste and stimulates language and communication, promotes bond and attachment. It is especially important for children which can be a remedy for discomforts and helps children with illnesses and enhances the parent-child relationship for adopted and foster children. All in all, it provides relief, stimulation, relaxation, bonding and attachment for the child.

Physical touch always communicates messages, especially emotional ones. It is an efficient way of breaking down communication barriers. Touch, such as an embrace, a kiss in our daily life, is a way of showing our love, and hand shaking can easily make two strangers familiar to each other on their first meeting. As the most extreme reduction of individual distance, touch is one of our most primitive and yet sensitive ways of relating to others, and plays a significant role in giving encouragement, expressing tenderness and showing emotional supports. It can be even more powerful than words sometimes, especially for establishing a link to people or conveying emotion.

Then how do people perceive touching behavior also depends on culture, gender, age, education and some special qualities such as occupation, social status, etc. The interpretations of touch are pleasant, and nonthreatening, or awkward, inappropriate depending on different cultures. Everyone wants to have physical contact with outside world. They just don't want to be invaded, molested or abused which is closely related to culture. Researchers have found that in the typical individualism culture, such as American culture, teachers touch very little, especially when the children grow older. Thus, teachers living in a really touch-deprived society may consider touch as a prohibited behavior. The more important thing we should remember is that how, where and when people touch others.

3.4.3 Paralanguage

We should point out that the term "paralanguage" should not be confused with kinesics. Kinesics is non-linguistic, and it is not necessarily related to vocal or written language, but paralanguage is.

The study of paralanguage is known as paralinguistics, and was invented by George L. Trager in 1958, while he was working at the Foreign Service Institute of the Department of State. The term was first used as a synthesis of the linguistic and psychological material collected on the categories of voice modification which could be applied to different situational contexts. According to Houston (1984, 185), paralanguage is the "study of those aspects of speech communication do not pertain to linguistic structure or content, for example, vocal qualifiers, intonation, and body language." The present book focuses on the discussion of paralanguage in terms of the communicators' tone of voice, pitch, rhythm, tempo, intensity (loudness), emotional content and vocal segregates such as an "uh-huh."

3.4.3.1 Classification of Paralanguage

According to the earliest typological classification of Trager (1958, cited from Pennycook, 1985), any human utterance could be fully accounted for in terms of voice set, the physiological and physical peculiarities which allow identification of mood, state of health, age, sex, body build, and so on. Voice qualities are recognizable speech events which include degree of control of pitch range, articulation, rhythm, resonance, and tempo. The vocalization is the specifically identifiable noises (sounds) such as laughing, crying, and whispering, as well as uh-huh (affirmation) or uh-uh (negation).

Literature review shows that most classifications divide paralanguage into three kinds of vocalization: (1) vocal characteristics; (2) vocal qualifiers; and (3) vocal segregates (Samovar et al., 2006, 162-163). Here we only discuss vocal qualifiers, vocal segregates, and silence.

1. Vocal Qualifier

The vocal qualifier refers to tone, volume, pitch, rhythm, tempo, resonance, of the spoken word and stresses, etc. (Dou Weilin, 2011, 173). These elements form a powerful subtle and vital part of communication between speakers. As Miller (1988, 13) stated, "The adage 'It is not what we say that counts, but how we say it' reflects the meaning of vocal intonation. Vocal intonation is probably the most understood and valid area of nonverbal communication. It includes the multitude of components (for example, rhythm, pitch, intensity, nasality, and slurring) that elicit the 'truth' of a message. The vocal variations are fundamental components of expressive oral communication. If vocal information contradicts verbal, vocal will dominate."

(1) Tone of voice. It refers to the rising or falling inflection that tells us whether a sentence is a question or a statement, whether the speaker is uncertain or confident, whether a statement is sincere or sarcastic. The voice rising or falling in tone plays a dominant part in making clear the emotions that lie behind or inspire meaning; we have no rally adequate method of conveying in speech what we feel other than of varying the expression in our voices. For example, you can say: "I am so happy," raising the pitch of your voice on so and keeping it raised until the second syllable of *happy*, which indicates an abundance of happiness, or you can keep your voice on one note until you reach the word *happy*, and raise the first syllable several tones, in which case you will indicate a feeling of wonder at your own happiness. There are obviously many other possibilities of accentuation of this phrase. Each variant conveys a subtle and individual emotional meaning. Another example, it is quite possible to say: "I hate you," all on the same note and without emphasis, but if you do so you will entirely fail to convey any sense of hatred; but if you raise your voice on *hate* your feeling will be at once conveyed to your listeners. Subtler shades of emotions can also be indicated by change of tonal emphasis.

When tone of voice is conflict with the meaning of words, people usually believe the tone of voice. Chinese is a tonal language with four tones: high and level tone, rising tone, falling-rising tone and falling tone. When a syllable is pronounced in different tones, it bears different meanings.

(2) Volume. It is another factor of paralanguage concerned with loudness or softness of speech. Generally speaking, loud voice can be perceived as aggressiveness or over bearing and soft voice can be perceived as timid or polite. Volume differs with situations. For example, Americans are very skillful in adjusting their volume levels according to the size of the audience and the physical environment. But it seems that the Chinese in America often has some difficulties in adapting to extra low voice than Americans are accustomed to. That is why some Americans who first to China wonder why Chinese like quarrelling on the street. They don't realize these people are actually talking loudly.

The volume of speech is also culture specific: Arabs speak very loudly because this is an indication of strength and sincerity. To speak softly implies that one is frail. For Israelis, increased volume reflects strong beliefs towards the issue under discussion. Germans conduct their business with a commanding tone that projects authority and self-confidence. On the other hand, in Japan, raising one's voice often implies a lack of self-control. A gentle and soft voice reflects good manners and maintains harmony, which are important values in Japanese culture.

(3) Pitch. It measures whether a voice uses sounds that are low or high. Some people use a wide range of pitch, talking now in a high voice and past in a low voice, while others make few pitch changes or talk in a monotone. Pitch can serve as an emotional marker. It is said that the English word "yes" can be uttered in more than fifty different ways to show different emotions, attitudes and meanings. The same is true of its Chinese counterpart "hao," "dui," or "ya." In English, a speaker raises the pitch at the end of a question, signifying a nonverbal question mark. Ending sentences with a high pitch in American English may indicate self-doubt and uncertainty. On the other hand, in French, sentences tend to end in a higher pitch than in English. The French speaker may be very certain of what he/she is saying, yet a listener from America may have a different impression.

(4) Tempo. It is also culturally patterned. For instance, American speech has a faster tempo than Chinese speech. This phenomenon can be explained in two ways. One is that speech tempo tends to increase with the development of industry. Industrialized countries have a faster speech tempo than non-industrial countries. The other is that the English language has much more polysyllabic words and carries less information per syllable than the Chinese language does. Namely, the same amount of information can be contained in few Chinese syllables. The rate of speech varies with the region in the US. Northerners speak faster than Southerners. Often these discrepancies in rate make people feel uncomfortable.

2. Voice Segregate (Vocalization)

Voice segregates are all the noises that seem not to serve any function but to interfere with the flow of speech, such as "uh-huh," "shh," "uh," "um," or "er," sucking in one's breath, or clicking one's tongue. These noises may be used as connectors between ideas; they may be used to indicate that someone is ready to say something or more time is needed to think over.

Some researches also call it as little words. The way the little words are said is very important. They may convey the negative meanings such as disagreement, doubt, complaint or positive meanings like agreement, affirmation, reservation, interest, etc. (He Daokuan, 1988, 155).

Related to the nonword vocalizers are fillers. For example, in English, "okay" and "you know" are often used as fillers. The words have a meaning, but the speaker who uses them does not attach the specific meaning to them. They simply build a bridge to what the speaker says next.

We should point out that the use of vocal segregates is universal, but the duration, the placement of them may vary in different cultures. In a speech or conversation, Westerners feel it more proper to decrease the use of vocal segregates, which may make them uncomfortable, while in some Asian cultures, it signals wisdom and attractiveness. Americans are used to laughing and yelling especially at sports games. Such behaviors are often interpreted in Europe as aggressive behaviors or can be seen as sign of uncultivated behaviors. Likewise, the British way of speaking quietly might be understood as secretive by Americans. Also, French males whistle at beautiful girls, but Chinese males find it disgusting to do so.

Research has already found that gender and personality can influence the use of voice. Argyle (1988) pointed out that men tend to have louder and lower pitched voices, which is not entirely due to anatomical differences. Similarly, Hall (2006) noted that men's verbalizations tend to be louder, lower pitched, and contain more speech disturbances (e.g., ums, repetitions, and incomplete sentences). In some cultures, vocal cues may distinguish between male and female responses, educational level or social status. In other cultures, verbal communication is readily supplemented by vocalizations, in order to demonstrate sincerity, politeness, good manners or to emphasize verbal messages conveyed.

3. Silence

Silence is also one type of paralanguage. Traditionally, silence has been negatively related to the merely absence of speech. However, "silence means something more than a void or an empty space" in communication (Armstrong, 2007, 1). It has a capacity to provoke diverse interpretations and ambiguities which, in turn, make it one of the highest forms of communication and yet one of the greatest sources of misunderstanding.

The definitions of silence vary greatly, depending on the theoretical frameworks and methodologies adopted for its study. Several ways to conceptualize silence come from a variety of disciplinary perspectives such as, sociolinguistics, literary theory, anthropology, and the arts, etc. Bilmes (1994) stated that "there are as many kinds of silence as there are of relevant sounds." He operationalized silence into two general types: the simple absence of sound, which is called "absolute silence," and the relevant absence of a particular kind of sound, called "notable silence." A subtype of the latter is absence of (relevant) talk and is labeled by Bilmes as "conversational silence."

Jaworski (1997) has worked on successive comprehensive works on silence in which he argued that silence is a diverse concept and its study merits an interdisciplinary (1), and it "can be said to have an important position in those branches of linguistics that deal with how people actually communicate with each other"(Jaworski, 1993, 1). However, within the framework of linguistics, silence has been traditionally ignored except for its function as a boundary-marking, delimiting the beginning and end of utterances (Saville-Troike, 1985, 3). As Poyatoes (2002) claimed, "Linguistics has wasted many research opportunities offered by silence... rarely have linguistics referred to silence as a component of interaction" (299).

The concept of silence crept into speech studies and linguistics in the 1970s. It was associated with negatively, passiveness, impotence and death and treated as absence: absence of speech, and absence of meaning and intentions (Bruneau, 1973, 18; Saville-Troike, 1994). This is due to the studies carried out by scholars, specifically Western linguists, who focused on lexicography and grammar. As Bruneau (1973, 19) asserted, "Much of the manner in which we have studied language function has denied the functioning of silence." Before the mid-1980s, linguists conducted projects and published writings on specific sub-topics of silence. Only in the 1990s, with the ongoing interest in pragmatics, did the linguistic study of silence make a slight shift, from ground to figure, for example, Bilmes' (1994) study—"*Constituting Silence: Life in the World of Total Meaning*," Zitzen and Stein's (2004)—"*Chat and Conversation—a Case of Transmedial Stability*?", etc. Ephratt (2008) summarized that there are two different routes that aroused linguists' interest in silence. Influenced by philosophy and literature, one route was an introductory and programmatic look at silence from a functional point of view (Jensen, 1973; Bruneau, 1973). The other was acoustics which introduced silence as a subject of study.

Until recent years, the fact that how people use communicative silence in interrelationship has aroused scholars' interest. Studies show that silence is a complex linguistic item whose meaning goes beyond the non-communicative absence of speech and whose function needs a comprehensive descriptive and explanatory treatment with reference to various pragmatic and sociolinguistic frameworks (Jaworski & Sachdev, 1998). Schultz (2009, 14) claimed that researchers and theorists conceptualize silence in several overlapping ways, so we can delineate it as a form of communication. In this way, silence has varied meanings across geographic regions, cultures, and individuals.

Within the field of sociologistics, the meanings of silence are often assumed rather than systematically investigated. It has been traditionally ignored except for its function of marking boundaries that delimit the beginning and end of utterances. In fact, even in interpersonal communication, silence can help provide an interval in an ongoing interaction during which the participants have time to think, check or inaugurate another line of thought. It may also be interpreted as evidence of agreement and disagreement, lack of interest, uncomfortable feelings, or contempt. The use of silence is different at high- and low-context cultures. The ignorance about silence as a way of communication is partly due to the fact that silence is associated with negative values in Western culture. However, talk and silence are fundamentally opposed, and it is useful to conceptualize silence and talk as interwoven. Silence contains sound and talk always contains silence. This also suggests that the binary thinking that often characterizes silence and speech is inadequate.

Sociocultrual theory situates the production of silence in classroom community demonstrating how it is shaped by its social and institutional contexts. Across the world, the youth are socialized to speak and remain silent at different time and for different times and different purposes (Saville-Troike, 1985). They are taught that talk and silence hold different values for communication between teachers and students, adults and the youth. In situations where talk is highly valued or expected, silence is marked. In other words, if the expectation is that communication occurs through talk, silence and silent students stand out. In contrast, in his discussion of the use of silence in the Igbo tribe of Nigeria, Nwoye (1985) explained, "silence in Igbo communication is a figure which reveals its meaning against the ground of speech" and suggests that in comparison to the United States, where talk is paramount, among the Igbo, the locus of communication is silence (191).

Cultural Difference

According to the sociocultural theory, silence can be viewed differently by people from different cultures (Giles, Coupland & Wiemann, 1992), and it holds multiple meanings for individuals within and across racial, ethnic, and cultural groups. For example, in low-context cultures where ideas are explicitly encoded into words, silence does not fit with the emphasis on precision and clarity. People view silence as communication that has gone wrong, which makes them feel uncomfortable. For example, American people can put up with a silence of only a few seconds, if the silence is more than ten seconds, it will make them nervous. But the high-context cultures have a different attitude towards the use of silence. Eastern cultures value silence more than the use of words. People in some Asian countries consider silence an integral part of business and social discourse, not a failure of communication.

For example, in Japanese culture, silence is regarded as virtue as well as a sign of respectability and trustworthiness. They think that silence during communication is necessary and desirable. In East Asia and Finland, silence is associated with listening and learning; it protects and shows respect for privacy and individualism of others. We Chinese like periods of silence and do not like to be hurried. The proverbs such as "silence is golden" emphasize the value of silence over words in our culture. As Giles et al. (1992) claimed that Chinese appear to perceive silence as more important, more enjoyable and being used to a greater degree for social control than Caucasian Americans. Such differences in beliefs about silence confirm that silence and talk are related to issues of control and affiliation in communication.

Silence in communication is also context-dependent. The use of it is regulated by a number of factors, such as the communicative goals, the setting, ambiguity of roles and expectations, and the relative power of participants, etc. Thus, silence can be seen "as positive or negative by members of any culture, as it is measured against what is expected in that context" (Tannen, 1985, 98). Accordingly, people in different cultures learn how to speak and the norms of silence and when, where and how they are expected to keep silent. For example, Turkish society traditionally socializes children not to talk much because it is widely accepted that being quiet is a well-behaved attitude for a child. Similarly, in classroom, the students are expected to listen, respond only when asked a question, and not ask questions, an act that might be perceived as a threat to the teachers' authority. In America, there also are implicit and stated rules for talk and silence that are taught to children when they enter the school. Silence is often assigned a limited number of meanings. Teachers grade classroom participation according to verbal contribution of students, and they insist on silence to signify order and authority. Students who practice silence are often thought of either as "good"(compliant) or "bad" (resistant or unintelligent), and their silence uses are rarely understood as intentional.

We have discussed the types of paralanguage, now it is clear that different cultures have different interpretations of paralanguage. The different ways of interpretation cause breakdown in intercultural communication. From above discussion, we can see that paralanguage meanings are conveyed by consistencies and inconsistencies in what is said and how it is said. Depending on the circumstance, a person's voice may or may not be consistent with the intended word meanings. But we should make every effort to avoid inconsistencies that will send a confusing message. Consistency among the words we choose and how we deliver them to create clear meaning should be the goal. We should remember that our tone should reinforce the verbal message we are relying on. Whether we are speaking casually or doing a formal presentation, our inflection should be appropriate. With informal speech, we should be conscious of the emotion in the voice; with a formal presentation, we should vary the tone subtle so that we are not putting the audience to sleep with a controlled monotone.

3.4.4 Proxemics

Human beings like animals in the wild regard a certain space as their own territory that is a fixed geographical area. This is another type of nonverbal communication involving space. How people use space and what they do in certain spaces tell much about themselves. Thus, each person has a space language just as he/she does a body language. Individuals usually follow predictable patterns in establishing the distance between themselves and those with whom they interact.

The term "proxemics" was coined by Hall (1966) who was the first scholar to systematically study proxemics. Hall divided it into three kinds of space: fixed-feature space, semi-fixed feature space, and informal space.

Fixed-feature space refers to those unmovable structural arrangements around us. When a house is built, the wall around it becomes fixed-feature space. We can only move in this space by destroying its structure. This kind of space is a dimension of architecture, which varies from culture to culture, such as the differences between the traditional palace or temple in China or Japan, the cottage, or Victorian style buildings in the United States.

Semi-fixed feature space is the arrangement of movable objects within a room, such as furniture and file cabinets. The use of this kind of space and material objects is also culture bound. In Germany, where privacy is often valued, a closed door in an office is the expected behavior. In North America, a closed door can indicate something else. So many managers attempt to leave the door or curtain open. Another example, in the evening, Syrian men converse sitting across a room from each other, with the furniture arranged to facilitate this arrangement. The Chinese prefer side-by-side seating arrangements for personal communication, rather than sitting with direct eye contact.

Informal space refers to the distance between the interactants in communication. It directly affects the way we communicate with others. Hall classified American cultural interpersonal distance into eight categories. We can put the categories into four discernible distances: intimate, personal, social and public. Intimate space is from 0 to 8 inches, such as hugging, kissing, and holding hands are included in this category. Personal space, from 1 or 1.5 feet to 4 feet, is the distance we occupy in interpersonal communication, usually with friends. Social distance, from 4 to 12 feet, characterizes comfortable interaction in the workplace between acquaintances or strangers. Finally, public space is any distance beyond 12 feet and usually in this distance public communication takes place.

Cultural Difference

Individual behaviors in each type of space are learned from their culture, so these distances often culturally determined and can have an impact on the overall communication and relationship building process. In some cultures, it may convey warmth and affection, while other cultures that are culturally more inclined to non-contact behavior might even see it as an intrusion of one's personal space which may be experienced as threatening and result in behavioral patterns of social avoidance or withdrawal in some instances. So some cultures can be classified as "contact cultures," while others may be defined more as "non-contact cultures." For example, Anglo-European cultures tend to maintain a distance of about three feet between themselves and others during conversations, while Latinos, Middle Easterners and most African cultures are comfortable with closer conversational distances. Asians on the other hand, usually prefer more space between speaker and listener (Lynch, 1999, 71). For the American communicator, an Italian seems to stand in his/her space, continuously grabbing him/her, talking over the top of him/her. But these behaviors are a normal part of everyday friendly Italian communication, thus, not all things in all cultures mean the same things.

Different cultural conceptions and uses of distancing lead to different patterns of communication distances. Jensen (1970) found that American males prefer to be approximately 18 to 20 inches away from conversationalists they do not well know, and about 22 to 24 inches if they are conversing with a woman. Conversely, South Americans, Greeks, and Arabs establish a much closer distance when interacting than Nouth Americans. Less space in the American culture may be associated with either greater intimacy or aggressive behaviors. The common practice of saying, "Excuse me" for the slightest accidental touching of another person reveals how uncomfortable Americans are if people get too close. Thus, a person whose "space" has been intruded upon by another may feel threatened and react defensively. In contrast, the Latin Americans, the Japanese and the Chinese prefer to keep a much closer distance, for them, Americans may be perceived as cold and distant. For the Germans, they prefer greater distances when interacting, while Chinese people are used to short distance in face-to-face communication. Sometimes, they think the closer they get together, the more intimate their relationship might be. It is quite usual for Chinese to walk hand in hand between the same sexes. But in America, friends with the same sex never keep such close distance. Such kind of behavior is considered homosexual in the West and is strongly disgusted.

Other aspects of space use include the way space is arranged. For instance, in order to display the individuals' power in high positions, people have their offices at an upper floor of the building, usually with a massive desk opposite the window with a great view. Also, the way the furniture is positioned in a room can have a great deal of influence on the employees' productivity. A round table usually encourages collaboration and suggests that all the members of the team are equals. Standing side by side, like in a waiting room will make communication harder.

Therefore, a culture's use of space is directly linked to its social norms. The more each participant understands the norms, the fewer the unnecessary misunderstanding in intercultural communication will be.

3.4.5 Chronemics

Chronemics, or time language, referring to how we give meaning to time and how it is communicated to others, is a powerful element of nonverbal communication (Lesikar & Flatley, 2005, 427).

Time is culturally different. People in different cultures have different conceptions and uses of time. For example, Americans say, "Time is money," "He who hesitates is lost," while Chinese say, "Think three times before you act." All reflect on how different each culture perceives time.

Time communicates role relationship and status. The "boss" may walk right into the subordinate office, while the subordinate knocks before entering the office of "boss." A secretary has to phone the boss to gain entry for the subordinate, and the subordinate may have to "wait to see the boss." Studies have showed that the person with low status waits longer than the one with higher rank before getting into office.

Time also communicates the urgency and importance of an event. If your phone rings at 2 o'clock in the morning, you probably feel urgent, even a sense of danger. Generally speaking, the phone in the morning is perceived as very important and the phone in the evening less important.

Samovar et al. (2006, 167) claimed that a culture's conception of time can be explored from three different perspectives: (1) informal time; (2) perceptions of past, present, and future (that is, time orientation); and (3) Hall's monochronic and polychronic classifications.

Informal Time

Time systems are the implicit cultural rules that are used to arrange sets of experience in a meaningful way (Du Ruiqing, Tian Dexin, Li Benguan, 2004, 212). When we say "time talk," or "time is money," we refer to the concept of informal time. Most of the rules for informal time, such as pace and tardiness, are not explicitly taught and function unconsciously. In order to understand the meanings of informal time, we should know its context and cultural settings. For example, an Irishman saying "I'll be back in a pint" can have many interpretations depending on the situation. While "tomorrow" is a specific designator in North America, the equivalent word in Arabic, Spanish may or may not literally mean the "next day."

People's reaction to punctuality is rooted in their cultural experience. In Latin America, one is expected to arrive late to appointment as a sign of respect. But the same behavior will be perceived as rudeness in Germany. The American boss can arrive late for a meeting without anyone raising an eyebrow, while if a secretary is late, he/she will receive a reprimand in the form of a stern glance. Argyle (1982, p.87) compared cultural differences in punctuality standards in the following way:

> How late is "late"? This varies greatly. In Britain and America one may be 5 minutes late for a business appointment, but not 15 minutes late, which is perfectly normal in Arab countries. On the other hand in Britain it is correct to be 5-15 minutes late for a invitation to dinner. An Italian might arrive 2 hours late.

The attitude to the pace of time also reflects cultural diversities. For example, Americans always seem to be in a hurry, and always have one more thing to do. But the Japanese, Arab and Chinese cultures treat time in a quite different way. As Brislin (1993, 211) illustrated how pace of time is reflected in the negotiation with Japanese: at the beginning, they want to have a long conversation with their American counterpartners so as to know them more, while Americans like to get down to business after a few small talks about the weather, their trip, baseball, etc.

Time Orientation

Time orientation refers to the importance the members of a culture assign to the passage of time.

The Harvard professors—the husband and wife team, Clyde and Florence

Kluckhohn and their fellow anthropologist Fredrick Strodtbeck (1961) conducted a study of human values during the mid-twentieth century in which five universal questions are examined. They stated that every culture must find a solution to each of these problems. One of these questions is about what the orientation towards time is. A culture's conception of time can be examined from three different perspectives: past-oriented, present-oriented and future-oriented. People in any culture must come to terms with the three orientations, but one tends to predominate in a particular culture.

The past orientation predominates in cultures placing a high value on tradition, worshipping ancestors or emphasizing strong family ties. People regard previous experiences and events as most important. In time of crisis, history can often offer precedents in which the wisdom of the ancestors is worth following. Apart from this, in such a country, the force of tradition and customs is usually strong, and sometimes it becomes rather an obstacle to fundamental changes or reforms.

The present orientation predominates where people pay relatively little attention to what has gone in the past and what may happen in the future. In this orientation, the past is seen as unimportant, and the future is seen as vague and unpredictable. People work and earn, in order to enjoy the present life. Mexicans are famous for their enjoyment in daily life.

The future orientation predominates where change is valued highly. In this orientation, the future generally is viewed as "bigger and better" while the past being "old fashioned," is scorned. Americans are dominated by a belief in progress. They are future-oriented. This implies a strong task or goal orientation. To them, time is money, therefore not to be wasted. They have an optimistic faith in the future and what the future will bring. They tend to equate "change" with "improvement" and consider a rapid rate of change as normal.

Monochronic and Polychronic Time

Hall (1959, 153) divided time into monochronic time or M-time and polychronic time or P-time to study how people use, structure, interpret and understand time. The two views of time influence the temporal concepts, such as appointment, schedule, etc.

The concept of monochronic view of time means that cultural members prefer doing one thing at a time. They tend to view time as inescapable, linear, and fixed in nature and it is quantitative, measured in units that reflect progress. The timing appointment is important to monochronic cultures. An American or Australian might allow five minutes delay for an appointment. But to Swedes, a ten o'clock appointment means ten o'clock on the dot. Good examples of time-driven countries include Germany, Austria, Switzerland and the United States. People of these countries are known for their punctuality.

In contrast, the concept of polychronic view of time means that cultural members prefer operating with several people, ideas, or projects simultaneously. They tend to view time more flexibly and have unlimited continuity. A number of Southeast Asian cultures view time cyclically rather than linearly, and thus they attach less importance to time consciousness. For example, people of Middle East and Latin America come late to appointments or do not come at all, which is not considered especially inconsiderate. Countries with typical polychronic view of time include China, India, Saudi Arabia, Latin America and Spain.

3.5 Conclusion

So far we have examined the cultural impact on nonverbal communication from intercultural perspectives. We should point out that like all other forms of communication, no single type of behavior exists in isolation. Specific nonverbal behavior can be understood only by taking the person's total behaviors into account. As a matter of fact, many aspects of our nonverbal behaviors may contain information that others use to form an impression of us. What is more, because of cultural variations in the form of nonverbal communication, it behooves us to know cultural attitudes to talk, noise, and silence. This knowledge can save us from both anxiety and ethnocentrism in intercultural communication. Another golden rule for effective cross-cultural communication is to always consult with other parties in order to determine what is acceptable and what is not. This may avoid much misunderstanding and miscommunication among people from different cultures.

Through the analysis of cultural differences in nonverbal communication, we know that nonverbal communication can not be separated from culture context. Thus, nonverbal communication study should combine with culture closely and put communicators' behaviors into specific context. We can see that the findings of abroad studies in this area may not suitable to the Chinese communication context, therefore, it is necessary to make further research in China.

Chapter Four

Nonverbal Communication and Intercultural Communication Competence

4.1 Introduction

This chapter will explore the relationship between nonverbal communication and intercultural communication competence (ICC) since the latter is considered as one of the ultimate purposes in language teaching and learning in China. After a brief historical review of intercultural communication study, some basic concepts related to ICC will be analyzed. And then a discussion about how nonverbal communication features have been incorporated into different models of communicative competence is presented. Finally, the relationship between nonverbal communication and foreign language teaching is discussed. The purpose of this chapter is to illustrate the importance of nonverbal communication in the development of ICC.

4.2 Development of Intercultural Communication

Nowadays, the progress of communication and transportation technology has made Marshall McLuhan's prophecy of a "global village" come into reality. Travel that once took months now takes hours. Business dealings that were once confined primarily to local economies have given way to an extensively integrated world economy. The walls that separate us are tumbling down and it is clear that various cultures of the world are far more accessible than ever before, and that the peoples of these cultures are coming into contact at an ever increasing rate. These contacts ultimately comprise interpersonal encounters. We can see that face-to-face intercultural communication is increasingly becoming the new norm in modern world. What can be difficult, however, is how to communicate effectively with individuals who speak other languages or who rely on different means to reach a common goal, which involves the study of intercultural communication.

4.2.1 Factors Influencing Development of Intercultural Communication

There are various factors which have influenced the development of intercultural communication, but three aspects are always discussed: (1) technological development; (2) economic globalization; and (3) widespread population migrations in the world (Chen & Starosta, 2007, 4-7).

4.2.1.1 Development of Technology

The development of new transportation and information technology has made people's dream traveling to every corner of the world come true. People can share space with local stories in the newscasts at the same time. Supersonic transports carry passengers from one continent to another in time for them to conduct business, attend conferences, or meet friends.

Communication technologies, including the Internet, the cellular phone, interactive cable TV systems, and information superhighway, permit our instantaneous oral and written interchange at the same time at any hour to most locations at home and abroad. We sit in our living rooms but feel connected to events that happen elsewhere in the world and find that we need to improve our understanding of persons and groups from the outside world. The improvement of information technology has greatly reshaped intercultural communication, creating common meanings and a reliance on persons we may or may not meet face-to-face in the future.

4.2.1.2 Globalization of the Economy

The progress of communication and transportation technology has made markets more accessible and the world business more globally connected in the past decades. The trend towards a global economy brings people and products together around the world. In the face of economic globalization, nations have to determine how to remain competitive in the presence of new trade communities and find ways to promote products and services. So better development of the national economy is based on effective intercultural communication and calls for skillful interaction in the future across linguistic and national boundaries.

4.2.1.3 Widespread Migrations of Population

With the development of technology and economy, there is a cultural migration among nations in the world. Most people leave their countries to find peace, employment, a better living condition or a new start in new places.

Canada and America have been the destination of choice for generations of refugees, job seekers, students and others seeking a change. Earlier immigrants to the United States considered America to be a "melting pot" of ethnicities, and this image now has been replaced by that of the "tossed salad" in which each ethnic group retains its own "flavor." In 2008, there are almost 303 million people in America. Of these people, nearly 66.8 percent are European Americans, 14.8 percent Latinos, 12.8 percent African Americans, 4.6 percent Asian Americans, and 1.0 percent native Americans. (Data adapted from the US Census Bureau, "Annual Estimates of the Population by Sex, Race, and Hispanic Origin for the United States: April 1, 2000 to July 1, 2007," from http://www.census.gov/propest/national/asrh/NC-EsT 2007-srh.html.)

Besides the United States, countries in Europe, Asia, Africa, and South America, have also become the destinations of people around the globe who want to seek more chances or challenges.

4.2.2 The Origin of Intercultural Communication Study

The history of intercultural communication among people of different cultural backgrounds is almost as long as human history itself. The emergence and conflicts among the primitive nomadic tribes, the bargains of merchants along the Silk Road during the Tang Dynasty in China are examples of communication across cultures, not to mention Marco Polo in China, Chinese monk—Jianzhen visiting Japan, the immigration of thousands upon thousands of "gold-diggers" to North America, Norman Conquest in 1066, and Columbus discovering the New World. So we can see that as a matter of fact, humans have had intercultural communication ever since the cradle of human civilization.

Intercultural communication study originated from the United States. According to Dodd (1989, 22-24), some scholars claimed that prior to World War II many people in America seemed to lack a kind of world perspective. They could learn from the experiences of travelers, missionaries, and the like. But the Second World War made American people aware that there was really another world out there. Not only did the war cause the soldiers to return home with stories of other countries or regions, but during the war, American leaders were forced with a practical strategic problem. How could the United States secure the cooperation with some island residents, for instance, when the leaders knew nothing about their language or culture? They invited some anthropologists to study and discover the culture of these places. Through these investigations, the study of culture became generally accepted, and many people began discussing the importance of culture. The national attitude towards the world began to change into a more global view.

After the Second World War, a number of programs focusing on world situations and US policies abroad influenced the development of intercultural communication studies. Especially, the establishment of the United Nations became a significant concern of US foreign policy. With the United Nations playing a prominent role in world events, the US government felt obliged to initiate new programs in interacting with leaders from other nations throughout the world. This situation made it urgent to learn about the political, social, economic, and cultural life of other nations. With the advent of the World Bank and other agencies, the need to understand the culture of many developing nations and interact meaningfully with citizens from these nations became one goal of some governments. In order to understand other nations' culture and communicate with other people, the United States set up the Information Agency, that is, the USIA (the United States Information Agency). In 1977, the name was changed to the International Communication Agency, which has the responsibility of providing information about the United States through various communication media for the world, such as, the "Voice of America."

The 1960s also marked a kind of cultural wakening in the United States. With the passage of the Civil Right Act in 1964, the nation seriously discovered its pockets of minorities, and many human rights issues and countercultures emerged. For example, African American people began to fight for their rights and freedom. The issues and the fights sometimes made Americans painfully aware that communication between groups and cultures were urgent.

Another important event having severe influence on intercultural communication was the Vietnam War. The overflow of refugees thrusted a new generation of Americans into cultural contact. Overnight, elementary, high school and college students were in classroom with counterparts from Cambodia, Laos and Vietnam. The continuing influx of political and economic refugees from Caribbean, Central America, and Mexico also caused various problems. How to avoid the conflicts among different cultural groups became a serious problem throughout the United States.

From these historical points, investigations began to increase, along with collection of essays revolving around intercultural communication. For instance, anthropologist Alfred Smith edited *Communication and Culture* (1966) a resource that brought together essays from a number of fields, including communication theory, social psychology, linguistics, anthropology, and sociology.

4.2.3 The History of Intercultural Communication Study

Although intercultural communication has a long history, the study of it has had a short history. It is still a brand-new discipline.

4.2.3.1 Before the 1960s—The Burgeoning Period

In 1958, Lederer and Burdick's *The Ugly American* first raised mass awareness of intercultural issues, but the term "intercultural communication" itself didn't appear until Edward T. Hall's *The Silent Language* (1959) was published.

Edward T. Hall was an American anthropologist and cross-cultural researcher. He is remembered for developing the concept of social cohesion, a description of how people behave and react in different types of culturally defined personal space. Throughout the growth of intercultural communication study, Hall's work has remained influential. *The Silent Language* placed a serious accent on "nonverbal" communication, and a significant contribution of the book is its discussion of unseen aspects of human communication. Hall coined the term polychronic to describe the ability of attending to multiple events simultaneously, as opposed to "monochronic" individuals and cultures who tend to handle events sequentially. Generally speaking, the publication of *The Silent Language* in 1959 marks the birth of intercultural communication.

Hall has made noticeable contributions to the study of intercultural communication. One of them is that he extended the study of culture from a macro perspective to a micro analysis and the study of culture to communication. He synthesized some crucial and fundamental issues in understanding culture and communication, cultural perceptions of interpersonal distance and time, and their relationship to numerous intercultural misunderstandings.

Hall was the first person who discovered the existence of covert culture. He pointed out that culture includes two aspects, that is, the overt culture and the covert culture, and the latter is the most difficult part to reveal. Hall also examined nonverbal communication which had not been noticed at that time. People usually consider that Hall was the father of intercultural communication study.

4.2.3.2 From the 1960s to the 1980s— The Developing Period

Hall's influence on the study of intercultural communication is far-reaching. His writings have attracted numerous scholars to the study of intercultural communication. Together with Kluckhohn and Strodebeck's (1961) discourse on cultural value orientations, another representative book reflects the continuous efforts made by scholars in the fields in the 1960s is Oliver's *Culture and Communication* (1962). In 1966, the first college class in this field taught at the University of Pittsburgh in Pennsylvania.

The 1970s witnessed the rapid development in the field of intercultural communication. Many books were published, such as, Stewart's *American Cultural Patterns* (1972). In this period, Indiana University awarded the first doctoral degree in intercultural communication. An academic journal entitled *The International Journal of Intercultural Relations* was first published in 1977, which influenced research in this field in the years that followed.

4.2.3.3 From the 1980s to the Present— The Flourishing Period

Scholars who received formal academic training in intercultural communication in the late 1960s and the early 1970s began to make their contributions in research and teaching by the 1980s. A lot of theories and methods on intercultural communication study appeared in this period.

The direction of the study of intercultural communication since the 1970s has been influenced by (1) the International and Intercultural Communication Annual (IICA); (2) the Speech Communication Association (SCA); (3) the International Communication Association (ICA)(Chen & Starosta, 2007, 12).

Recently, three additional journals, *The Howard Journal of Communications*, *Intercultural Communication Studies*, and *World Communications*, a publication of the World Communication Association, have begun to specialize the issues in communication research (Chen & Starosta, 2007, 13).

4.2.3.4 Intercultural Communication Study in China

The history of intercultural communication study in China is much shorter than that in the United States and Europe. It was first introduced into China during the early 1980s by some English teachers, who took an interest in intercultural communication study for the purpose of changing traditional teaching method into communicative approach in EFL in China. The EFL field at this time realized the weakness of traditional grammar-based teaching and tried to adopt the prevalent communicative approach in classroom. The short history in China can be divided into three periods.

The first period is from 1979 to 1987, and it mainly aroused attention to language teaching and the field of language and culture. It was commonly agreed among English teachers that the goal of EFL is to develop students' communicative competence in using the target language; the learning of a foreign language was believed to be the learning of a culture. The communicative functions of everyday English and the knowledge of cultural backgrounds were listed as teaching items in the national syllabus.

The years of 1988 to 1994 marked the second period, while foreign language teaching was still growing and intercultural communication was taught as a course for English majors in many universities. *College English Curriculum Requirement* mentioned that "College English" is not only a language course that provides basic knowledge about English,, but also a capacity enhancement course that helps students to broaden their horizons and learn about different cultures of the world. The introduction of intercultural communication was just in time to satisfy the need for this. Intercultural Communication as a new discipline began to draw attention of Chinese researchers.

The third period began when the 5th International Conference on Cross-Cultural Communication "East and West" was held in China in 1995; and it was in this conference that the China Association for the Intercultural Communication was established. Chinese scholars' study has grown from academic interest to theoretical research and practical implementation. Publications on intercultural communication by Chinese as well as foreign scholars are no longer difficult to come by. More recently, intercultural studies have been applied to other fields. Intercultural training and consultation are now gaining popularity in more developed cities like Shanghai, Beijing, Shenzhen.

With the arrival of 21st century, the intercultural communication study to foreign language teaching is booming. Chinese scholars have focused on researches on intercultural communication academically and practically with the fast pace of political and economic development in China. The newly issued *College English Curriculum Requirement* in 2004 in China listed that intercultural communication as an important content of the syllabus. The same has been written into the *English Teaching Syllabus for English Majors* in 2000 by the National Foreign Language

Teaching Advisory Board. A boom of teaching materials and course books, along with more in-depth researches into intercultural communication, can be expected in the near future.

4.2.4 Defining Intercultural Communication

The term "intercultural communication" was first used by Edward T. Hall (1959) in his book—*The Silent Language*. In its most general sense, intercultural communication occurs when a member of one culture produces a message for consumption by a member of another culture. According to Samovar, et al. (2006, 48), "Intercultural communication is communication between people whose cultural perceptions and symbol system are distinct enough to alter the communication event." Collier and Thomas (1988) stated, "Intercultural communication is contact between persons who identify themselves as distinct from one another in cultural terms." We can see that intercultural communication has a wide range, which refers to all kinds of human communications. We can put its definition into a simple way, that is, it refers to communication between persons from different cultures. However, it can also refer to communication between persons of the same cultural group but with differences in personality.

Due to the comprehensiveness of culture and the complexity of communication, intercultural communication takes various forms. The labels international, interracial, interethnic, intracultural communication are often used in the discussion of intercultural communication.

International communication takes place between nations and governments rather than individuals. The dialogue in the United Nations, for example, would be termed international communication. Interracial communication occurs when the sender and receiver exchanging messages are from different races, while interethnic communication refers to the communication of people from different ethnic groups. For example, Cubans living in Miami, Mexicans in San Diego, and Chinese in San Francisco might be all citizens of the United States, yet they are from different ethnic groups. If a Tibetan communicates with a Han in China, it is interethnic communication, as they are from different ethnic groups. If an Afro-American interacts with a white American, it is interracial communication due to their different physical characteristics. Interracial communication may or may not be intercultural.

Intracultural communication is defined as communication between and among members of the same culture, so if we examine communication between two Japanese or between two Germans, we are looking at intracultural communication.

We should point out that some people also translate the terminology—intercultural communication into "cross-cultural communication" which emphasizes a comparison between cultures while intercultural communication focuses on the process of communication. That is, the term "cross-cultural communication" traditionally implies a comparison of some phenomena across cultures. For example, when we examine the use of self-confidence in Japan and China, we are making a cross-cultural comparison. If we examine how Japanese use self-confidence when communicating with Germans, we are investigating intercultural communication. In this book, we use intercultural communication as the terminology since we mainly focus on the dynamic changes in communication between people.

4.2.5 The Importance of Intercultural Communication

4.2.5.1 Prerequisite for Language Learning

The ultimate goal of language learning is to improve one's communicative competence, so it is significant to find out how to achieve the goal. Since language and culture are interwoven together, it is important for language learners to understand the cultures of other nations, and have intercultural awareness, otherwise, intercultural communication will be impossible.

People used to assume that learning the rules of English grammar and a large amount of vocabulary was sufficient in English learning. The more grammar and vocabulary a learner had, the higher the level of proficiency was. It has shown, however, that mastering a lot of language rules doesn't necessarily mean effective communication among people. For example, if someone says "he have a book" instead of "he has a book"; the grammatical mistake doesn't affect the communication purpose. But if a person asks an English lady how old she is, no matter how correct his/her grammar and pronunciation might be, the English lady may not be tolerant of his/her blunders, because such a question could put her in an embarrassing situation. In English culture, people take age, salary, religious beliefs, etc., as privacy.

The communication repertories people possess can vary significantly from culture to culture, which can lead to all sorts of difficulties. Through the study of intercultural communication, these difficulties at least can be reduced and at best nearly eliminated.

4.2.5.2 Demand of Current Situation in China

"Global village" is a term used to describe the shrinking world brought about by the rapid development of telecommunication technology and transportation networks. The advent of the global economy is changing the fundamental nature of the governments, business, organizations and populations. We are no longer constrained by state boundaries but have become part of an interdependent international network in the global business environment setting.

China is the world's largest market with a population of 1.3 billion. With the development of the Reform and Opening-up Policy, international exchange and co-operation are being dramatically expanded. Especially after the entry into WTO, increasing waves of intercultural contact have occurred between Chinese and the world in business, education, arts and personal lives.

Since 1978, the total number of Chinese who went overseas for further education has reached one million. And more and more foreigners visited China for business and tourism. The 29th Olympic Games held in Beijing in August 2008 provided an invaluable opportunity for China to show herself to the world and for the world to get to know the real China. As a result, skills in intercultural communication have acquired significant and practical values for the growing numbers of people who choose to work, study, travel, or live abroad.

4.2.5.3 Basic Requirement for Successful Career

One main purpose of Intercultural communication study is to improve one's intercultural communicative competence, which will ultimately lead to personal success, especially for individual on a managerial or professional level. Good communicative competence does not only depend on the basic knowledge but also the ability in intercultural communication. With the knowledge of the communicative ways of other cultures, we may know more about the norms and values and communicate effectively with people from different cultures in the future career.

To some degree, many international business failures have been ascribed to a lack of intercultural competence on the part of business practitioners. We may say that without intercultural communicative competency, there will be less chance for being involved in foreign business negotiation and academic exchange.

4.3 Basic Concept

In order to better understand the concept of intercultural communication competence and the various ways to conceptualize the concept by cultural scholars, it is helpful to explore briefly the nature of competence, intercultural competence, and intercultural communication competence. The relationship between nonverbal communication and second language learning will also be analyzed in this section.

4.3.1 Competence

In literature, various terms are used to name the abilities needed for the age of globalization. In addition to intercultural competence, other terminologies such as global and international competence and multicultural competence are also employed. All of these expressions use the word "competence." For this reason, a brief discussion of the notion of competence follows.

Spitzberg (2000) stated that competence is considered as an ability or a set of skilled behaviors. But any given behavior or ability may be judged competent in one context, and incompetent in another. Accordingly, competence cannot inhere in the behavior or ability itself. It must instead be viewed as a social evaluation of behavior. This social evaluation is composed of two primary criteria of appropriateness and effectiveness. Appropriateness means that the valued rules, norms, and expectancies of the relationship are not violated significantly. Effectiveness is the accomplishment of valued goals or rewards relative to costs and alternatives.

Bowden and Marton (1998) outlined four possible approaches to competence: (1) behaviorist (basic performance); (2) additive (performance plus knowledge); (3) integrative (performance and knowledge are integrated); and (4) holistic (including self-perception and views in the integrated performance and knowledge) (105-106). According to Bowden and Marton (1998), competence includes the element of performance regardless of the approach used to view competence. They view competence in two ways: in the first sense, competence refers to sets of independent, observable units of behaviors in the workplace; in the second sense it refers to the capabilities of seeing and handling novel situations in powerful ways, capabilities that frequently integrate disciplinary and professional knowledge (113-114). This definition goes beyond the basic definition of competence and incorporates integration and application of learning and focuses on how situations are handled.

Havelock, Hasler, Flew, McIntyre, Schofield and Toby (1995) defined competence as "the possession of the abilities required to manage a particular problem in a particular context" with the development of competence demonstrated by the range of contexts in which the person works and the attributes and abilities are needed in each of these contexts (39-40).

Some researchers consider that the word "competence" includes distinctions between conscious and unconscious, acquired and learned, and general and specific. For example, according to Maslow's (1970) model, conscious and unconscious aspects are expounded further by the delineation of skill development under one of four leaves: unconscious incompetence, conscious incompetence, conscious competence, unconscious competence, in which skills are second-nature (Beebe, Beebe, & Redmond, 1999). Boys (1995) also stated that competence is a mixture of the unconscious as well as the conscious, the unarticulated as well as the articulated (cited from Edwards & Knight, 1995, 38).

Some communication scholars describe competence as a characteristic of the association between individuals, not an individual attribute. Lustig and Koester's (2003) definition concurs with other scholars who stress the contextual element of competence. They pointed out that competence is dependent on relationships and situations and is ultimately a social judgment that people make about others (64-65). In relation to assessment, they noted that while "judgments of competence are influenced by an assessment of an individual's personal characteristics; they cannot be wholly determined by them, because competence involves an interaction between people" (64). Communication scholars, like Spitzberg and Cupach (1984) claimed that the fundamental competence is an individual's ability to adapt effectively to the environment over time to achieve goals (35). After a wealth of literature on competence, they confirmed that no other aspect of competence seems universally accepted as the ability to adapt to the changing environment and social situations (35) and the adaptability is as the core of all competence constructs (36).

Klemp (1979) defined competence as generic knowledge, skills, traits, self-image, or motives that are causally related to effective behavior referenced to external performance criteria (42). This definition includes traits, self-image, and motives which are not cited in other definitions. The researcher further stated that competence tends to be measured individually, when in reality, individuals utilize numerous competencies at once (49). This has implications for the measurement of competence, that is, competence should be measured as a whole as opposed to separating measures of just knowledge or just skills alone. Other researchers also agreed that competence needs to be integrative and holistic and thus, assessment should be holistic as well. For example, Pottinger and Goldsmith (1979) viewed the division of global behavioral objectives as too simplistic. According to them, such divisions assume that acquisition of micro-skills and abilities adds up to overall competence (27). Thus, oversimplification may yield reliable observable outcomes but "provides no insights into the skills and abilities that cause these outcomes" (Pottinger and Goldsmith, 1979, 28). They advocated the use of multiple measures in assessing competence by stating that "how one defines the domain of competence will greatly affect one's choice of measurement procedures" (Pottinger and Goldsmith, 1979, 30). Since competence varies by setting, context, individual, using a variety of assessments ensures a stronger measurement.

Chen and Starosta (1996) argued that there remains a debate about whether competence refers to "performance" or "knowledge" or whether it is an "inherent ability" or a "learned ability." The exploration of the definition of competence raises numerous issues and questions. For instance, how to avoid oversimplification to measure students' outcomes in communication? How to identify and assess the unconscious competence? In which context is intercultural competence viewed and assessed? These questions show the complexity of this topic and demonstrate the myriad of issues with which teachers may need to wrestle in order to assess intercultural competence more effectively.

4.3.2 Communicative Competence

Intercultural communication competence is often considered to be a subfield of communication competence, so it is helpful to view communicative competence before the discussion of intercultural communication competence since many issues are similar to both.

To use a language and to interact with others through a coherent discourse require the acquisition, development, and application of what has been termed communicative competence, which is the knowledge system underlying the appropriate use of language in context.

The concept of communicative competence was originally developed by Dell Hymes (1972), reacting against the perceived inadequacy of Noam Chomsky's (1965) distinction between competence and performance. Hymes argued that children must learn not only language rules for the use of language. Their utterances must be culturally feasible and appropriate to the situation (see Section 4.4.1). Communicative competence is not a simple mastery of how-to rules for language use. Such competence "deals with how we know that a given situation requires a given speech variety and communicative approach" (Johnson, 1979). In a similar way, Gee (1993, 108) referred to primary discourse: "to which people are apprenticed early in life… as members of particular families within their sociocultrual settings." As members of groups, people learn other ways to use language throughout their lives, making them use multiple discourses. Gee calls these secondary discourses.

Then culture frames communication by directly influencing its forms and content. The use of routine language, for example, varies from culture to culture. In this regard, Forgas (1988) noted that those communicative episodes are both highly predictable and culturally specific: culture provides an individual with shared cognitive schemes that shape language use and broader communicative conduct. The most straightforward example is the difference in greeting behaviors from culture to culture.

Communicative competence within a cultural system can vary widely form person to person. Some people use language more effectively because their knowledge system is more complex. An individual can also possess different levels of communicative competence across cultural system, such that greater effectiveness and proficiency will be present when that person uses language in one cultural context compared to another.

In general, specific issues related to communicative competence evolve around the topics of communicators' consciousness, communication contextuality and competence measurement (Spitzberg & Cupach, 1984, 73). Communicators' consciousness includes objective self-awareness, self-consciousness, self-monitoring and interaction involvement. In regard to consciousness and communication, Spitzberg and Cupach (1984) noted that it is not enough to address consciousness but rather, to examine the relative degree of awareness and the effects of various levels and forms of awareness on communication (83).

Context in communication relates to the debate over trait versus state. In regard to this debate, Spitzberg and Cupach (1984) eschewed several scholarly works that are based on the assumption that "certain skills domains are universal assets for competence." They viewed this dichotomy (trait vs. state) as not necessarily mutually exclusive but rather, recast the debate in terms of "competence-related traits," recognizing that certain traits may lead to competence in some situations and not others (90-93).

4.3.3 Intercultural Competence

Cultures can be different not only between continents or nations, but also within the same company or even family. That is, every human being has its own history, its own life and also its own cultural affiliation (such as geographical, ethnical, moral, ethical, religious, political, historical). An understanding of "cultural" competence underlies an understanding of "intercultural" competence. Cultural competence is related to the language-culture ability individuals develop for use in their native societies. As we enter our native language cultures so early in life, we do not normally think about native cultural competence. Yet we are "culturally competent" and able to perform in acceptable and intelligible ways within our societies. When contact with people from different cultural backgrounds, they will meet many challenges since the monolingual-monocultural individuals are unaccustomed to dealing with people from other cultures and may be confused, repulsed by the differences they encounter. It is obvious that native competence alone is not adequate for sustained and satisfactory interaction, only intercultural competence can help people communicate with others from different cultures easily and effectively.

Defining intercultural competence is rather complex and difficult. Lynch (1999, 49) described it in terms of behaviors, attitudes and policies that are congruent, converge and which result in effectiveness in intercultural situations, Barrera and Kramer (1997, 217) used the term broadly to "refer to the ability of service providers to respond optimally to all children, understanding both the richness and the limitations of the socio-cultural contexts in which children and families as well as the service providers themselves may be operating." Lynch (1999, 49) considered cultural competence as the ability to think, feel and also to act in ways that acknowledge, respect and also build upon ethnic, cultural and linguistic diversity in multi-ethnic and/or multicultural situations.

There are many different words and phrases that have been used in the research as a synonym for intercultural competence, such as cross-cultural adaptation, intercultural sensitivity, multicultural competence, transcultural competence, global competence, cross-cultural effectiveness, international competence, cultural competence, and cross-cultural adjustment, etc. Kim and Ruben (1992) stated that the use of "intercultural" is preferable because "the term is not bounded by any specific cultural attributes" (404). Bradford, Allen and Beisser (2000) confirmed that many scholars seem willing to use intercultural communication competence in preference to other labels. Based on the definition of intercultural communication, the term "intercultural communication competence" will be used in this book.

Now we can use Fantini, Arias-Galicia and Guay's (2001) statements to summarize the two concepts: cultural competence and intercultural competence. The former refers to the "language-culture ability individuals develop for use in their native societies" (4). They referred to cultural competence as an "acceptable and intelligible" performance within one's society. The later, on the other hand, refers to the "multiple abilities that allow one to interact effectively and appropriately across cultures" (8).

4.3.4 Intercultural Communication Competence

Language and culture are inextricably bound, so intercultural communication is complex and potentially problematic. Even speaking the language does not guarantee effective intercultural communication. Intercultural communication competence (ICC) is important in all social encounters in culturally diverse situations. In fact, it is a social skill required almost everywhere and in all situations other than in mono-cultural settings. Even in so-called "mono-cultural" situations, various sub-cultural variations necessitate the ability to relate to and communicate with others different from oneself.

Chen and Starosta (1999) defined "intercultural communication competence" as "the ability to effectively and appropriately execute communication behaviors that negotiate each other's cultural identity or identities in a culturally diverse environment" (28). They outlined three key components of intercultural communication competence: intercultural sensitivity, intercultural awareness, and intercultural adroitness, defined as verbal and nonverbal skills needed to act effectively in intercultural interactions.

Wiseman (2001) argued that ICC is comprised of knowledge, skills, and motivation needed to interact effectively and appropriately with persons from different cultures. Motivation is a unique element in this definition. Wiseman (2001, 10) further listed researches on behaviors related to ICC including: being mindful (Gudykunst, 1992), interaction involvement (Cegala, 1984), recognition of nonverbal messages (Anderson, 1994), appropriate self-disclosure (Li, 1999), behavioral flexibility (Bochner & Kelly, 1974), interaction management (Wiemann, 1977), identity maintenance (Ting-Toomey, 1994), uncertainty reduction strategies (Sanders, Wiseman, & Matz, 1991), appropriate display of respect (Ruben, 1976), immediacy skills (Benson, 1978), ability to establish relationships (Hammer, 1987).

Kim (1992) used a systems-theory approach to examine ICC. She defined the construct as the "adaptive capacity" comprised of cognitive, affective, and operational/behavioral dimensions. So adaptability is seen as the core of ICC which refers to "the individual's capacity to suspend or modify some of the old cultural ways, and learn and accommodate some of the new cultural ways, and creatively find ways to manage the dynamics of cultural difference/unfamiliarity, intergroup posture, and the accompanying stress" (1992, 377). According to Kim, the elements of cultural difference, intergroup posture and accompanying stress are the challenges inherent in all intercultural encounters and the nature of ICC should be viewed in this context. Kim (1992) advocated separating intercultural communication competence from cultural communication competence since the content of the later is culture-specific and varies from culture to culture, whereas the content of ICC "should remain constant across all intercultural situations regardless of specific cultures involved" (373). Spitzberg and Cupach (1984) concurred with Kim on the role of adaptability as a critical competence that is context-independent. They noted that adaptability "implies that different behaviors and skills are applied in different contexts and situations" (90).

Byram (1997) argued that a comprehensive definition of ICC should include the social context and nonverbal communicative competence (34). He (1997) proposed a comprehensive framework that includes the components of knowledge, skills and attitudes. Knowledge is divided into two parts: (1) knowledge of others and of social processes of social groups; and (2) knowledge of self and of critical cultural awareness, which involves an ability to evaluate practices and products of one's own and others' cultures. Skills include: (1) skills to interpret and relate; and (2) skills to discover and/or to interact. Intercultural attitudes are defined as relativizing self (one's values, beliefs and behaviors within a larger perspective) and valuing others' values, beliefs and behaviors (Byram, 1997, 73). Of the three components, Byram viewed attitudes as fundamental to ICC. Based on the previous research, Byram (1997) concluded that there are a variety of issues that need to be taken into account when defining ICC. Those issues include: emphasis on knowledge of cultures and cultural practices versus the skills of "conscious analysis" of intercultural interaction, the role of non-verbal communication in ICC, the breadth in which the concept of ICC should be defined, focus on psychological traits versus "capacity to act," and the influence of social and political factors on defining and assessing ICC (Byram, 1997, 30).

From the above discussion, we can see that scholars' efforts in intercultural communication study have provided interesting insights into attitudes and behaviors which contribute to effective intercultural interactions and successful cultural adaptation. However, a number of limitations have hindered the study of ICC. Spitzberg (1989) concluded, "Indeed, the literature reveals an unwieldy collection of terminologies, a general lack of specific or practical predictive statements, and a deficit of conceptual explanatory integration."

In sum, intercultural communication scholars conceived of ICC not only as effective and appropriate interaction between people, but as effective and appropriate interaction between people who belong to particular environments. For the purposes of the present study, ICC is considered very broadly as an impression that behavior is appropriate and effective in a given context. We adopt Chen and Starosta's (2007) definition: ICC is the ability to effectively and appropriately execute communication behaviors to elicit a desired response in a specific environment (241). This definition shows that competent persons must not only know how to interact effectively and appropriately with people and environment, but also know how to fulfill their own communication goals using this ability.

4.3.5 Construct of Intercultural Communication Competence

Research and literature on ICC was initially focused on the discussion of what factors and elements could predict an individual's success, especially on overseas assignments. Thus, a discussion of ICC has usually involved a list of dimensions or components or elements.

The researchers in communication, education, psychology use different approaches in developing lists of components or predictors. Lustig and Koester (1993) identified at least four different approaches to research on ICC: trait approach, perceptual approach, behavioral approach, and culture-specific approach. Collier (1989) also provided different approaches to ICC, including intercultural attitudes approach, behavioral skills approach, ethnographic approach, and cultural identity approach. Collier (1989) concluded that different approaches emphasize different aspects and perspectives on intercultural competence and that research can benefit from the "clarification of conceptualizations" (298).

A review of the intercultural literature suggests an ICC construct various components, including: three domains (Wiseman & Koester, 1993), four dimensions (Fantini, 2000), multiple manifestations (Kealey, 1990; Kohls, 1979), various developmental levels and proficiency in a second language (Fantini, 2000).

Domains

Three domains include (1) the ability to establish and maintain relationships;

(2) the ability to communicate with minimal loss or distortion; and (3) the ability to attain compliance among the parties involved to accomplish something together. Lacking any one of these ingredients, the interaction fails. These domains are equally important to success in one's own culture.

Dimensions

The dimensions of ICC include: personality strength, communication skills, psychological adaptation, and cultural awareness (Chen & Starosta, 2007, 244-252). The first three dimensions are familiar with Bloom's (1969) educational taxonomy with the terms "cognition, behavior, and affect." However, Bloom's construct omits awareness, which is not equally important, perhaps the most important of the four dimensions.

Personality attributes refer to the traits that constitute an individual's personality. These traits stem from our unique experiences within a culture and reflect our heredity partly. The main personal traits that affect ICC include self-concept, self-disclosure, self-awareness, and social relaxation. Communication skills are the verbal and nonverbal behaviors that enable us to be effective in interactions with others. Such behaviors in intercultural communication include message skills, behavioral flexibility, interaction management, and social skills. Psychological adjustment refers to the ability to adapt to a new culture. It entails a complex process through which we acquire the ability to fit in the new cultural environment. We become more competent in intercultural communication when we display psychological adaptation, which includes four elements: (1) stress; (2) feelings of frustration; (3) feelings of alienation, and (4) ambiguous situations caused by the new environment. Cultural awareness refers to understanding the conventions of the host culture that affect how people think and behave. Each culture shows different thinking patterns. It emphasizes the importance of cultural knowledge for effective intercultural communication and requires understanding of the "cultural map." If a map is accurate, we read it, and we won't get lost; if we know a culture, we'll know our way around in the life of a society.

Manifestations

The qualities of intercultural identify behavioral traits are: flexibility, patience, humor, empathy, openness, respect, non-judgmentalness, and tolerance for ambiguity, among others. These empirical findings are substantiated in research about intercultural effectiveness (Kohls, 1979, 72).

A Development Process

Developing ICC is a life-long process. One is always in the process of "becoming." Each intercultural experience presents new challenges. And no matter how long one works towards developing ICC, in all likelihood adult learners will never attain a level of competence comparable to that of host culture natives.

The Role of Language

Proficiency in a second language constitutes a critical component of ICC. It is inconceivable that second-language proficiency be omitted from any intercultural effort. But Bennett (cited from Fantini, 1997, 16-21) stated that a person with proficiency in a second language but little or no understanding of its culture may misunderstand and even offend his/her hosts because of the lack of cultural ability. It is more difficult to imagine a person without a second language attaining any significant degree of success in another culture. Accordingly, ICC development is limited and constrained by an inability in the target tongue; conversely, it is facilitated and accelerated by ability in the host language.

4.3.6 Effective Intercultural Communicator

We have discussed some basic concepts related to intercultural communication competence, and the construct of it. Now we summarize that despite different theoretical approaches, paradigms, definitions and philosophical foundations, researchers are in consensus about some characteristics shared by most people who are capable, skilled and effective communicators in intercultural communication. It is generally agreed upon that communication effectiveness is significantly improved when the interventionist (Lynch, 1999, 77):

- respects individuals from other cultures;
- makes continued and sincere attempts to empathetically understand the world from others' point of view;
- is open to new learning;
- is flexible;
- has a healthy sense of humor;
- tolerates ambiguity well;
- is sensitive to own prejudices;
- approaches others with a desire and an openness to learn;
- is genuinely interested in others;
- sees differences not in terms of inferiority but as learning opportunities.

As abovementioned, language and culture are closely related, intercultural communication becomes a complex and problematic activity. The miscommunication often takes place because we always assume that people who share a common culture or language also share the same attitudes, beliefs, values and behaviors. It must be emphasized that culture is not the only important or salient variable when differences or potentially conflicting situations arise in diverse settings. Socio-economic status, educational background, religion, gender, age and world-view are some of the determinants that influence who and what we are, and also why we react in a particular way in certain situations.

But we should point out that being an effective intercultural communicator does not imply becoming a member of another culture by adopting another group's values, attitudes, beliefs, customs, or manners of speech, dress or conduct. According to Green (1982, 52) such over-identification is none other than patronizing and manipulation. Abandoning one's own culture and substituting another is a sign of disrespect for one's own culture. Being an effective intercultural communicator does not mean that individuals should be easily grouped and categorized without variability among such groups. It does not imply knowing everything about all different cultures. It is rather an active demonstration of respect for differences, an enthusiastic eagerness to learn about other cultures, an acceptance of different viewpoints on reality and a flexibility and willingness to adjust, change and reorientate where required (Lynch & Hanson, 1999).

4.4 Nonverbal Communication in the Models of Language Proficiency

So far we have discussed the intercultural communication study and some basic concepts related to ICC in the past decades. Now it is time to examine the relationship between the ability of effective communication and nonverbal communication.

The issue of nonverbal communication in intercultural communication competence has been noted by Le Roux (2002). In reviewing nonverbal communication and its impact on the culturally diverse classrooms, Le Roux put forward that educators need to investigate nonverbal communication patterns in culturally diverse groups. This process will help educators better understand the specific needs of culturally diverse students and facilitate the implementation of culturally sensitive communication strategies which will help reduce the threat of conflict and aid in conflict resolution when problems arise.

Thus, this section will analyze the position of nonverbal communication in some frequent-used models of language ability known as communicative competence, which has been considered as one of the most influential theoretical developments in language education. Different models of language knowledge and language use will be illustrated so as to expect more models to emerge as researchers try to open the Pandora's Box.

4.4.1 Hymes' Communicative Competence

In Chomsky's (1965) view, competence refers to speaker-hearer underlying knowledge of his/her language, and it is a kind of internalized grammar which is implicit in actual language performance, while performance is the actual use of the language in concrete situations, which is the manifestation of the competence. According to Chomsky (1965) only under the idealization that a speaker-listener perfectly knows the language of a completely homogeneous speech-community and is not affected by such grammatically irrelevant conditions as memory limitations, distractions, shifts of attention and interest, and errors in applying his/her knowledge of the language in actual performance (1965, 3-4).

Hymes (1972) criticized Chomsky's notion of competence and performance and their relationship. He argued that Chomsky's view of competence is too idealized and limited to describe language behavior in actual situations and his view of performance cannot reflect competence completely because it is confined to the linguistic competence and doesn't account for socio-cultural factors involved in the process of interaction. Social life influences not only the outward performance but also the inner competence, and performance should be associated with language use in the concrete situation. It is necessary to distinguish two kinds of competence: linguistic competence and communicative competence. The former deals with producing and understanding the grammatically correct sentences while the latter deals with producing and understanding the sentences which are appropriate for the situation related.

Hymes further argued that communicative competence is not a simple mastery of how-to rules for language use. It is composed of two primary criteria: appropriateness and effectiveness. In Hymes' view (1972), the appropriateness of language use should be taken into account since the speaker knows intuitively what is socially appropriate or inappropriate and can adjust the language to sociocultural factors. He defined communicative competence as "a knowledge of rules for understanding and producing both the referential and social meaning of language," and a competence concerning "when to speak, when not, and as to what to talk about with whom, when, where, in what manner" (1972, 277).

To Hymes (1972), there are certain rules of use without which the linguistic or grammar rules are useless. Among many things needed for communicative competence, are also the rules of nonverbal communication of target language. Thus, he highlighted the rules of nonverbal communication as important as other grammar rules for learning a second language.

In 1987, Brown also emphasized the need to include nonverbal behavior in the definition of communicative competence: we cannot underestimate the importance of nonverbal communication in second language learning and in conversational analysis. Communicative competence includes nonverbal competence—knowledge of all the varying nonverbal semantics of the second culture, and an ability both to send and receive nonverbal signals unambiguously (1987, 212).

Earlier models of language ability were either linguistic or psycholinguistic. Such models focused exclusively on the linguistic components of language skills or mental processes needed to realize these skills. These models had a fairly narrow vision of linguistic ability and were concerned with verbal aspects of language, thus ignoring the nonverbal aspects altogether (Bachman, 1990). From the 1980s, three different models of language knowledge and language use (communicative competence) have been proposed, which will be examined in the following based on the three dimensional frameworks that opt for the components, functions and rules of using nonverbal communication (see Figure 4.1).

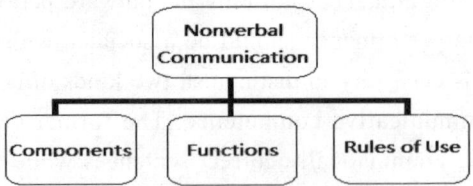

Figure 4.1 Three dimensions of nonverbal communication

4.4.2 Nonverbal Communication in Canale and Swain's Communicative Competence Model

In the 1970s and early 1980s, a more comprehensive model was proposed by Canale and Swain (1980). The 1980 model comprises minimally grammatical competence, sociolinguistic competence, and strategic competence and does not seem to have assigned a specific place for the components of the nonverbal communication;

nonetheless, the model is explicit about the compensatory function of nonverbal communication strategies. As part of strategic competence, nonverbal communication strategies can be called into action "to compensate for breakdowns in communication due to performance variables or insufficient competence" (30), such as the use of role-playing strategies for the communication of difficult concepts. Canale and Swain (1980) further concluded that, "Strategic competence will be made up of verbal and nonverbal communication strategies that may be called into action to compensate for breakdowns in communication due to performance variables or to insufficient competence" (Canale & Swain, 1980, 30). In 1983, Canale further stated that strategic competence is composed of mastery of verbal and nonverbal communication strategies... (1) to compensate for breakdowns in communication due to insufficient competence... and (2) to enhance the effectiveness of communication (10-11).

Other researchers also acknowledge that nonverbal communication is an important aspect of strategic competence. For example, Savignon (1983) stated, "A gesture may serve as a coping strategy by either filling in for a word or expression or sustaining rapport throughout a momentary silence" (44). Mime is included among the communication strategies suggested by Tarone (1981, 286). For instance, when someone faced a breakdown in communication because he/she was unable to recall the word "applause," he/she replaced the word by clapping his/her hands to illustrate the idea he/she wished to communicate. Dörnyei and Scott (1997) also mentioned "mime" as a strategy for "describing whole concepts nonverbally, or accompanying a verbal strategy with a visual illustration" (190). As Bachman (1990) confirmed, "Nonverbal manifestations of strategic competence...are clearly an important part of strategic competence in communication" (100). As for grammatical competence, it is not only concerned with the rules of grammar but also knowledge of the paralinguistic and kinesic features of the language such as intonation, facial expressions, and gestures, in other words, the mastery of the language code (verbal or nonverbal).

In 1983, Canale began to modify the earlier model and introduced a model that tried to account for both psychological and contextual factors. He defined communicative competence as "the underlying systems of knowledge and skill required for communication" (Canale, 1983, 5), which is shown in the following figure 4.2.

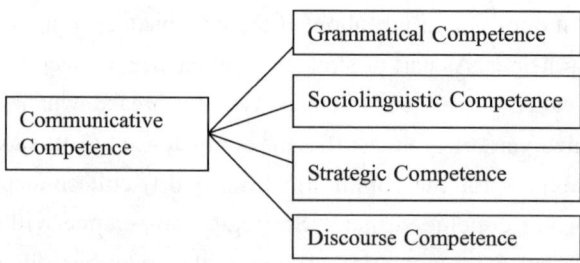

Figure 4.2　The model of communicative competence (Canale, 1983)

The components of Canale's model, except for the grammatical competence, have witnessed drastic changes when compared with Canale and Swain's (1980) model. Sociolinguistic competence, for instance, helps form two separate components of sociolinguistic and discourse competence. It refers to the sociocultural rules of appropriate use of L2; that is, how utterances are produced and understood in different sociolinguistic contexts. It includes appropriate use of kinesics and proxemics such as eye contact, respect for personal space, clothing and ornamentation, how and where people touch others, and gestures. Discourse competence is defined as rules concerning cohesion and coherence of various kinds of discourse in L2 (e.g., use of appropriate pronouns, synonyms, conjunctions, substitution, repetition, marking of congruity and continuity, topic comment sequence, etc.). Canale also extended the use and the function of nonverbal communication strategies in that he considered them not only as compensatory strategies that are called upon when grammatical and sociolinguistic L2 competence fail to function, but also as elements that boost the effectiveness of communication (e.g., slow speech for rhetorical effect).

4.4.3 Nonverbal Communication in Bachman's Model of CLA

In 1990, a more comprehensive model of communicative competence was proposed by Bachman, who stressed the importance of describing "the processes by which various components interact with each other and with context in which language use occurs" (81). Bachman (1990) suggested using the term "communicative language ability (CLA) to combine in itself the aspects of both language proficiency and communicative competence. He developed three central components for CLA to define ones' competence in communicative language use: language competence, strategic competence, and psycho-physiological mechanisms. Bachman (1990) associated the three components of communicative language ability with language use context and language users' knowledge structures. In 1996, Bachman and Palmer defined language competence as "a domain of information in memory that is available for use by the metacognitive strategies in creating and interpreting discourse in language use" (1996, 67-75).

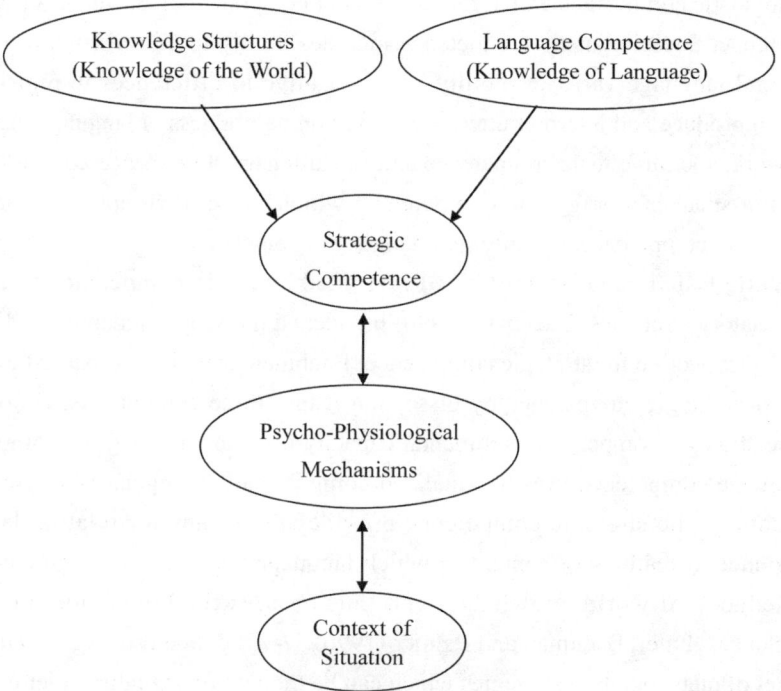

Figure 4.3   Components of communicative language ability in communicative language use (Bachman, 1990, 85)

The first component refers to language competence containing organizational and pragmatic competence. The organizational competence was further divided into grammatical competence and textual competence. Bachman's grammatical competence is consonant with Canale and Swain's (1980) grammatical competence in that it comprises abilities to control the formal structure of language. The textual competence refers to the knowledge of conventions for cohesion and coherence and rhetorical organization. It also includes conventions for language use in conversations, involving starting, maintaining, and closing conversations. Bachman's (1990) textual competence is thus believed to contain Canale and Swain's (1980) discourse competence, as well as the strategic competence. Pragmatic competence mainly focuses on the relationship between what one says in his/her communicative acts and what functions he/she intends to perform through his/her utterances. This concerns the illocutionary force of an utterance, or "the knowledge of pragmatic conventions for performing acceptable language functions" (90). Illocutionary competence enables a speaker to use his/her language to serve a variety of functions; it also helps a hearer interpret the illocutionary force of an utterance. This ability is accounted for by the sociolinguistic competence which forms the other component of Bachman's pragmatic competence. Sociolinguistic competence includes ability to be sensitive to regional and social language varieties; ability to be sensitive to differences in register; and ability to produce and interpret utterances based on naturalness of language use. In his framework, sociolinguistic competence and illocutionary competence are put together to form a speaker's pragmatic competence, which, in turn, composes, along with grammatical competence, the speaker's language competence.

While Canale and Swain (1980) restricted strategic competence to a set of compensatory strategies, Bachman (1990) broadened the scope and envisaged a much broader perspective for strategic competence. Bachman provided a broader theoretical model of strategic competence by dissecting it into three components. He believed that the strategic competence is a mental capacity for implementing the competences of language competence in contextualized communicative language use. According to Bachman, the strategic competence provides the means for relating language competence to features of context in which language use takes place (soicocultural knowledge, real world knowledge) and thus ensures the interaction among the competences. Later, Bachman and Palmer (1996, 67-75) defined strategic competence as "a set of metacognitive strategies which can be thought of as higher order executive processes."

The feature that distinguishes Bachman's (1990) model from other models is its in-depth analysis of the components of each competence. Bachman mentioned paralinguistic features and placed them within the grammatical competence which are governed by sociolinguistic competence and illocutionary competence for contextual and functional appropriateness, with strategic competence providing the link between these competences. That is, paralanguage is seen as mastery of the language code (verbal or nonverbal), or as part of sociolinguistic competence, which includes appropriateness of kinesics and proxemics.

In the models of communicative competence, paralanguage is viewed as a few gestures used as strategies to overcome linguistic deficiencies. If paralanguage is as important as has been dicussed in communication, it surely needs to be granted a far more significant place. Since strategies in these models have never been represented parsimoniously—strategies can be linguistic, sociolinguistic, discourse, or paralinguistic—it is proposed that strategies be considered as a means of producing "actual communication" (Canale, 1983) and paralinguistic competence be regarded as a primary facet of communicative competence. As Brown (1980, 202) said, "communicative competence includes nonverbal competence—knowledge of all the varying nonverbal semantics of the second culture and an ability both to send and receive nonverbal signals unambiguously."

4.4.4 Nonverbal Communication in Wen's ICC Model

With the development of economy, communication between people with different cultural backgrounds has become more and more frequently. The ability to communicate with people effectively becomes a basic requirement for people who want success. Then how to improve people's ICC becomes an important project for researchers who focus on the study from the intercultural perspective. The research on communicative competence becomes relatively stable and more interdisciplinary. Wen Qiufang (1999), a Chinese researcher, made a systematic analysis of the communication competence and put forward a model of cross-cultural communication competence which consists of communicative competence and cross-cultural competence. Her model is illustrated in Figure 4.4.

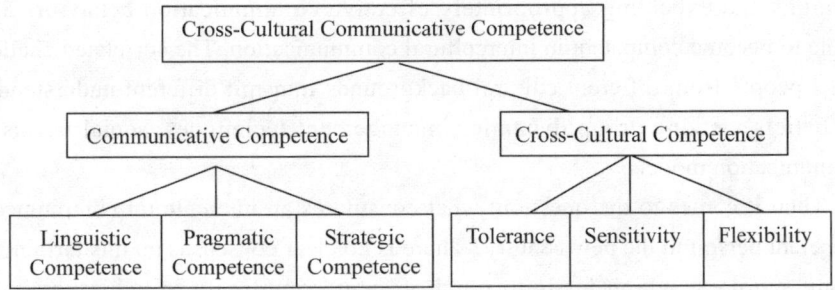

Figure 4.4　Wen's model of cross-cultural communicative competence (Wen, 1999, 21)

In this model, Wen integrates the concept of pragmatic competence which was put forward by Bachman (1990) in the category of language competence into communicative competence. Her integration is comparatively simple and reasonable.

4.4.5 Nonverbal Communication and a New Model of ICC

Confucian said, "Human beings draw close to one another by their common nature but habits and customs keep them apart." Culture gives meanings to behaviors, diverse hand gesticulations; consequently, culture affects every aspect of nonverbal communication. When we first expose to a new situation where manners, language and behaviors are all strange, we may experience culture shock with changeable meanings from other societies. What is absolutely adequate in one culture may be impolite or even disgusting in other societies. As Arasaratnam and Banerjee (2007) stated that many studies show that the failure or misunderstandings in intercultural communication are largely caused by the misinterpretation or misuse of nonverbal behaviors. Accordingly, learning the art of switching cultural channels to avoid the pain and discomfort of misinterpretations of nonverbal communication is essential for successful interaction in intercultural situations which entails just as much understanding of nonverbal messages as the verbal ones. The better our intercultural communication skills, the easier it will be for us to take our place in international society. Most important of all, the widespread population migrations in modern society have changed the demographics of some nations and new intercultural identities and communities have been born. All civilizations depend on each other for different reasons. The growth of interdependence of people and cultures in the global society of the 21st century has forced people to become a competent person in intercultural communication.

Chen and Starosta (1996) claimed that the abilities of negotiating cultural meanings and executing appropriately effective communication behaviors allow people to become competent in intercultural communication. The correlated challenge is that people from different cultural backgrounds transmit different understandings and beliefs viewing group dynamics, management techniques, social norms and communication models.

Then it comes to the question: what constitutes an intercultural communicative competent person in the new century? There is no clear consensus on this terminology among scholars, which leads to much greater complexity in achieving expert agreement on the nature of this concept. In recent years, some common, general terminologies have even begun to emerge on what constitutes an interculturaly competent person; however, these terms often lack specificity.

Aghayeva (2011) argued that three significant positions are included in a meaningful measurement of intercultural communication. Firstly, intercultural communication should be judged at the level of social acts and not just language interpretation. Accordingly, the accepting of words and sentences is not so essential, and what accounts is the social dimension. Secondly, intercultural communication is a socially structured action or message, so the meaning of communication cannot be diminished by words. Thirdly, intercultural communication does not go on in a power vacuum, or equal-power dealings. Intercultural communication is situated in the context of imbalance of power and inequality in resources between the east and the west, the north and the south, men and women, the majority and the minority.

Based on the previous discussion, we set up a model of intercultural communication competence which shows the complicated components of ICC in the modern world.

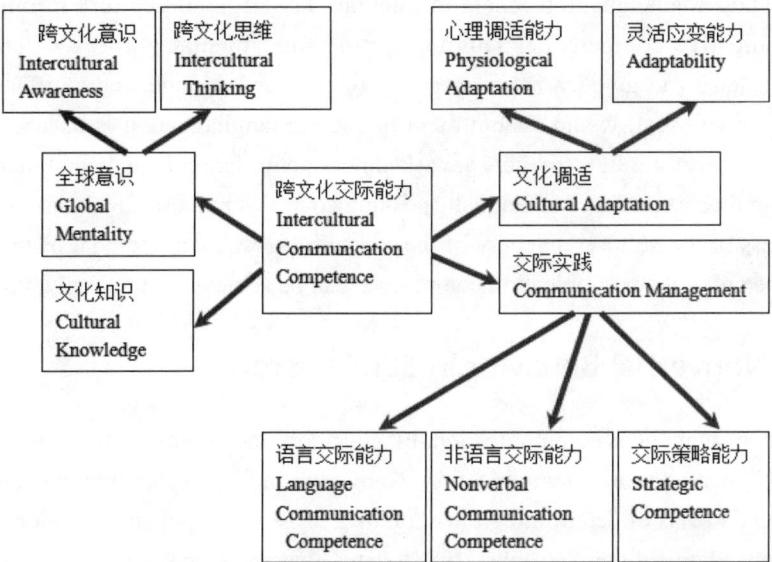

Figure 4.5   A new model of the components of intercultural communication competence

4.5 Nonverbal Communication and FL Teaching and Learning

From the different models of communicative competence we can easily access the significance of nonverbal communication. Then what is the relationship between language acquisition and nonverbal communication in FL teaching and learning?

4.5.1 FL Learning is a Process of Enculturation

The above discussion shows that language-based communicative competence is essential for L2 learners to participate in the target language culture. Learners are not only expected to acquire accurate forms of the target language, but also to learn how to use these forms in given social situations in the target language setting to convey appropriate, coherent, and strategically effective meanings to the native speakers. Therefore, learning a foreign language becomes a kind of enculturation. The L2 learner acquires new cultural frames of reference and a new world view, reflecting those of the target language culture and its speakers.

Since the target language culture is different from the learners' own culture, it is necessary for language teachers to integrate language and culture in improving communicative competence. This is also the fundamental purpose of language learning, for it can give learners experience of another language, and a different way of coping with reality, and enable them to use the language as it is used by native speakers. Therefore, EFL teachers are asked not only to familiarize their students with the cultural characteristics of English-speaking countries but also to increase students' awareness of the cultural diversity of these countries. As such, the goal of improving their intercultural communication competence can be achieved more easily.

4.5.2 Nonverbal Behavior in ELT Classroom

Since language is communication, FL educators should pay more attention to the whole phenomenon of communication. Nonverbal messages can be a more explicit and candid means of determining intention than merely the spoken word alone in FLT classroom. Woolfolk and Brooks (1983) stated that nonverbal behaviors often have effect on the demeanor of teachers and students. The success of both the student and teacher depends upon the effective communication between them, communication would be failure without the proper use of nonverbal behaviors. Stevick (1982) agreed that all of these unnoticeable things (nonverbal behaviors) carry important messages which create a profound effect on the students' feelings of welcome and comfort with the teacher (6).

On the one hand, in FLT classroom, teachers give more impressions by nonverbal behaviors than the knowledge of subject and verbal messages as the language of body and motion can send clear and distinct messages. Teachers' nonverbal behaviors communicate teachers' warmth and affect, indicate approval or disapproval, define the relationship with students, show relative power and status, reveal teachers' emotional status, regulate and pace verbal exchange, show the values, attitudes, and influence students' performance. Teachers' effective use of nonverbal cues can help them become better speakers, controllers, and entertainers and help to express teachers' emotions, convey interpersonal attitudes, present personality, and amplify verbal communication (Liu Jun, 2001, 30). It can also assist in a wide range of classroom practices by adding an extra dimension to the language, such as reducing teachers' unnecessary talking time, increasing learners' participation, building confidence, reducing fear of silence, helping make an efficient classroom management, improving classroom atmosphere, avoiding misunderstandings, and improving intercultural competence, etc. Thus, nonverbal behavior is a more effective communicative tool for improving teacher-student relationships than verbal communication in classroom.

On the other hand, students' nonverbal behaviors can also provide some cues for effective teaching because their ability and comfort with processing instruction can be interpreted from their nonverbal cues, which, in turn allows teachers to advance the discussion based on the type of observed cues. As Angelo and Cross (1993) stated that "through close observation of students in the process of learning…teachers can learn much about how students learn and, more specifically, how students respond to particular teaching approaches"(3). Therefore, students' nonverbal clues are also critically important. Their real-time feedback influences teachers' subsequent communication and allows teachers to alter the course of action if needed. In a study by Webb, Diana, Luft, Brooks and Brennan (1997), "expert" and "non-expert" teachers were evaluated for their ability to judge students' comprehension, they found that "expert" or more experienced teachers are in fact more accurate. Similarly, Neill and Caswell (1993) found that inexperienced teachers "…show an unfortunate and almost total lack of awareness of the extent or function of nonverbal pupil behaviors…"(55), and they suggested that such classroom awareness only develops with experience. Thus, classroom observation is "discrete teaching skill that needs to be learned" and "teachers learn to observe in the classroom on their own with little direction or training" (Neill and Caswell, 1993, 37). Webb et al. (1997) concluded that "from observation and interpretation of students' body language and facial expressions, the perceptive teacher can decide whether there is a need to check for comprehension, provide more or a different kind of instruction, or assign more practice" (89). As Angelo and Cross (1993) stated:

> As they are teaching, faculty monitor and react to student questions, comments, body language, and facial expressions in an almost automatic fashion. This "automatic" information gathering and impression formation is a subconscious and implicit process. Teachers depend heavily on their impression of student learning and make important judgments based on them… . (6-7)

Therefore, there is a clear need for teachers to be sensitive to nonverbal cues as a means of real-time assessment. These nonverbal cues can help teachers to refocus their teaching and help students learn more efficient and effective. A failure to observe and recognize may make students bored and frustrated. "Only when we can accurately perceive what is occurring can we reflect upon what the student is learning and upon what interests and feelings they bring with them to the learning situation" (Radford, 1990).

4.5.3 Nonverbal Communication and Language Acquisition

Earlier approach to language teaching and learning was oriented to the development of grammatical accuracy rather than communicative skills. With the development of linguistic science and teaching methodology, the idea of improving learners' ability to communicate successfully has become more and more popular. The effect of nonverbal communication on language teaching has aroused the interest of researchers. Many studies show that much more understanding will be achieved if nonverbal communication is in company with verbal language, the classroom will be more lively with teachers' vivid and alive nonverbal behaviors. In other words, nonverbal communication is a juncture of all behaviors, and will be helpful for students' command of knowledge and easily memorize what they have learned.

The relationship between nonverbal communication and language acquisition has been investigated by researchers. As Stam (2006) argued, we can get a clearer and more complete picture of the learners' progress in learning another language by investigating not only their speech but also their gestures. Gullberg (2006) also suggested that the analysis of second language learners' use of nonverbal behaviors in communication can offer valuable insights into the processes of language acquisition. Stam (2006), Yoshioka and Kellerman (2006) have found that the speakers of verb-framed languages, like Japanese and Spanish, as well as those of satellite-framed languages, like Chinese and English, inappropriately transfer their L1 gestures of motion verbs to their L2 signing. Krashen (1981, 10) further pointed out that nonverbals help teachers to provide intake, "that subset of linguistic input that helps the acquirer acquire language." Intake is supplied through teacher-talk, the language that accompanies classroom activities may be verbal or nonverbal. FL teachers use simplified input as a natural part of trying to make themselves understood. Hatch (1983, 66) included the use of gestures in her identification of the five general areas in which input is simplified.

Nonverbal communication has its most direct instructional impact on the affective domain of learning. It is related to students' likes and dislikes, attitudes, values, beliefs, appreciations, and interests. It is known that affective learning is a valued goal of teaching. No matter what disciplines we teach, we share the goal of creating life-long learners. For example, English teachers hope that students retain their ability to analyze a play or a novel but also hope to motivate them to do something related to plays and novels after they complete the literature class. In any discipline, we are interested not only in cognitive learning, but also in creating positive student affect to the content area. Anderson (1979) found that one-fourth of the variation in both students' liking for the content area and students' desire to take future courses in the content area was a function of the teacher's nonverbal behavior. Over half of the variation in students' liking for the instructor was the result of the instructor's nonverbal communication.

Therefore, if teachers know how to use nonverbal behaviors more effectively, their relationship with students will be improved. In order to adapt to the new situation of national higher education, deepening the educational reform and fitting the needs of society, the Ministry of Education of China released the new *College English Course Teaching and Learning Requirements* in 2007, which claims that the objective of college English teaching should contain the basic English knowledge, learning strategies, and intercultural communication competence which includes verbal and nonverbal communicative competence, etc. Therefore, college English teachers should fully realize the importance of nonverbal behavior in classroom which can not only improve teacher-student relationship, but also set up a good image for the students. For a vivid smile, an encouraging gesture, or a gentle expression in teachers' eyes can be effective tools of teaching effectiveness.

4.6 Conclusion

With the development of globalization, the cultural diversity of today's school classrooms presents tremendous and demanding challenges to teachers. It is necessary for teachers to understand the historical development of intercultural communication, and the components of ICC since they are the main goals of language teaching as Bowden and Marton (1998) stated that "the basic principles and intentions of competency-based education have remained essentially unchanged since the 1960s" with a "focus on outcomes, greater workplace relevance, outcomes as observable competence, assessments as judgments of competence, improved skills recognition"

(99). For the purpose of this chapter, some basic concepts related to intercultural communication competence, the status of nonverbal communication in the models of communicative competence have been discussed. Based on these analyses, a new model of intercultural communication competence has been set up. And the relationship between nonverbal communication and second language teaching and learning has been illustrated, which implies that nonverbal communication is a pivotal tool for teachers in the diverse classroom and plays an important role in language acquisition as Helmer and Eddy (2003) confirmed that nonverbal communication in a culturally diverse classroom can be an issue of concern. This is because students from different cultures may misinterpret nonverbal cues, escalating conflict or creating a barrier for effective communication and that nonverbal communication is often culturally biased and unconscious. And, educators may unwittingly employ nonverbal communication which serves as the foundation for creating conflict with culturally diverse students in classroom.

Part III

Research on Classroom Nonverbal X-Factor

Chapter Five

Chinese Teachers' Classroom Nonverbal X-Factor

5.1 Introduction

This chapter will explore Chinese teachers' nonverbal behaviors in classroom. Based on the illustration of some issues related to this area, it examines each component of teachers' nonverbal behaviors in classroom, though few nonverbal behaviors are made in isolation from others. And then two researches conducted by the author will be presented. One is about students' attitudes to teachers' appearance and the other is related to students' attitudes to teachers' facial expression, smile and gestures. The purpose is to make teachers more aware of their nonverbal cues and to demonstrate how he/she communicates with his/her students using this medium. It hopes to offer a candid view of how nonverbal communication theory is realized in classroom settings and to provide teachers with a greater insight into communication in a diverse classroom setting.

5.2 Background Information

In the 21st century, economic globalization in China has engendered a multicultural learning environment in education that challenges both faculty and students. The classroom is more than a place where knowledge, skills, and competencies are taught and shared. It is a miniature community where students and teachers interact, exchange their ideas and cultures, and influence each other. Diversity in classroom is further complicated by nonverbal communication, which impacts on students' attitudes towards faculty members. Because today's classrooms are changing and undergoing rapid shifts in composition, culture, and orientation, the nature of learning is also changing to be more participative, interactive, and team-oriented. To ensure that effective learning is taking place in global/multicultural classroom settings, an improved faculty-student nonverbal relationship is critically important.

Obviously, adequate knowledge of the subject matter is crucial to success for teachers; however, it's not the only crucial element. Creating a climate that facilitates learning and retention demands good nonverbal and verbal skills. Besides the verbal skills, other elements can also influence the communication in classroom. Firstly, the decor of the classroom, the color of the walls, the origin of the lighting, the existence of the natural light, the temperature of the classroom, the height of the chairs and tables and quality of the transmission of sound in the classroom are important factors for good communication. Secondly, the distribution of classroom space, the location of the desks, the distribution of the students at the desks and the distance between the students and the teacher are also key factors for effective communication. Thirdly, the appropriate use of body language by the teacher is one of the most important elements in the nonverbal communication: the teacher must adequately handle haptics, chronemics, kinesics, proxemics, olfactics, paralanguage, oculesics and physical appearance. Therefore, nonverbal messages are an essential component of communication in the teaching process. Teachers should be aware of nonverbal behavior in classroom for three major reasons: (1) an awareness of nonverbal behavior will allow the teacher to become a better receiver of students' messages; (2) the teacher can become a better sender of signals that reinforce learning; (3) this mode of communication increases the degree of the perceived psychological closeness between the teacher and students (M. Ali & S. Ali, 2011).

5.2.1 Previous Research on Teachers' Nonverbal Behavior

Although research on nonverbal communication didn't originate in education, it is necessary to provide a review of nonverbal communication in education and what has been reported about the development and impact of this process on the teacher and students' interaction.

5.2.1.1 Teachers' Nonverbal Behavior and Students' Achievement

Researches on nonverbal communication have been incorporated into the classroom setting for several decades. Some studies present data relating teachers' effective nonverbal communication with students' academic success in some context, especially teachers' immediacy with students' learning outcomes, for example, with students' motivation on learning (Allen, Witt & Wheeless, 2006; King & Witt, 2009), nonverbal immediacy and affective learning (Plax, Kearney, McCroskey & Richmond, 1986), with instructional outcomes (Powell & Harville, 1990), and students' cognitive learning (Richmond, Gorham, & McCroskey, 1987; Sanders & Wiseman, 1990; Titsworth, 2001), etc.

A number of studies analyze the connection between teachers' nonverbal communication and students' achievement. Klinzing and Aloisio (2004) illustrated a significant number of studies and collated research data spanning half a century. The authors made the important finding that teachers' nonverbal expressiveness is "comparable with other variables found to be related to achievement" (9). They pointed out that there were significant positive effects on students' achievement in those studies which examined frequent gesturing (Rosenshine, 1970), occasional teachers' gaze (Breed, 1971), high rates of eye contact and dynamic voice tone (Driscoll, 1969) and high enthusiasm (Ware & Williams, 1975, 1977).

Some researchers have found similar connection between nonverbal communication and learning and even claimed that nonverbal communication is more powerful than verbal communication when it comes to learning. For example, McCroskey et al. (2006, 425) argued that "the instructional research to date suggests that nonverbal factors may have a much stronger impact on learning than do verbal factors" since nonverbal communication can arouse students' feelings and attitudes towards what they are learning and towards who is teaching. Teachers with strong nonverbal skills have been found to influence learning outcomes. The influence extends into other domains beyond the typical "measurable" learning objectives. Students have increased "affinity" for the teacher and a greater liking for the subject being taught and better perceptions of themselves as learners. The teachers also provide their students with more "referent power"—are seen as positive models. In simple words, nonverbal communication can stimulate students' "affective meaning," which means that the students develop an emotional connection with the subject and with the teacher.

Currently, there has been a growing interest in searching for the teachers' gestural behavior in the classroom communication and its implications in relation to the teaching and learning processes. Comadena, Hunt and Simonds (2007) made a review of the impact of teachers' nonverbal behavior on the development of students in classroom. They pointed out that research has consistently demonstrated that the specific nonverbal language used by the teacher will have a direct impact on both the psychological attachment of the student to the teacher and the ability of the teacher to connect with the student. They stated that in education context nonverbal communication serves as the foundation of creating intimacy and allows students to feel connected to the teacher. This connection can have marked implications for students' overall academic performance.

Mackay (2006) conducted a survey of the development and use of nonverbal cues in classroom. The results show that students often respond first to the teacher's nonverbal body language. Specifically, Mackay made the following observations:

> The mood and tenor for the day or lesson is established in the first few minutes. At the outset of every class, students and teacher both instinctively assess how they should act and respond to each other. A teacher's facial expression, eyes, voice, movement and gesture all convey confidence and control, or lack of these. As students become familiar with the teacher's ways their responses don't change unless the teacher gives due cause. (54)

Mackay asserted that the teacher's nonverbal communication can have a powerful influence over the class. The changes in nonverbal communication patterns can garner students' attention, especially if this change occurs after consistent patterns of nonverbal communication which has been established over time.

5.2.1.2 Effective Teacher and Their Personality

Researches found that teachers' personality can be reflected by their nonverbal behaviors in classroom. A landmark study titled "Half a Minute: Predicting Teacher Evaluations from Thin Slices of Nonverbal Behavior and Physical Attractiveness" conducted by Ambady and Rosenthal (1993), in which three studies were included. In studies one and two, based on ten-second video clips, subjects were asked to rate college teachers and high school teachers' nonverbal behaviors and physical attractiveness. In study three, they investigated whether strangers' ratings of teachers would predict nonverbal behavior and physical attractiveness from study one and two if even more thinned slices of the video were shown. The clips were reduced from ten seconds to five and two seconds. The results are surprising:

> There were no significant differences in the accuracy of judgments based on video clips 10s, 5s, and 2s in length. In addition, there were no significant differences in the accuracy of judgments from the two samples of teachers... Moreover, judgments based on 30s exposure (three 10s clips of each teacher) were not significantly more accurate than judgments based on 6s

exposure (three 2s clips of each teacher). (437-438)

Ambady and Rosenthal summarized that based on nonverbal behaviors shown in very brief silent video, we can evaluate our teachers as acceptable, active, attentive, competent, confident, dominant, empathic, enthusiastic, honest, likeable, calm, optimistic, professional, supportive, and warm. They concluded:

> Teachers with higher ratings tended to be more nonverbally active and expressive. They were more likely to walk around, touch their upper torsos, and smile. Less effective teachers were more likely to sit, touch their heads, and shake rather than nod their heads. These results suggest that teachers with higher ratings showed more nonverbal expressiveness and involvement than less effective teachers. (436-437)

Boyd's (2000) study revealed that when effective teachers interact with the at-risk African-American-male middle school students, they frequently were in close proximity, changed their voice inflections, established eye contact, invaded students' territories (were within two feet), and gestured to students. With different perspectives, Sime (2008) and Lörscher (2003) examined teachers' nonverbal signs and their teaching implications to the foreign language classroom. Sime (2008) found that the teacher's gestures contribute to the classroom interaction by enhancing comprehension, facilitating the learning processes and indicating the teacher's reactions to the learners' output. Lörscher (2003) observed the teacher's nonverbal signs in German schools and noticed that the teacher's gestures were often used to provide positive feedback, to highlight information and to replace the verbal elements when the lexemes were unknown to the learners. This particularly occurred with a high intensity at the beginner level and within phases in which fictitious communication took place, for example, in moments of role play when learners were expected to act out a story. Lörscher (2003) asserted that the teacher's nonverbal signs occur in connection to the verbal signs to interpret, comment or modify the verbal utterances in the spoken discourse.

From above discussion, we can see that researches on nonverbal communication in classroom are plentiful, but there is inconsistent data on the effect of nonverbal communication used by teachers and the impact on students' learning within the higher education environment. In the past decades, FL teachers have found ways to use nonverbal as effective teaching strategies and in classroom management and have explored ways to include the nonverbal in presenting the target culture. However, no empirical studies have yet been conducted to identify and categorize the various nonverbal strategies FL teachers typically use to convey meaning in their day-to-day instruction. Therefore, much work remains to be accomplished in identifying and implementing the important roles of nonverbal behaviors in FL classroom in different context.

5.2.2 Research Method of Nonverbal Behavior in Education

As mentioned above, research on nonverbal communication in education systematically began from the 1970s. Compared with other areas of research, the slow progress was due to the difficulties of measuring nonverbal communicative behaviors although several research procedures had been proposed.

Okon (2011) discussed one useful method in nonverbal research in education—the microteaching which followed the technological advances in video recording. It is basically a data-based feedback intervention for teachers' self-inquiry and skill training. Typically, a class session is videotaped and the recording serves as the empirical data for further analysis. The videotaped material captures an unbiased evidence of teachers' behaviors and teaching situation. Microteaching was conceived as a tool for instructional evaluation instead of focus on nonverbal aspects of behaviors. With microteaching sessions, teachers can receive feedback on how to improve their conduct in their teaching and in their interactions with students. The analyses focus on the teacher's position towards the entire classroom, appearance, dress, poise, use of voice, body and hands, movement in the classroom, teacher's enthusiasm, eye contact, etc. Microteaching is a categorized research method in education due to its qualitative and reflective actions.

Thin slices research is another nonverbal research that measures decoding sensitivity via judgments of brief instances of nonverbal behavior. The process of conducting thin slices research involves exposing brief samples of nonverbal behaviors to judges and asking them to rate their impressions of these target figures. These ratings are then correlated with different diagnostic or predictive criteria of the target people.

Stamatis (2012) summarized the methods in the research of nonverbal communicative behaviors in education, including:

(1) Eliciting the views of participants in the research questionnaire. Under this method, students are asked to describe and evaluate nonverbal communicative behaviors of the teacher in classroom. This process is not very reliable because the

views of individuals have been shaped over time and not instantaneously.

(2) Exploring of nonverbal communicative behaviors with physical observation in the classroom. This method was developed in early 1990 and it requires physical presence of the researchers and the record of their observations in the classroom.

(3) The video-typing of nonverbal communicative behaviors in the classroom. Today, the technique of video-typing for the collection of research data of nonverbal communication and behavior has been highly developed and the technique of video-analysis is due to the evolution of technology and possibility to manage the data indefinitely.

However, Stamatis (2012) pointed out that despite extensive observations, the difficulties of accurate interpretation of nonverbal signals are always remaining since it is extremely difficult to ascertain exactly the thoughts, feelings or intentions of the speaker, because these data are not completely measurable. The data are also volatile, subjective and often involve elements of pretense. And the focuses of micro-analytic method are mainly the head, and the face, hands, body position, the mood and voice. Therefore, the researcher must take into account the contradictory signals and ambiguities created by leaky individual verbal and nonverbal signals to resolve any deceiving attempts (Pease, 2006). What is more, the researcher also pays attention to the investigation of nonverbal communicative behaviors which shows a difference depending on the situation or a person. For example, a change in the tone of teachers' voices when they were addressed to "good" or "bad" students or when they were teaching a new concept or when they were making comments to students who disturb the class, etc. Students understand all these micro-differentiations or discriminations of educators, which affects their view of the personality of the teacher and therefore, their attitudes and general behaviors in class (Richmond & McCroskey, 2000).

Now we can make a conclusion that nonverbal behavior in educational environment can be measured in three distinct ways: asking participants about their impression; conducting behavioral observation in the classroom and videotaping ongoing nonverbal behavior in the classroom. According to Okon (2011), asking students about their teachers' behaviors seems to be the most economical and maybe practical method of researching nonverbal behaviors within educational setting.

5.2.3 Nonverbal Behavior as Teaching Strategies

Literature in FL education has provided many examples in which nonverbal behaviors are used as effective teaching strategies for classroom management with the following purposes: (1) vary the tempo; (2) control participation; (3) signal changes; (4) indicate who is to respond; (5) cue choral response; (6) mark beginnings and ends of lessons; and (7) give students an idea of what to expect, etc.

Researchers explore various strategies in the use of nonverbal behaviors in teaching. Richardson (1979) advocated to use nonverbal cues to promote dialogue and stimulate classroom interaction. For example, the teacher can establish eye contact to pair students for group work, be silent to encourage reluctant students to participate, and smile and nod to encourage and support students. Allen and Valette (1994, p.152) suggested using gestures to convey the meanings of specific words such as descriptive adjectives, prepositions of place, and action verbs. For example, when students hear the word "grand" and see the teacher using an accompanying gesture which illustrates the adjective, the gesture may activate the concept of "tall" and students can infer from the gesture that "grand" means "tall." Thus, nonverbal behavior can facilitate comprehension by activating concepts already stored as mental representations in the students' memories since nonverbal behaviors enhance comprehension by providing additional contextual information.

Teachers can develop a standard set of hand or arm gestures in classroom to help teaching. For instance, the teacher swinging the arm upward could cue the students to form a question while swinging the arm downward requests a response. Other signals may indicate when students should listen, repeat, answer or speak louder. Schachter (1981) has devised a set of hand signals used to indicate certain types of errors in classroom. An error in tense, aspect, or voice is signaled by a basketball "T" time out signal. The signal for an agreement error is the letter "A" formed by the forefingers and the middle fingers. The "V" for victory signal indicates an error in pluralization. When students see a reversed "P" signal, they know they have made a preposition error. To indicate an error in word order, the teacher forms an "O" with the fingers of both hands. A crossing of the index fingers in an "X" indicates an error with articles, etc.

5.3 The Functions of Teachers' Nonverbal Behavior

The primary function of teachers' verbal behavior is to give content to improve students' cognitive learning, while the primary function of teachers' nonverbal behavior is to improve students' affect or liking for the subject matter, teacher and class, to instill in them the desire to learn more about the subject matter, etc.

Researchers have reported that depending on different situational needs in classroom, the teacher's nonverbal behavior has different impacts on students. Ehrman and Dörnyei (1998), Sime (2006), for instance, have identified three functions of nonverbal communication. The first is cognitive function. Given its intercultural and interlinguistic variation, nonverbal communication can be treated as part of what learners can acquire in a target language (Gullberg, 2006; Pennycook, 1985; Neu, 1990). The second is the emotional function. Rosa (2004) believed that in order to teach effectively, teachers need to pay attention to how they combine verbal elements to convey particular meaning to students. She recommended proactive use of eye contact to individual students. Nonverbal communication tools, like tone of voice, body posture, facial expression, and gesture can help a teacher to establish a presence in classroom and therefore motivate students to engage actively in class activities (Sime, 2006). These tools help boost the students' learning capacity and their ability to recall information (Allen, 2000; Lazaraton, 2004). The third is organizational function, which has implications for how conflict will be managed. Rosa (2004) backed the use of gestures for classroom management and endorses the use of paralanguage (voice tone, pitch, volume, tempo, intensity and silent pause) in establishing and sustaining learners' attention.

In Chapter Two we have discussed that nonverbal communication can function to repeat, contradict, substitute, complement and regulate verbal, this is especially true of nonverbal communication in classroom. Generally speaking, the functions of teachers' nonverbal behaviors in classroom include:

5.3.1 The Disciplinary Function

One of the major functions of nonverbal communication in classroom is its disciplinary function and is reported as having many related functions which help teachers in managing classrooms. The teacher signals whose turn it is by dropping their pitch, gestures, relaxing and leaning slightly, and ending a vocal phrase by looking directly at the student expected to respond. The teacher can shorten the student's response and by nodding his/her head rapidly, opening mouth as if to talk, verbalizing during the first pause that is accompanied by eye contact. As Gower and Walters (1983) stated, the main uses of eye contact in classroom are to show a student who is talking that the teacher is taking notice; to check that everyone is concentrating; to indicate to a student that the teacher wants to talk to him/her. Or the teacher wants the student to do something, to encourage contributions when the student is trying to elicit ideas. The teacher only knows students having something to say by looking at them; and holds the attention of students not being addressed and encourages them to listen to those doing the talking and to maintain attention (cited from Snyder, 1998).

Nonverbal communication is also used to check whether the students understand; puzzled expressions quickly tell the teacher what is to be revised or repeated. Ledbury, White and Darn (2004) suggested that teachers watch learners as well as listen to them, particularly while they are performing tasks to look for signs of being bored or being lost. Thus, eye contact is not only to be considered as a tool for the teacher to convey messages but as a means to interpret the messages students can display nonverbally via their eyes, mimics and gestures.

5.3.2 Reflecting Teachers' Confidence

Facial expression and eye contact can play an important role in reflecting teachers' confidence. A teacher needs to be convincing and trustworthy in order to be credible in the eye of the students. Cruickshank, Jenkins and Metcalf (2005) stated that regardless of a teacher's knowledge, experience, education level, or position, a teacher is credible only when his/her students believe he/she is. Since eye contact and facial expressions are considered as signs for reflecting teachers' self-confidence, they have an impact on teachers' credibility and trustworthiness.

A teacher who never looks students in the eye seems to lack confidence and gives the students a sense of insecurity (Gower & Walters, 1983). Pollitt (2006) claimed that eye contact is an important key in the sense that if a teacher does not look the students in the eye when speaking to them, it may show a lack of confidence in oneself, hence, the teacher is likely to have problems with discipline (cited from Zeki, 2009).

5.3.3 Establishing Teacher-Student Immediacy

Ward and von Raffler-Engel (1980) have testified kinesic synchrony between the students and the teacher. When the teacher acts disinterested, unenthusiastic, or bored, the students act the same way. But when the instructor is lively and enthusiastic, the students are lively and enthusiastic too. Thus, teachers' nonverbal behaviors have a close relationship with students' emotions.

The use of eyes, mimics and gestures is also believed to help establish rapport.

In classroom, teachers seldom verbalize their feelings, yet students can know the teachers' attitudes to them in the teaching process by inferring these affective data from teachers' nonverbal behaviors. Factor-analytic studies indicate that positive affect is communicated through a cluster of nonverbal behaviors, labeled immediacy behaviors (Anderson, 1979). Nonverbal behaviors closely associated with the immediacy cluster contain eye contact, smiling, vocal expressiveness, physical proximity, gesturing, etc. Immediacy behaviors communicate feelings of warmth and support and engender feelings of interpersonal attraction. Teachers who use nonverbal immediacy behaviors show greater liking and affect to students and can arise higher student affect.

According to McCroskey and Richard (1992), increased teachers' immediacy can result in: (1) increased students' affinity for the teacher. Immediate teachers are liked far more than non-immediate teachers. This is the most consistent finding from all of the researches of this area; (2) increased students' affect for the subject matter, which is the essence of affective learning. Immediate teachers can prevent some negative education outcomes, for instance, the "turned off" students reject future classes in a subject, devalue school attendance, and may ultimately "drop out" from formal schooling; (3) increased cognitive learning among students; (4) increased students' motivation; (5) reduced students' resistance to teachers' influence attempts. Immediate teachers have more referent power, thus students tend to comply with the wishes of those teachers without such compliance becoming an issue in the interaction between teachers and students.

On the other hand, teachers who are cold, negative and aloof to students since they dislike teaching or dislike the immature undergraduates will probably have trouble feigning immediacy with students. Therefore, teachers' sincere positive attitude is a crucial prerequisite for the successful communication of immediacy. Rossman (1989) added that teachers need to coordinate their body language, speaking voice, eye contact and wardrobe to create a convincing, but not confusing impact on the learner.

5.4 Teachers' Nonverbal Communication in Classroom

Nonverbal communication is a complex process involving people, words, tone of voice and body movements, and few gestures are made in isolation from others. The more tools that can be added to the teaching arsenal, the better the chance that the instructional effort will be a success. This part will illustrate what teachers' behaviors mean in the educational environment to make teachers more aware of his/her nonverbal cues to demonstrate how he/she communicates with his/her students using this medium.

In Liu Jun's (2001) study, five component parts of development of nonverbal communication in classroom were reported: "paralanguage, facial expression, eye contact and visual behavior, gesture and body movement, and space." (30) and each has specific purpose of "expressing emotions, conveying interpersonal attitudes, presenting personality, and amplifying verbal communication" (30) and functions differently depending on the context of the classroom environment and the specific subject that is being studied. The following list is generalized relative to culture, gender, type of academic institution, and course subject. It has been accumulated from a variety of sources and in most cases adapted specifically to classroom conditions.

5.4.1 Appearance

As has always been suggested in the nonverbal literature, impression formation takes place very early in a relationship. In the workplace, one's personal appearance is not thought of as an element of etiquette, but it sends a strong signal to managers, colleagues, and customers. As Thourlby (1978) claimed, people make important decisions based on appearance, such as level of success and educational background. Cardon and Okoro (2009) reported that surveys of employers consistently illustrate the importance of dressing up in many organizations, including academic institutions. For example, 41% of employers stated that employees who dressed more professionally were more likely to be promoted. Some studies described the long-lasting impressions formed by professional attire and appearance. Therefore, employees are advised to dress for success to build their careers.

In the educational environment, although physical appearance is not considered a particularly rich nonverbal indicator in classroom, it is still an important element in teaching and learning. Because of its significance, the dress/attire aspect of nonverbal communication has been of immense interest to researchers for some time. Zweifel (2003) argued that the pedagogical activities of teachers and their nonverbal messages (i.e., dress/attire) combine to make the learning experience exciting and create a lasting impression. Molly (1975) stated that clothing/attire is a nonverbal communication that reveals an individual's educational level, social position, economic background, and social background, and it impacts students' judgments of credibility, likeability, and interpersonal attractiveness. Merritt (2008) reported that the "attractiveness of the teacher is in connection with expressiveness and without detriment to the quality of the cognitive content of teaching. It was observed that the more the teacher attracts the students' attention with his physical appearance and presentation of the lesson the more they enjoy the lesson and learn it easily, even if it contains a lot of difficult concepts." Hogan and Stubbs (2003) conducted a research by asking university students how likeable their professor was after a few seconds of the first impression. Students who thought the professor congenial in the first few seconds found the entire class throughout the semester more enjoyable than did the students who stated they did not like the professor after the first impression.

There have been ongoing discussions as to whether faculty members should wear business attire to their campuses in order to represent themselves as professionals. Researchers have reported that the teachers' appearance sends important messages in the classroom setting, and their personality reflected through dress and attire positively or negatively impacts teacher-student relationships in classroom and creates a lasting impression for the students. Many times the student-to-teacher relationship is dependent on their personal appearance and these initial impressions determine the communication that follows. An instructor's attire influences the way students perceive that instructor. When teachers dress very formally, it makes students feel as if the teacher is competent, organized, prepared, and knowledgeable, but not receptive to their needs and not likely to communicate with them. The teacher who always dresses formally may communicate that he/she doesn't want much student interaction, even though the dressing behavior may simply reflect the teacher's clothing preference. The teacher who dresses casually is perceived as open, friendly, outgoing, receptive, flexible, fair and more immediate, but perhaps not as competent as the teacher who dresses more formally.

Studies of the effects of attire/clothing on observers' perceptions have shown that formal or professional dress is positively perceived, both in academic and business settings (Harris, James, Chavez, Ftiller, Kent, Massanari and Wash, 1983; Bassett, 1979). According to Cooper's (1988) survey, in the American students' opinions, the teachers dressed formally are very capable of the class organization, and most knowledgeable, and prepared best for class, while the teachers dressed casually are most friendly, sympathetic, fair to students, enthusiastic and flexible. Wasley (2007) illustrated that the administrators at Tri-State University in Indiana have required faculty and staff members to present themselves professionally and to conform to workplace dress codes at all times. It was not acceptable for any faculty or staff to come to campus dressed inappropriately. Male faculty members were required to wear ties and dress shirts, tucked in, with business or dress khakis; and, if the slacks had belt loops, a belt must be worn. Hair was to be kept trimmed above the ears, any facial hairs had to be well manicured, and the wearing of earring was prohibited in the classrooms.

However, the negative effect of appearance also has been known. As revealed by Cooper's (1988) story: one 8-year middle school student in America made comments on one of his English teachers in such a way: she is very beautiful. We cannot force our attention to the class, because she always wears close fitting clothes. All of the students in my class can not tear ourselves from her attractive appearance and as a result, we can hardly learn anything in her class. Accordingly, we can suggest that the teacher may dress formally for a week or two until credibility is established, then dress more casually to project the image that one is open to students' interaction.

We should point out that different cultures have different norms towards physical attractiveness. The attractive appearance and artifacts in one culture may be considered as improper in another culture. Both teachers and students in intercultural classroom teaching should be aware of cultural difference in physical attractiveness and artifacts. Whatever the teacher's motivation, the students' perceptions are what counts.

5.4.2 Gesture

The effectiveness of gestures in teaching has been supported by many researchers. Some studies have found that lessons which are characterized by the use of gestures are more effective than the same lessons without the usage (Perry, Berch, and Singleton, 1995; Goldin-Meadow, 2004). Church, Ayman-Nolley, and Mahootian (2004) pointed out that teaching with gestures can facilitate students' learning. As aforementioned, gestures and other nonverbal behaviors are forms of input to classroom L2 learners (Lazaraton, 2004). In Chapter Three, we have discussed gestures a lot, here we mainly analyze some specific gestures of teachers in communication.

Hand Movement

Cohen (2007) claimed that nearly 12.5% of our brain space is devoted to the use of the hands. Hand movements can convey messages. Teachers often use hands to give away signals. The movements of hand can indicate anxiety, conveying confidence and assuredness. Lyle (1990) stated one hand or two are resting on the hip bones, drawing attention to the erogenous zone. Borg (2008, 111) remarked, "the palms up position wins hands down" and we associate the use of open palms with openness, honesty and friendliness. If teachers want to present themselves as open, it is important to use the hands with the palms facing up (White & Gardner, 2012, 55).

Another type of hand gestures is joining the hands together and pointing them upwards to look like a church steeple, which is associated with the portrayal of confidence. Borg (2008) pointed out when the teacher places the two palms together and his/her elbows rest on the table, which convey the message of confidence.

One other type of hand movements is the "thumbs up" signal, which is used to indicate approval. It also conveys confidence (Borg, 2008). The teacher uses it when he/she speaks to the whole class, and also directs messages at specific students at the same time.

Head Movement

Pleasing facial expressions are often accompanied by positive head movements. The teacher who uses positive head nods in response to a student's comments is perceived as friendly, concerned about the communication between teacher and student. A teacher who rarely nods, or uses more negative head movements than positive ones quickly stifles teacher-student communication. Not many students volunteer to talk when they realize that their teachers will not respond in a positive or at least encouraging fashion. Positive head nods are a means of stimulating classroom student-teacher interaction, and help teachers to know whether the students have understood the teaching content.

5.4.3 Facial Behavior

Facial behavior refers to the look on a person's face. Facial cues are the first information that we give to or receive from others. People's faces disclose emotions and telegraph what really matters to them. We can get information about the type of the person, personality traits from face. As Wainwright (2003, p.11) stated, considering the muscles in the human face, it is not surprising that we can produce a wide range of facial expressions. "There are many subtleties in changes of expression which can be shown, for example, the great variety of smiles between the Mona Lisa's partial smile and an open grin."

Facial expressions and the use of eyes are two powerful facial behaviors to convey messages in classroom communication.

5.4.3.1 Facial Expression

Facial expression between teachers and students is one of the most important types of nonverbal signals in classroom. The lively facial expressions can promote a supportive and non-threatening classroom atmosphere, which aid students' positive attitudes and corresponding achievement. For example, when the teacher raises a question, an expectant expression he/she shows can encourage students to think carefully and answer actively. Sometimes an unconscious frown can make sensitive students correct their answers immediately. A smiling teacher is thought to convey warmth and encouragement in all cultures, and will be perceived as more likeable, friendly, warm and approachable. But the teacher who has a dull, glum, boring facial expression is perceived by the students as uninterested in them and the subject matter, less animated and less immediate than those with a pleasing facial expression. This type of teacher is likely to have more classroom disruptions because students become bored with the teaching style. Therefore, teachers must have pleasing facial expressions that show that they are interested not only in the subject matter, but also in their students.

Facial expressions can convey messages to complement or contradict verbal messages. It needs to point out that in some cultures, facial expressions tend to complement verbal speech and are more prominent to convey messages than in others. Despite the importance of facial expressions in the total communicative context, teachers and students must guard against unsubstantiated generalizations or to react merely on facial expressions alone.

5.4.3.2 Eye Behavior

Ergin and Birol (2005, cited from Zeki, 2009) pointed out that the real communication between two persons begins when they establish eye contact. If a person looks you in the eye (builds eye contact with you), it can be interpreted as that person cares for you or is interested in you. However, a person who avoids eye contact might be hiding something, which is a sign for lack of confidence. Thus, the eyes are the most powerful means of reflecting one's individuality as a whole. The behavior, the attitude, and integrity have also been the prominent features of critical appreciation through one's eyes. Whatever goes or occurs in one's minds, gets reflected into the eyes. An analogy that brain is a land of micro Processor and the eyes are treated as Monitor is a better illustration. The eyes can command, process and program up to further micro level and thus can be suitably crowned on the top of the software teaching Gears (Bissa & Sharma, 2009).

1. The Functions of Eye Contact in Classroom

In classroom, eye contact performs a very significant function. It can provide information, regulate interaction, exercise social control, and facilitate goals and a constant channel of communication. It can be shifty and evasive; conveys hate, fear, and guilt; or expresses confidence, love, and support (Miller, 1988, 12). Teachers can use eye contact for the enhancement of students' learning in various ways. Students can get attentive when teachers make regular eye contact with them during teaching-learning process. Due to regular eye contact, students remain alert in class and this enhances their retention rate of learning material, which eventually results in improving their learning outcomes. Miller (1988, 13) stated, "Teachers can have individual contacts with every student in the classroom through eye contact. Attitudes of intimacy, aloofness, concern or indifference can be inferred by the way a teacher looks or avoids looking at a student." Wainwright (2003) highlighted the following six different functions of eye contact:

- seeking information;
- showing attention and interest;
- inviting and controlling interaction;
- dominating, threatening and influencing others;
- providing feedback during speech;
- revealing attitudes.

Based on the previous researches, we can categorize the functions of eye contact in the following ways:

A Management Role

Ledbury et al. (2004) reported that eye contact can establish a management role in classroom. Teachers need to be present in the classroom before learners and welcome them individually with a combination of eye contact and their names as they enter the classroom. Eye contact can set the tone of a lesson. When the lesson starts, the teacher can check whether the students are ready or not through eye contact. Researches show that there is a strong link between the amount of eye contact people receive and their degree of participation in communication. As Parker (2006) indicated, "by maintaining eye contact with students when speaking or listening to them, the teacher is asserting that he/she expects conversation and is interested in what the student is saying." Thus, teachers can nominate and invite response by eyes to encourage students to take part in conversation.

Establish Rapport with Students

Eye behavior is a significant indicator of the relationship between students and teachers. The use of eyes and other gestures is believed to help establish rapport. Regardless of a teacher's knowledge, experience, education level, or position, a teacher is credible only when his/her students believe he/she is. The level of credibility and honesty has been found to be related to the amount of eye contact exhibited by a speaker.

In classroom, teachers want those who to whom they are talking to look at them and to have eye contact with them. If that doesn't occur, it is taken as rejection of their teaching content and personal rejection as well. Eye contact is an important key in the sense that if a teacher does not look the students in the eye when speaking to them, it may show a lack of confidence in himself/herself and gives the students a sense of insecurity; hence, the teacher is likely to have problems with discipline. It also suggests to the student that the teacher is not interested in him/her and not approachable. When there is little eye contact between teachers and students, students do not know when to talk, when to ask question or how to approach the teacher. This is a common complaint on college campus that the instructor never looks at students when lecturing. So eye contact and facial expressions have an impact on teacher's credibility and trustworthiness.

We should point out that the teacher has little eye contact with students may be the result of his/her cultural upbringing. In some cultures, it is considered inappropriate for teachers and students to have direct eye contact. On the other hand, if a teacher has an eye contact with only a selected few alert and interested students, other students might consider this to be biased and favoritism.

Time and Effort Saving

Ledbury et al. (2004) reported that eye contact is time and effort saving since it can send specific messages to students, such as praise, encouragement and disapproval. It can be used to check whether the students understand or not, and their puzzled expressions can quickly tell the teacher what is to be revised or repeated. Teachers watch learners as well as listen to them, particularly when they are performing tasks to look for signs of being bored or being lost. So eye contact is not only the tool to convey messages but also as a means to interpret the messages students display.

Although eye contact in classroom has multifunctions, it should be noticed that there would be a cause of misunderstanding between the teachers and students from different cultural backgrounds. Teachers from predominantly westernized cultural backgrounds typically insist on eye contact in order to keep their students' attention and involvement in class. This, however, could result in intercultural conflict, especially if students of a particular cultural group were taught that eye contact is indicative of disrespect for elders or symptomatic of challenging and rebellious behavior. The incongruence of eye contact messages in multicultural classrooms should therefore be a cause of great concern to any multicultural classroom teacher. Any culturally responsive teacher will realize the need to interpret any communicative message within that particular cultural context. Understanding and proper use of eye contact, by teachers, can change the complicated learning environment of the classroom. Therefore, teachers need to coordinate their body language, speaking voice, eye contact and wardrobe to create a convincing, but not confusing impact on the learner. Only a competent teacher can use it successfully and fruitfully in teaching-learning process.

2. Smiling

One expression of eye is the smile which has long been associated with liking, affiliation, and immediacy. The teacher who smiles and has positive facial affect is perceived as more immediate and likeable than the one who does not. Students react more favorable to the teacher who smiles than to the teacher who frowns a lot or does not smile much. Similarly, teachers react more favorable to the student who smiles than to the student who frowns or does not smile much. Thus, smile in classroom is used as a responsive mechanism. Sime (2008) observed that teachers' smiles tend to appear when they provide positive feedback to the learners' output. The smile turns out to be a sign of approval of the students' answers and/or comments. On the other hand, the smile can be seen in regard to the students' reaction to some of teacher's verbal behaviors. Keith, Tornatzky and Pettogrew (1974) found that teachers who smiled more often and who managed to smile for longer periods of time conducted classes where their students spent more time thinking, answered questions more often, and discussed topics more readily and their responses were more spontaneous. However, researchers also warn that teachers need to be careful when and why smile. Neil's (1989) study showed that students perceived the smiling teachers as being "weaker than frowning teachers."

The teacher's smile can provide different pedagogical objectives according to different interactive moments in classroom. As discussed in Chapter Three, smile can be divided into the real smile and the false smile. The true smile was observed during classroom interactive moments when the teacher agrees with the students' answers or in moments that deal with jokes. It was often displayed during informal interaction between teachers and students. The false smile could be seen as a polite instrument of social contact that could be named as social smile. Such a smile could be observed in interactive moments when the teacher gives a reprimand or when he/she disagrees with some student's comment.

Dantas (2007, cited from de Araújo Nóbrega, 2012) analyzed the teacher's smile in the EFL classroom interaction. She found that the smile is used to increase classroom interaction through a convivial strategy (a balance between the instructional and the spontaneous discourse), as well as to promote a funny learning environment, thus favoring students' learning, and also to reprimand students (exerting power and saving the face) for not doing their homework. Although her work gave emphasis on the teacher's smile in relation to the EFL learning, she also noticed that the teacher's smile helps to lower the affective filter between teachers and students, favoring oral interaction among students.

Now we can conclude that teachers need to be convincing and trustworthy in order to be credible in the eyes of the students since eye contact and facial expressions are not only reflecting teachers' self-confidence, but also impacting on teachers' credibility and trustworthiness and teacher-student relationship.

5.4.4 Posture

Teachers' posture refers to the standing or sitting in relaxing professional manner in classroom. Researchers have found that positive posture can arouse students' positive attitude and show that the teacher is receptive and friendly. Being comfortably upright, squarely facing the students, and evenly distributing the weight are to change students' mood, draw students' attention, or reinforce some ideas. For example, Richard, Graham and McCroskey (1987) examined how teachers use their bodies in classroom and found that teachers who lean forward, use purposeful gestures are perceived as likeable and approachable by their students. Neill (1991) also found that a teacher leaning forward towards a student can be interpreted as teacher's enthusiasm for the answer. While the same posture with a frown would be interpreted as a threatening manner. As Miller (2005a, 47) confirmed, "we lean forward when we like someone and we lean away from individuals we have negative attitudes toward."

People from different cultures perceive the posture differently. A teacher sitting on top of a desk or perching on the arm of a chair in class is seen as extremely rude by many Muslim cultures, whilst sitting in a position where one's head is higher than an elder (such as a teacher) is totally unacceptable by Samoans (Lynch, 1999, 72). The Chinese teachers, known as Confucian scholars are the souls of belief, knowledge and authority. Their image of power certainly ought not to be damaged by the unserious posture in Chinese traditional culture. However, nowadays, college students prefer college English teachers especially young teachers being casual and friendly.

5.4.5 Touch

Physical touch in classroom is a subject of significant debate. It is a form of useful communication in establishing and maintaining an effective teacher-student relationship. The teacher can use it to reinforce a student for a job well done, to substitute for the verbal reprimand or control without ever saying a word. For example, the teacher who walks up and touches the child on the shoulder whose misbehaving has gotten his/her attention. The child knows that he/she should stop what he/she is doing.

Although touch is extremely important for social interactions, the term is rarely used in researches on communication skills (Stamatis, 2012), and there is very little expressive touch in classroom today. Teachers are reluctant to touch students because of the insinuations that other might make. Students, above the lowest grade levels, have always been reluctant to touch teachers because of the status differential. Touch should be an acceptable form of communication in the educator-student relationship, but teachers should know the appropriate touch in classroom.

Appropriate body contact means calmness, directness, belief and favor. Touching a student on the arm, hand, shoulder should be acceptable. This type of touch can be a very effective means for communicating a message without ever uttering a word. Back, head and hands are intermediate areas, but the head and hands, which are frequently touched by teachers of very young children, become less acceptable from ten or eleven onwards, especially for girls. It might be expected that all groups of students dislike angry types of touch, such as being hit or having their heads twisted round. What is more, we should know that it is not common for college teachers to touch students. Most college students do not like teacher's touch, except for some necessary or particular situations such as encouraging touch combines with words, which would be more effective than verbal encouragement alone sometimes.

Some researches have been conducted on touch as communication strategy from pedagogical perspective. Bertsch, Houlihan, Lenz and Patte (2009) argued that teachers can use touch as a pedagogical strategy for classroom interactions instead of using commands. Some researches have shown that affectionate touch can improve bonding and attachment relationship between teachers and students (Wellman, Phillips & Rodriguez, 2000). Teachers and students can both feel better and improve mutual understanding than when they keep physical distances from each other since proximity and touch are two important factors to construct trustful, friendly, anti-biased and cooperative perceptions and relationships with others. More recently, Stamatis (2009, cited from Stamatis, 2012) carried out an investigation to determine whether or not the use of touching behavior is a valuable teaching strategy that can help improve the interactions between preschool teachers and children. 20 preschool teachers were trained to give positive touching behavior to kids, such as the approaching, caressing the head or hugging more than in the past. The finding highlights the improvement of classroom climate and the interpersonal relationships between preschool teachers and preschoolers. Stamatis (2012) concluded that teachers and children felt more comfortable, experienced less insecurity and developed their expressive and communicative skills. Some studies have shown that deliberate and appropriate student/instructor touching in classroom can be academically beneficial (Neill & Caswell, 1993; Thompson, 1973).

5.4.6 Silence

In educational settings, silence has two directions: the teachers' silence and the students' silence. Teachers' silence is relatively marked while students' silence is relatively unmarked, underlying linguistic form (Jaworski & Sachdev, 1998). Teachers' silence plays an important role in classroom. Gilmore (1985, 147) illustrated that the teacher's use of silence does affect the student's behavior which, in turn, affects his/her academic achievement. However, the main focus of the literature has been on students' silence in classroom with little attention about teachers' silence. In this part, we focus on the discussion of the functions of teachers' silence.

5.4.6.1 Silence as a Teaching Method

Teachers' silence is considered as a teaching method which is built on the "silent teacher" in the well-known approach: the Silent Way which was originated in early 1972 by Caleb Gattegno (Richard & Rogers, 1986; Al-Humaidi, 2008). It "represents Gattegno's venture into the field of foreign language teaching…building on the premises that the teacher should be silent as much as possible in the classroom and the student should be encouraged to produce as much as language as possible" (Richard & Rogers, 1986, 99). Richard and Rogers (1986, 99) stated the main theories underlying the Silent Way as follows:

● Learning is facilitated if the learner discovers or creates rather than remembers and repeats what is to be learned;

● Learning is facilitated by accompanying (mediating) physical objects;

● Learning is facilitated by problem-solving involving the material to be learned.

Al-Humaidi (2008, 1) observed aspects of Silent Ways and pointed out that "it has been used creatively for various purpose from teaching pronunciation to story-telling."

Like other teaching methods, this method was also challenged in the 1980s and early 1990s, as Richard and Rogers (1986, 111) claimed "the actual practices of the Silent Way are much less revolutionary than might be expected" since "…the method exemplifies many of the features that characterize more traditional methods, such as Situational Language Teaching and Audiolingualism…", thus, it should be combined with and couldn't be separated from other methods.

The dynamics of silence as a teaching methodology are proved in La Forge's (1975) classroom observation which lasted for more than five years. The key of La Forge's argument is his categorization of silence: silence on the part of the teacher, silence on the part of the learner, and silence during evaluation period after the given tasks. To La Forge, the meaning of silence is "a psychodynamic phenomenon" magnifying "what goes inside and between folks" (La Forge, 1977). The former type of silence is referred to silence within learners and the latter is between teachers and learners. In La Forge's study, he provided three different activities which have been proved that there is a direct mapping between psychology and silence. Teacher's silence has three different psychological reactions on learners shown in the following figure.

ACTIVITY		LEARNERS' REACTIONS
TYPE 1 ACTIVITY	T E A C H E R S'	Provoking → ANXIETY to Speak
TYPE 2 ACTIVITY		Provoking → WILLINGNESS to be INDEPENDENT EGO LANGUAGE
TYPE 3 ACTIVITY	S I L E N C E	Provoking → WILLINGNESS to be RESPONSIBLE for a one-to-one SPEAKING RELATIONSHIP with the teacher and each of the peers

Figure 5.1 Silent teacher—a positive methodology in language settings (Adopted from Al-Halawachy, 2008, 76)

The above figure shows that teachers' silence can provoke learners' anxiety to speak, willingness to be independent, and responsible for developing relationship with others in classroom.

Kaufman (2008) created a silent teaching method: the Silent Discussion which is adopted for many years in his teaching. It simply goes in this way: the students are assigned to do the exercise in which they are distributed with a handout instructing them to answer some questions by writing their answers on separate pieces of paper without uttering any single word or without writing their names. When the students are done, they pass their papers around to the left. Then, they read that paper in front of them and write a one-paragraph response to it and start passing around the papers to the left. This activity takes 45 minutes. All the papers are circulated and each student gets his/her original paper back. He/she has to decipher this by the style of writing and even the views. The students read all the responses and write one last response and at this moment verbal discussion starts. Kaufman (2008) concluded the benefits of the Silent Discussion: "although some students who may have the most to offer in terms of personal experiences and perspectives are often inhibited from sharing their wisdom with the class…the silent discussion works on multiple levels to ensure that all students gain their voice."

Al-Halawachy (2014) confirmed that this activity of Silent Discussion "implicitly guides to the path of psychology empowering the role of silence as a teaching method which offers the students a comfortable safe space to voice their views." So what teachers need to do is to cultivate a learning environment for students to make them feel comfortable to speak their views in classroom.

5.4.6.2 Silence as a Controlling Tool

The power relations in classroom can be constructed and reproduced through silence. Teachers' silence always marks their dominant status over the students'. This is how they get and focus on the students' attention, interrupt them, or relieve the moments of tension. Students' silence is subordinate, although it need not be submissive, as in the case of stylized sulking which is a sign of the students' reluctance to submit to their teachers' authority. For example, sometimes, the silence seems to mean "pay attention to me" and/or "what you are doing is not acceptable to me." Simply, silence display is a means to get attention and class cohesion for a new lesson or activity, marking the beginning of a new game.

The value of the teacher's silence as a power within educational processes has been confirmed in some studies. Several researches have testified the use of silence as a power in classroom. Hilsdon's (1996) study showed how teachers use silence as a mechanism for exerting power over students. "One can observe that teachers' authority power is being exercised when students are listening to teachers imparting their knowledge" (cited from Botas, 2006). Edwards and Redfern (1992, quoted in Jaworski and Sachdev, 1998, 277) also found that silencing orders have been used to control the minority children in educational setting in both Britain and Canada. What is more, silence is not only used for "maintaining an orderly interaction" or "only to initiate but also to regain and maintain the orderliness of the lesson structure" (Gilmore, 1985, 147).

5.4.6.3 Silence as a Facilitator

Silence in classroom can be used as facilitators, such as slowing down the tempo of speech in student-led discussions (Kurtz, 1988; quoted in Schratz & Mehan, 1993), and "wait-time" (Rowe, 1974). The slowing down the rate of speech and increasing the lengths of pause can improve the quality of classroom interaction. Rowe (1974) examined the enhancing role of increased silent periods for communication, which was called "wait-time" and the quality of instruction. Wait-time was defined as the length of a pause between teacher question and student response, between student question (or response) and next teacher response (or question). In his research, Rowe (1974) well documented and studied two types of wait-time in monocultural classroom setting: (1) the teacher's pause between the end of his/her question and the beginning of the student's response, and (2) the teacher's pause between the end of the student's response and the teacher's beginning of his/ her response to it.

The findings of Rowe's (1974) study reveal dramatic changes on several measures of students' performance following the training of teachers to increase wait-time from 1 to 3 seconds. For example, the length of student response increased from a mean of 7 words to a mean of 27 words; the mean number of appropriate unsolicited responses increased from 5 to 17; the mean of failure to respond dropped from 7 to 1; the mean of incidence of evidence-inference statements increased from 6 to 14; the average incidence of soliciting, structuring, and reacting moves increased from 5 to 32; number of speculative responses increased from a mean of 2 to a mean of 7; the incidence of student-student comparisons of data increases; the frequency of student-initiated questions increases from a mean of 1 to a mean of 4 (Rowe, 1974). Rowe stated that "the increase of the amount of wait-time indicates that teachers' expectations toward the performance of weak students improve." Another study conducted by Mohatt and Erickson (1981) showed that the students who were given a wait-time of 4.6 seconds by an Indian teacher were more responsive than those who were given a wait-time of 2.0 seconds average by a non-Indian teacher.

In sum, given that teaching and learning are primary objectives in the classroom setting, the facilitative use of silence for learning and teaching is likely to account for the greatest variance in the use of silence in classroom.

5.4.7 Proxemics

Proxemics in classroom refers to the distance between teachers and students. The process of teaching and learning is a process of communication and the spatial distance between teachers and students is a critical factor in the communication process. The space in classroom is limited and certainly affects positively or negatively on classroom activities.

5.4.7.1 Classroom Management

There are many elements which can determine the communication in classroom, but the arrangement of classroom space may have the largest impact. The following presents the typical classroom managements and their advantages and disadvantages in classroom interactions.

Part III Research on Classroom Nonverbal X-Factor

1. Traditional Classroom Management

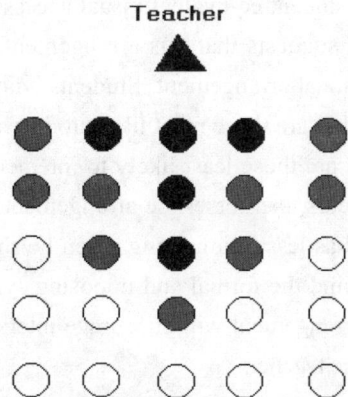

The circles represent students' seats. Students sitting in the dark areas have more chances of communication with others, while those sitting in the gray areas interact less frequently than those in the dark areas. The most less frequent participation in communication are those students who sitting in the white areas. The explanation for this is that the students sitting in the dark areas have the best visual contact with the teacher and they are comparatively closer to the teacher. But students who are quite anxious about communicating with others and who are shy, may try to avoid interaction in classroom, thus, they usually sit in the white areas. Therefore, if the teacher wishes to dominate the interaction in classroom, the traditional arrangement is probable the best because students are seated side by side and the primary focal point is the teacher. And most interactions will go from teacher to student and form student to teacher.

2. Horseshoe Classroom Arrangement

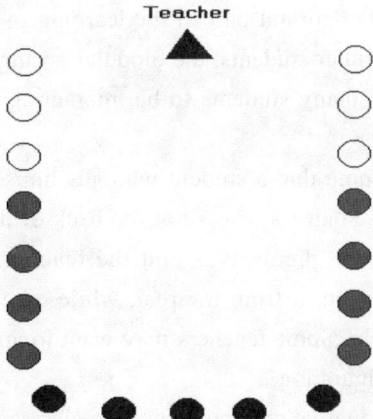

(Different colors of seats have same meaning as above)

This arrangement is used when small number of students in one class. Such an arrangement provides each student equivalent visual access to most other students and the teacher. Some research suggests that this arrangement results in great and wider participation than the traditional arrangement. Students who are at the opposite end of the horseshoe from the teacher are those most likely to interact, while those at the right and left hand of the teacher are those least likely to interact. If the teacher wishes that the full-class interaction occurs, the horseshoe arrangement may be the most desirable since a teacher is perceived as less intimidating when he/she is seated in a circle with the students rather than behind the formal and imposing symbol of his/her large desk. The horseshoe classroom arrangement will encourage interaction both among students and between students and the teacher.

3. Modular Classroom Arrangement

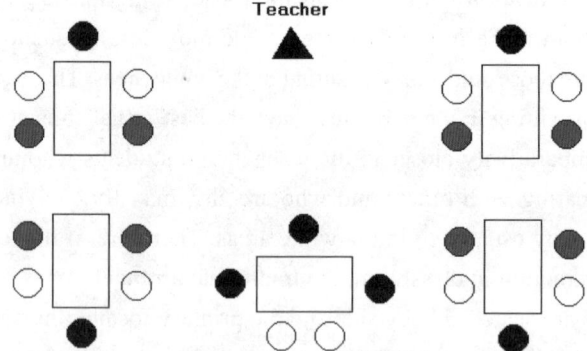

This classroom arrangement can provide more interaction among smaller group of students, but at the same time it can make interaction with the teacher more difficult. If the very important part of the learning in the class is dependent on student's interaction with other students, the modular arrangement may be preferable. This arrangement permits many students to be interacting at the same time without interrupting one another.

The teacher may assume that a student who sits himself in dark areas wants to be involved in classroom. Students who sit at the back of the room want to maintain maximum distance between themselves and the teacher. Some teachers may be content with minimal disruption from the rear, while others will assume that these students need the most help. Some teachers may want to arrange students' desks in a circle or open square configuration.

In order to foster productive communication in classroom, teachers must provide flexible changes that are beneficial for group interaction. As Miller (1988, 22) stated, "The most advanced curriculum and the highest hopes have little chance of success without a supportive physical learning environment." Several guidelines for improving the learning environment of the classroom are presented as follows:

- Offering a variety of stimul;
- Providing a secure, comfortable feeling;
- Being adopted to fit the activity;
- Giving some privacy and individuality.(Miller, 1988, 22)

Based on the above discussion, we can see that teachers should adopt different ways to arrange the classroom based on the different requirements of teaching. For example, when we have a small number of students in one class, we can use the horseshoe classroom arrangement to achieve a full-class interaction. When we have several small groups of students in classroom, we choose the modular classroom arrangement, especially, when we want to train students' cooperation with each other and their team-work spirit.

5.4.7.2 Teacher's Classroom Movement

As we know, a person who uses interpersonal space with another interactant communicates how he/she perceives that person. In classroom, the teacher who stands behind the desk or podium and rarely approaches students or allows them to approach her/him is perceived by students as unfriendly, unreceptive, unapproachable, non-caring and non-immediate. This does not help to improve teacher-student relationships.

In China, the classrooms are usually divided into territories where a teacher and students occupy given areas of traditional space. Distance establishes the status of interaction. The traditional classroom arrangements are static, with the teacher's desk at the front of the room and students seated in rows. The arrangements of desks and furniture influence the potential meaning of a learning context. Where and when a teacher chooses to travel in a classroom signifies meaning. To move forward or away from students signifies relationships.

In fact, most students prefer their teachers moving around the classroom to just standing at the very front between the blackboard and the platform. Some students think the teacher who walks around the room or stands closer to them is perceived as friendly, easy-going and can make students more involved in activities. On the other hand, in most cases, we can find that teachers do stand further away from poor students or put them in the far end of the classroom, especially in primary schools or middle schools in China. The teachers who stand or walk among the students during teaching are viewed more positively than those who stand at the front of the classroom, and are seen friendlier and are more effective than those who stand further away from the students.

According to our classroom observation, when a student gets absent-minded or does something irrelevant to the teaching content, the teacher, if permitted, usually moves forward to the student if he/she does not want to interrupt the communication in classroom. The teacher's approach may bring back the student's attention and resumes his/her classroom learning. This indicates that the closer the teacher is to the student, the better the student responds both in attitude and in academic performance. In other words, there is a decrease in students' participation as the distance between teachers and students increases and as the directness with which they face each other decreases. If a teacher just stands behind the teacher's desk throughout the process of teaching, he/she neglects the fact that "motionless teachers can bore students."

Now we can conclude that teachers' proper personal distance can make students feel more comfortable, and positively make themselves aware of the things going on in classroom. And also students may feel at ease in appropriate personal distance and take interest in the teaching-learning process. It should be noted that the appropriate spatial distances and arrangements are limited by a myriad of variables, including the conversational topic, the nature of the relationship, and the physical constraints present in classroom. Therefore, teachers should adapt their personal distances to the teaching contexts. For example, when the teacher is giving a lecture, he/she should walk off the stage to join the crowd of students and make moderate interaction with them instead of standing on the stage all the time which can hardly draw students' attention. When a student is answering a question, the teacher can lean a little bit to him/her to listen attentively, showing interest and attention on the teacher's part. If the teacher finds certain student does not concentrate on, the teacher can go close to the student to wake up the absent-minded student. To the students' misbehaviors, the teacher can use a wide variety of verbal and nonverbal reactions to them, such as walking closer to the offending students and using a physical cue, such as a finger to the lips, to point out inappropriate behavior.

5.4.8 Use of Time

In classroom, time distribution can play a significant role. How teachers use their time indicates the value and importance they place on something. Spending little time on a topic or passing by it can indicate no interest in it or little knowledge about the topic, and students can frequently relate what a teacher's preferences are and what the teacher dislikes.

Appropriate use of time in classroom can make students less likely notice time. At the beginning of every class, the teacher can use five minutes to do a warm-up. He/she can ask students to make a short report about weather, news, or to tell a humor or just sing a song in English. This "warming-up" time can not only make each student have an opportunity to practice oral English, but also form an English atmosphere quickly. This is much better than teaching as soon as class begins. During teaching process, how much time for teachers to spend on a student is another aspect of the use of time. It is a rule that more difficult questions need more time to think, and less able students want more time to be cared about.

Punctuality is another aspect of teachers' use of time. If teachers expect students to take the classes seriously, they should always be on time or a little early. By being a little early, it gives us an opportunity to interact with students as they enter the room. If the teacher is consistently late to the classes, it sends the message to the students that he/she is not interested in the content area or concerned about the students. Therefore, students may begin being late for the class. Thus, punctuality is important for the teacher. Different cultures and different individuals may have different attitudes towards the punctuality. Teachers in Chinese colleges are required to enter the classroom several minutes earlier for preparation before the class begins. It is also common that students are required to be on time for class. Those students who are punctual to class can impress teachers positively, while students who are frequently late for class may be perceived as irresponsible, lazy, or uninterested.

5.4.9 Paralanguage

The full and correct use of paralanguage in class is very powerful to the effective teaching and learning. Here we mainly focus on teachers' nonverbal sounds in classroom.

Nonverbal sounds in classroom include such vocal elements as intonation, tone, pitch, rhythm, volume, pace, etc. These elements form a subtle and vital part of communication. Effective teachers are good at varying their voice or conveying different messages in different situations for different purposes. For example, in presenting material, effective teachers are inclined to employ emphatic intonation and few ungrammatical pauses, and skim quickly the less important. They use proclaiming tone when referring to aspects of the theme which have already been covered once.

When there are key points in the process of teaching, or there are some problems needing being emphasized, they usually raise their tones and slow down the speed. While in the process of statement, the mid-pitch and low-pitch can be alternatives, and the speed can be raised. When the students seem tired, the teacher may change his/her tone in time to make them excited again.

The inflection of tone simply refers the "rise and fall" of the tone of the voice of the teacher. It is significant in conveying and transmitting the "real" messages through the words uttered by the teacher. The word may have one plain meaning in its natural articulation and presentation but when it is uttered in different tones and inflection, it may give different messages and sometimes quite contrary to that of its actual explanation in that situation. Thus, a word may have two messages in general way of communication: one is from its verbal of which it stands literally and the other is nonverbal which is understood and appreciated due to the tone and its inflection. When the inflection is associated with face expressions and body gestures, the composite presentation can ensure maximum learning, retention and recalling of the contents. The teacher's presentation with a loud voice, a high pitch and a fast rate is more likely to draw students' attention than the quiet voice, low pitch and low rate.

Nonverbal sounds also indicate a person's emotional states. They represent a person's demographic traits and show personal characteristics. For example, when the teacher asks a question and calls on one more talented student, who answers the question correctly, the teacher usually responds with some positive verbal reinforcement enhanced by vocal pitch or tone, expressing the acceptance and liking of the student's answer. In the same situation, if the teacher calls on a less talented student whose response is incorrect, not only might the teacher verbally reject the response, but he/she might also modify the answer accompanying vocal cues. As Hopkins (2004) pointed out that the voice rising and falling in tone "plays a dominant part in making clear the emotions that lie behind or inspire our meaning; we have no rally adequate method of conveying in speech what we feel other than of varying the expression in our voices."

Richmond (2002) found that students felt that the monotone voice projected the image of boredom, non-caring, and non-immediacy. And they learned less when the teacher had a dull and monotone voice and less interested in the subject matter and liked the class less. Students like the teacher to have a lively, animated voice. Richmond (2002) concluded that among all voice qualities, teacher's monotone voice draws the most negative criticism from both teachers and students who said that they perceived the person with monotone voice as boring and dull.

So far we have discussed teachers' isolated nonverbal behaviors in classroom. It is clear that teachers' nonverbal behaviors have various meanings and can influence students greatly. It can be used as a means to both prevent the development of conflict in classroom and to mitigate conflict that may arise in classroom. Language learning is facilitated only when teachers provide students with nonverbal cues. Therefore, teachers should use whatever tools, such as pictures, demonstrations, gestures, pantomimes, or chalkboard drawings to assist their students to infer what the teaching is saying so as to improve student-teacher interaction and to make the classroom a more exciting environment. The teacher's delivery style should also be animated and dynamic, which can keep the class interested in the subject for longer periods of time.

We should point out that even though nonverbal communication may be effective in facilitating classroom management, the issue of culturally diverse student populations may require teachers to examine nonverbal behavior to meet the unique needs of diverse student groups. Only in this way, can teacher employ it strategically to improve classroom management and learning outcomes for all students.

5.5 Investigations on Chinese Teachers' Nonverbal Behavior

Literature review shows that the study of nonverbal communication in education is still considered to be relatively "new," especially in university level. As Radford (1990) confirmed that while college-level course work has been offered in nonverbal communication since the 1970s, the majority of communication studies still focus on verbal and written communication. Particularly, research in China is far from enough, and some researches were carried out in the researchers' own teaching and learning environment. So in this part, the present author intends to explore nonverbal behavior used by Chinese English teachers in a university.

Two investigations conducted by the author are presented in this section. The primary focus of the first one was to examine students' perceptions of teacher dress/attire in classroom. The second one was carried out to identify the teachers' most frequently used nonverbal behaviors including facial expressions, eye contact, gestures, and to find out the impact on the learners' learning in ELT classroom.

5.5.1 Students' Perception to Teachers' Appearance

This investigation was conducted to explore students' perceptions on teachers' appearance. Although appearance is not thought of as an element of etiquette, it sends a strong signal to students and influences students' attitude to the teacher. In order to teach effectively, the teacher must have students' full attention by various ways.

5.5.1.1 Methodology

The purpose of this survey is to assess the impact of the teachers' appearance on the students' perceptions of teachers' performance and professionalism. It was conducted in the spring of 2013 in Linyi University, Shandong Province, among non-English majors. The questionnaires were administered by their teachers during the normal class hours of the respondents. About 229 students took part in the questionnaire. 8 of the returned responses were incomplete, so the final sample consisted of 221 subjects. Among them, 129 were females and 92 were males. Their ages ranged from 19 to 24. The description of the subjects is shown in the following table.

Table 5.2 Description of the respondents

	Respondents for investigation (221)	
Gender	Female (129)	Male (92)
Average Age	22	23

The survey questionnaire (Appendix A) was modified from the work of Carr, Davies and Lavin (2009) on the effects of business faculty attire on the quality of instruction. The specific questions are, "Do you think the teacher's appearance (attire/ dress) may influence your perception on his/her_____?"

① Preparation for class
② Enthusiasm for teaching
③ Knowledge of the subject matter
④ Concern for students
⑤ Ability to prepare students for a successful career
⑥ Professionalism
⑦ Credibility
⑧ Level of expertise
⑨ Ability to communicate in the classroom setting effectively
⑩ Overall performance

Ten evaluation items were used by the students to rate their teachers. One of the advantages of this instrument—aside from its ease of administration—is easy to be conducted on large groups of students. And the rating scale of perception followed the

Likert technique of scale construction. The Likert-type scale is the most widely used method of scale construction due to "its relative ease of construction, its use of fewer statistical assumptions and the fact that, in contrast to other scaling technique, no judges are required" (Doukas, 1996). Students were also asked to respond to the five-point scale with "1" being strongly agree, "2" agree, "3" neutral, "4" disagree, and "5" strongly disagree.

5.5.1.2 Results

After collecting the statistics, the researcher entered the original data into the computer and processed it by the program SPSS (Statistical Package for the Social Science). The descriptive statistics and frequency distributions related to survey items can be seen in Table 5.3.

Table 5.3 Descriptive statistics and frequency distributions related to survey items

Teacher's dress influences my perception of his/her...	M	SD
Preparation for the class	2.45	1.06
Enthusiasm for teaching	2.82	1.16
Knowledge of the subject matter	3.22	1.17
Concern for the students	3.38	1.00
Ability to prepare students for a successful career	2.43	1.01
Professionalism	1.80	0.97
Credibility	2.56	1.06
Level of expertise	2.86	1.17
Ability to communicate in the classroom setting effectively	3.22	1.08
Overall performance	2.91	1.14

The table demonstrates that most students perceived that it is less likely that a teacher's dress/attire is related to his/her professionalism. While a large number of students were more likely to perceive that a teacher's knowledge of the subject matter, concern for the students and ability to communicate effectively could be reflected by the teacher's appearance in classroom, with the means of 3.22, 3.38, 3.22 respectively. Many students perceived that a teacher's appearance may show his/her enthusiasm for teaching, level of expertise and overall performance.

And then different attitudes to teachers' attire/dress between genders were also compared, which is shown in Table 5.4.

Table 5.4 Descriptive statistics and frequency distributions related to gender and survey items

…	Male		Female		
Teacher's dress influences my perception of his/her…	M	SD	M	SD	P
Preparation for the class	2.45	1.05	2.43	1.06	0.865
Enthusiasm for teaching	2.77	1.16	2.75	1.16	0.968
Knowledge of the subject matter	3.28	1.21	3.14	1.18	0.666
Concern for the students	3.40	1.10	3.18	1.05	0.332
Ability to prepare students for a successful career	2.53	1.14	2.37	0.94	0.467
Professionalism	1.97	1.16	1.76	0.87	0.334
Credibility	2.74	1.09	2.46	1.03	0.160
Level of expertise	2.82	1.25	2.86	1.17	0.963
Ability to communicate in the classroom setting effectively	3.53	1.09	3.02	1.06	0.004**
Overall performance	3.10	1.24	2.69	1.08	0.048*

The survey rendered two significant results related to the gender of the respondents. According to the survey, the female respondents were less likely to view a teacher's ability to communicate in classroom effectively by their appearance, with p = 0.004. Additionally, females were less likely to perceive a faculty member's overall performance by his/her dress/attire, with p = 0.048, while the male respondents were significantly more likely to attribute a teacher's ability to communicate in the classroom setting effectively and overall performance with their appearance.

5.5.1.3 Discussion

Although the merits of professional appearance and the perceptions of important attributes of teachers are debatable, the survey results suggest that teaches' appearance does influence students' perception of teachers' effectiveness. Students perceived that there was a connection between teachers' appearance and knowledge of the subject, teachers' ability to communicate in classroom. They also perceived that teachers' appearance was related to the teachers' concern for students. But how students perceived a teacher's preparation for class, ability to prepare students for a successful career and credibility showed no significant results. Another finding is that the perceptions of a teacher's ability to communicate in the classroom setting effectively and overall performance were impacted by the gender of the students.

Appropriate dress is not the single quality that creates student perceptions, but it is one of many nonverbal elements that may affect the educational process. It is important for teachers to realize the communicative power of their appearance in classroom setting. As Carr et al. (2009) argued that teachers should attach importance to the fact that all what is conveyed in classroom plays an important part in educational process, be it spoken or unspoken. Moreover, as today's classrooms of university become increasingly global, students' attitudes and perceptions towards teachers undergo constant change. Teachers must continue to monitor these changes in a constant effort to both keep pace and remain effective in classroom.

5.5.2 Students' Perception to Teachers' Other Nonverbal Behaviors

The focus of the second investigation is to explore Chinese students' attitude and gender differences to teachers' nonverbal behaviors in classroom. Through the analysis of Chinese teachers' nonverbal behaviors, the research intended to enable students to be aware of why particular moments in class were significant, to help them better understand certain events and teachers' behavior in class. The outcome was to develop students' awareness and understanding of what happened, why it happened and what it led to.

5.5.2.1 Methodology

Subjects

The researcher purposely chose 120 students including 60 males and 60 females among the 221 students who participated in previous research to complete the questionnaire.

Another 20 students among the 221 students were chosen as the volunteers to write self-report about their perceptions of their teachers' nonverbal behaviors in classroom which lasted for two months.

Instruments

Two instruments were used in this study. The first was a questionnaire (Appendix B), used to examine Chinese students' attitudes to teachers' nonverbal behaviors, such as facial expressions, eye contact, proxemics, paralanguage; and chronemics, with gender as the main dependent variable for the purpose of statistical analysis.

The second tool was the students' self-report called "critical moment reflection" report which was required in the autumn of 2013 in Linyi University. The critical moment was related to any of their teachers' nonverbal behaviors that students thought to be important with their own justification once a week after the classes. Students were given some explanations to show what the critical moment referred to and required to write the report within two days of the class time.

5.5.2.2 Results

1. Findings and Discussion from the Questionnaire

The empirical data of Chinese students' attitudes to teachers' nonverbal behaviors is based on the questionnaires administered to the 120 students, which is shown as follows: (SA=Strongly Agree; A=Agree; N=Neutral; D=Disagree; SD=Strongly Disagree)

Scenario		SA	A	N	D	SD
1. Smiling teachers teach more effectively than those who are always serious.		36(30%)	84(70%)			
	M		60	M	M	M
	F	36	24	F	F	F
2. It is easy to speak in front of those teachers who encourage students by nodding their heads.		56(43.33%)	48(40%)	16(13.33%)		
	M	34	26	7	M	M
	F	22	22	9	F	F
3. I feel nervous when the teacher indicates a particular student with their raised finger while asking questions.		70(58.33%)	50(41.67%)			
	M	26	16	M	M	M
	F	44	34	F	F	F
4. It is hard to speak in front of those teachers who stare at their students coldly.		70(58.33%)	50(41.67%)			
	M	25	35	M	M	M
	F	45	15	F	F	F
5. I avoid eye contact when I do not know the answer of the question asked.		92(76.66%)	16(13.33%)	12(10%)		
	M	40	17	3	M	M
	F	52	6	2	F	F
6. I pay more attention when the teacher makes eye contact with me in class.		100(83.33%)	10(8.33%)	10(8.33%)		
	M	48	5	3	M	M
	F	52	5	7	F	F
7. Teachers make eye contact only with the talented students.		82(69.25%)	28(23.33%)	8(6.66%)		
	M	32	21	7	M	M
	F	46	7	7	F	F

续表

Scenario	SA		A		N		D		SD	
8. I become motivated when teacher appreciates my involvement through his/her facial expressions.	78(65 %)		21(17.5%)		21(17.5%)					
	M	36	M	8	M	10	M		M	
	F	42	F	13	F	11	F		F	
9. I never take those classes seriously whose teachers are unpunctual.	72(60%)		36(30%)		12（10%）					
	M	28	M	16	M		M		M	
	F	44	F	20	F	12	F		F	
10. I see my wrist watch when the teacher takes over time in class.	67(55.83%)		24(20%)		4(3.33%)		9(7.5%)		16 (13.33%)	
	M	39	M	16	M		M	4	M	1
	F	31	F	11	F	10	F	3	F	5
11. Sitting close to the teacher in the front row helps me understand the lecture more.	75（62.5%）		45（37.5%）							
	M	34	M	26	M		M		M	
	F	41	F	19	F		F		F	
12. I feel bored in those classes where the teacher teaches in a monotonous tone.	60(50%)		36(30%)		24(20%)					
	M	36	M	24	M		M		M	
	F	24	F	12	F	24	F		F	
13. Poor teachers make meaningless sounds again and again in explanation.	84(70%)		15(12.5%)		21(17.5%)					
	M	41	M	8	M	11	M		M	
	F	43	F	7	F	10	F		F	
14.Teachers' movements in the classroom keep students active.	96(80%)		24(20%)							
	M	40	M	20	M		M		M	
	F	56	F	4	F		F		F	

Figure 5.5　Students' perceptions of teachers' nonverbal behaviors

This table shows that all the students liked teachers' smile. Analysis showed that the female students' (59% of them strongly agreed) motivation to teachers' smile was greater than the males but many of them felt difficult to speak in front of those teachers who stared at them coldly. Females (75% of them strongly agreed) were highly demotivated to such teachers than the males. This is accordance with some researchers' finding that the act of smiling has been shown to produce a more positive response for women than for men (Hall & Halberstadt, 1986; Henley, 1977).

Students (47% of them strongly agreed) were encouraged to speak in front of those teachers who encouraged their students by nodding their heads. In this regard, male students' (more than 57% of them strongly agreed) motivation to teachers' head nod was greater than the females, whereas majority of the students (58.33% of them strongly agreed.) felt nervous and embarrassed when the teacher indicated the particular student with their raised finger, females (73% strongly agreed) were slightly more demotivated to such teachers than the males.

More than 90% of the students avoided eye contact with the teacher when they didn't know the answer, but the number of female students (88%) was bigger, and they thought that the teacher had much eye contact with talented students. That is to say, eye contact is more important to female students than male students. Students, especially female avoided eye contact when they didn't know the answer of the question asked but they (95% of them) paid more attention when the teacher made eye contact with them. More than 82.5% of the students, especially female students, become motivated when the teacher appreciates their involvement through facial expressions.

Students (90%) did not take those classes seriously, whose teachers were irregular and unpunctual. They had different perceptions on teachers' punctuality; female students were more conscious than the males in this matter. Students (75.83%) looked at their wrist watch when the teacher took over time in class, but male students (65% of them strongly agreed.) were found less patient than the females in classroom.

All the students agreed that sitting close to the teacher can help them understand the lecture. More female students were more likely to sit close to the teacher than male students. More than 80% of the students didn't like the teacher's monotonous tone in teaching and 82.5% of them thought the meaningless sounds the teacher made could make them feel bored and thought the teacher was incapable in teaching. But there were small number of them (20% and 17.5% respectively) didn't care the teacher's paralanguage. They held the neutral attitude to it. As for teachers' movements in classroom, all the students agreed that this can keep students active.

To sum up, this survey shows that students had both the positive and negative impact from their teachers' nonverbal communication. (1) Students were highly motivated to the teachers who smiled at them, made them laugh in classroom, and illustrated the subject matter but felt difficult to deal with the teacher who stared at them coldly and indicated a particular student with their raised finger. (2) Students became more active if the teacher kept moving in classroom and made the frequent eye contact with them. Therefore, teachers should smile and nod their heads to encourage students in learning, and keep them alive by moving around classroom, keeping eye contact while asking questions so as to involve them in discussion.

The findings of this survey are confirmed by Hassan's (2007) study which showed that the college students are not only conscious of their teachers' nonverbal behaviors but are also biased towards certain types of nonverbal cues and behaviors. The results also show that the level of consciousness varies in gender differences, that is, female students exhibited a higher level of what Hall (2006) called interpersonal sensitivity than male students. That is, female students who tend to more readily notice, are better decoding than male students and are influenced by nonverbal cues. So they are more sensitive to teachers' nonverbal behaviors than male students.

2. Findings and Discussion from Students' Self-Reports

After the collection of the self-reports, the researcher read and analyzed them all. The analysis focused on the content which involves identifying, coding, categorizing, classifying and labeling the primary patterns/occurring themes in the data (Miles & Huberman, 1994, Patton, 2002). While analyzing, the researcher adopted Kvale's (1996) "meaning condensation" and "meaning categorization" approaches and Creswell's (2003) six steps generic process of data analysis.

Based on careful analysis, the researcher found that the topics of teachers' eye-contact, facial expressions, and gestures have aroused out of the critical moment reflection reports due to their frequency of mention by students. The researcher was attracted by the frequency and the saliency that students mentioned and attempted to examine the topics more closely by analyzing with what students have associated eye contact, facial impressions, and gestures.

Category 1: Facial Expression and Eye Contact

Students' perceptions about the meaning of facial expression and eye contact reveal several meanings.

(1) A Source of Information, Motivation, and Classroom Atmosphere

Research has indicated that teachers' facial expression and eye contact can be used to check whether the student concentrates, who is talking that the teacher is taking notice and to encourage contributions, participation (Ledbury et al., 2004). This is similar to the findings of this study. Most students reported that teachers' facial expression provides much information and motivates them. And the teacher's eye contact makes them feel important and confident. As some students reported:

S1: The teacher's facial expression can provide much information to us. For example, when the teacher entered the class I noticed her facial expression, she was very excited. Her smile made us feel easy and made the classroom lively.

S2: Today I made some mistakes when I answered one question. I was so nervous and was afraid of being criticized by the teacher. But he smiled at me and waited me to give a proper answer. Teacher's smile makes me feel so comfortable and encouraged.

S3: Our teacher maintains eye contact with classmates and this is motivating me. I feel as a part of the class. Teacher's regular eye contact makes the classroom's environment alive.

S4: The English teacher has a vivid facial expression in class. We can get much information from her facial expression. And sometimes her facial expressions are so rich which make us feel happy, anger, and sad with her. I like our English teacher.

S5: I like the way the teacher teaches us since she always smiles and has eye contact with us. It makes us believe we are each important and valuable. I feel myself deeply responsible for the class and I will try to do my best.

(2) A Reflection of Teachers' Mood and Confidence

Students reported that the teacher's facial expressions and eye contact can indicate whether the teacher is happy or not. The result is a bit surprising since eye contact is often used for reading students' mood whether they are puzzled or lost (Ledbury et al., 2004) but not for the interpretation of teachers' mood by students. It shows that facial expression and eye contact can suggest whether the teacher has self-confidence, whether the teacher is sure of what he/she is saying. This is supported by Pollitt's (2006) views that a teacher who never looks students in the eye seems to lack confidence and gives students a sense of insecurity.

S1: Today, the teacher was a little bit stressful since she used less eye contact with us than usual. Well, all teachers should present their characters clearly so students can understand what the teacher wants or how we should behave.

S2: Today, our teacher seemed not happy. We could understand it from her facial expressions and eye contact easily. She did not have eye contact with us as usual. Moreover, even when she looked at us, her eyes and her look were not as powerful as before. I understand that something bad happened and she was sad.

S3: I am very much affected by our teacher' look in classroom. It takes my attention and makes me to listen to what he is saying. His eye contact shows me that he has self-confidence and trusts his knowledge.

S4: By looking us directly in the eye, our teacher encourages us to pay attention, to respond and to respect her. Good eye contact shows that teacher has confidence in herself and what she is saying. However, when the teacher avoids eye contact, students may get the impression that the teacher is too anxious or unplanned.

(3) A source to Maintain Attention and Understand Topic Better

Some researchers claim that eye contact is used to hold the attention (Gower & Walters, 1983; Snyder, 1998). The similar results were found in some students' reports. What is more, students reported that teachers' facial expression and eye contact can also help them understand the topic better. This is a surprising result because few researches indicated such a use of facial expression and eye contact.

S1: I am very much affected by my teacher's eye contact as it takes my attention and makes me to listen to what she is saying. It shows me that the teacher has self-confidence and I trust her knowledge. It makes me believe in her and what she is saying. I think if a teacher avoids eye contact, he/she may be too anxious or unplanned for the lesson.

S2: The teacher's eye can encourage us to pay attention, to respond attentively. His facial expression shows that he has confidence in himself and what he is saying.

S3: In classroom, the teacher looks students in the eye. I am very much affected by this, and it takes my attention and makes me to listen to what she is saying, and the topic discussed.

S4: Teachers' facial expression and eye contact are very important. They can make us pay attention to the lesson. I like teachers who have more facial expressions. I think teachers who have never had eye contact with students may make students have difficulty in understanding the topic.

S5: First I am going to start with the teacher's eye contact. She uses eyes very effectively. When her tone of voice is up, she also opens her eyes. I mean the teacher's eyes and her tone go parallel with each other.

Category 2: Gesture

Teachers' gestures in classroom play an important role in language teaching as aforementioned. In this study, several themes generated by teachers' gestures were found from students' self-reports.

(1) A Source of Motivation, Enthusiasm and Confidence to Learning

Researches show that a lively and animate teaching style makes the material more interesting, facilitates learning and provides a bit of entertainment. For example, using gestures in teaching can make some complex grammar points easier to understand. Without gestures, the teacher may be considered as boring, stiff and inanimate. These have been confirmed by the students' self-reports.

S1: Once again I realized that teaching is like acting! The teacher is a kind of actor. The teacher's gestures are important for us to understand the lesson. I like the English teacher's rich gestures which make the lesson more interesting and motivational.

S2: The teacher's gestures are very friendly, so we feel safe, confident and comfortable. Her body language makes me think that she is enthusiastic for teaching and she cares for us. I can ask questions easily when I am confused.

S3: Compared with other courses, English class is more lively and actively since our English teacher has rich body language in teaching. By gesturing, the teacher makes the classroom very lively which is very good to our psychological situation. This makes us more motivated, encouraged and enthusiastic to learn.

S4: I like the teacher's gestures. It makes me feel that the teacher is easy to communicate with. I am encouraged to speak out in class when I have a question. The teacher always nods her head as she listens to my speaking. This gives me more confidence and motivation.

(2) A Means of Maintaining Attention, Creating Lively Atmosphere, and Emphasizing

The results show that teachers' gestures can capture students' attention, help them comprehend the lesson effectively. Students like the teacher who uses head, shoulder, and hands to emphasize the content and give them additional meaning which can generate their interest, especially when the topic is difficult to understand.

S1: Although the topic of today's lesson was boring and uninteresting, the teacher presented it in a very confident active posture and voice which gave us a message that our teacher has a confidence in herself. This made me feel that we can succeed throughout the semester. What is more, the way our teacher used her hands, facial expressions and voice made us stay awake and pay attention to her.

S2: During this week, I noticed that every time the teacher had something important to say, he switched off the OHP. This was such a good way to get all of our attention, because as soon as he switched it off, all my focus went to him. It forced me to concentrate, rather than trying to read the notes on the board and missing important information the teacher taught.

S3: I like the teacher using mimic voice, which really likes the animal sound. We all laugh and feel happy. His gestures are very friendly, so we feel safe and confidence. This makes us easily to ask questions when we are confused. I like the atmosphere of the classroom.

S4: In classroom, I observed that when the teacher wanted to emphasize the important points of a topic, she really spent a big effort when she stressed some of the words (her lips become an oval shape). Sometimes, she started walking around the desks and said the important points again and again.

The investigation shows that there is a different interpretation of teachers' eye contact, gestures compared with previous researches conducted at elementary school levels which indicate that the purpose of using eye contact, gestures is to control over and make students silent. University students mostly perceive eye contact, gesture, facial expression as a source of motivation, concentration, enthusiasm and a tool for taking and maintaining attention. As cognitive scientists state that meaningful learning could occur if students' attention is captured because information processing begins with students paying attention to the stimuli (Cruickshank, Jenkins & Metcalf, 2005). From the students' self-reports, we can find that they were motivated and feeling comfortable, confident and important by the teachers' nonverbal behaviors which gave them a sense of safety. Teachers' nonverbal behaviors can also create a comfortable and relaxing atmosphere. This enables them to have self-confidence which leads to an increase in the participation and contribution to the lesson. The self-confidence and lively atmosphere make students easily to ask questions which can improve their understanding of the topics in discussion.

5.6 Conclusion

This chapter has focused on the discussion of teachers' nonverbal behaviors in classroom. It illustrated how nonverbal communication is used as a teaching strategy and how it is closely related to students' development. The main function of teacher's nonverbal behavior is to improve students' affect or liking for the subject matter, the teacher and the class. And they are used as controlling, disciplinary and facilitative tools by teachers. To understand how teachers' nonverbal behaviors work in classroom, this chapter further explores them in details in terms of teachers' appearance, facial expression, eye contact, gesture, paralanguage, time and space language, especially teachers' silence which has not been examined enough in the past years.

In order to understand Chinese teachers' nonverbal behaviors in classroom at university levels, this chapter has provided two investigations. The first focuses on Chinese students' perception to their teachers' appearance. The results show that teachers' appearance does influence how students perceive the effectiveness of teaching. They thought that teachers' appearance was related to teachers' ability to communicate, concern for students, and knowledge of subject matter. The second investigation was conducted on students' perceptions on teachers' other nonverbal behaviors. The results suggest that teachers' nonverbal behaviors in classroom have both the positive and negative impact on their learners' motivation. The male students and female students had different perceptions on teachers' nonverbal behaviors. Teachers' nonverbal behaviors can influence students' perceptions of their personality, teaching effectiveness, and confidence, and help students get more information, encouragement, and attention.

Chapter Six

Chinese Learners' Classroom Nonverbal X-Factor

6.1 Introduction

This chapter will extend to the examination of students' nonverbal behaviors and how these behaviors influence teachers' perceptions and reciprocate behaviors. Based on the analysis of the limitation of previous researches, communicative effectiveness, and the reciprocate relation between teachers and students, it further explores each component of students' nonverbal behaviors in classroom. After that, two investigations are presented. The first one was conducted on the relationship between students' immediacy and teachers' perceptions of their credibility. The second is to explore the reasons and meanings of Chinese students' silence since it is a very common phenomenon in classroom. The main purpose of this chapter is to provide students with great insight into their nonverbal behaviors as Nuessel (1985) stated, "A full appreciation and complete understanding of another language requires the student to become aware and attentive to all the channels of communication available for encoding and decoding linguistic information. Foreign language fluency demands competency in nonverbal language."

6.2 Background Information

Most teachers would like to think that they are the center in classroom, and they can immune from students' behaviors, but in fact they are not. Students communicate using both verbal and nonverbal messages to convey various nonverbal messages in classroom. For example, some students remain active and interactive. They sit upright on their chairs, leaning slightly forward. They maintain eye contact with teachers while simultaneously nodding their heads and uttering vocal assurances. They laugh at the teacher's jokes and even seem to enjoy them. These nonverbal messages have been shown to stimulate feelings of attentiveness and responsiveness. They are a pleasure to teach. In another way, they are more communicatively competent and engage in more eye gaze, more object-focused gesturing, and less body-focused gesturing than individuals low in interaction involvement. For those students, they have been found more positive affect and greater ego strength during conversations and negotiations. However, some students remain passive and apathetic in classroom. They sit in a slouching position with their heads bobbing back and forth, eyes closed, and snoring, etc. They remain "too cool to care" and laugh at the teacher rather than his/her jokes. These students are less than a pleasure to teach. Their nonverbal messages show their boredom, lack of interest, and apathy. In a word, it is unquestionable that these negative and positive nonverbal messages influence teachers' behaviors greatly in classroom.

6.2.1 Limitations of Previous Research

In classroom research, studies of relationships between students' and teachers' behaviors have been largely correlational in nature. The results indicate systematic relationships between positive teachers' behaviors and positive students' behaviors, and between negative teachers' behaviors and negative students' behaviors. Although the nature of this correlational research did not enable the investigators to identify the role of students' behaviors in the determination of teachers' behaviors, the results of previous investigations indicate that students influence their teachers in various ways.

However, many studies investigated student-teacher classroom interaction have been directed almost entirely towards the immediacy of teachers, little is known regarding students' influences on teachers. What is more, the results of the previous researches have been somewhat inconsistent, and they appear to support a general trend that positive teaching behaviors are associated with more with students' growth than negative teachers' behaviors. In an extensive literature review, Nussbaum (1992) confirmed the fact that research needs to address the effects of students' communication behaviors on teachers since "teachers are viewed as the source and students as the receivers, and no attempt is made to account for mutual influence."

6.2.1.1 Ignorance of the Dynamic and Reciprocal Relationship

One limitation of previous research is that it has not considered the classroom as a dynamic process. Gardiner (1969) stated that communication "is dynamic in that it stresses continuous changes in the source, receiver, purpose, strategy, message, and performance." Jenkins and Deno (1989) confirmed the reasons of the paucity of evidence regarding the effect of students' behavior on teachers' behavior: "Change in student behavior is the primary, if not only, reason for education; therefore, most research efforts are directed toward the ways in which student behavior can be altered."

Some researches examine teaching and learning as a linear, one-directed relationship and often ignore the transactional, reciprocal aspects of how students' behaviors influence teachers and their teaching. To some extent, teachers' actions towards students are actually reactions to students' behavios. As Nussbaum (1992) stated both communication and education fields have virtually ignored the circular interaction of students and teachers in classroom. One aspect of the circular interaction element of instructional communication is feedback which is defined as "any information that the source gains from his receivers about the probable reception of his message. Smile, frowns, attention, inattention, questions, and comments are all examples of feedback" (Bettinghaus, 1968, 207). Bettinghaus (1968) claimed that the source of a message must be concerned with feedback so that decision can be made to structure message appropriately. Teachers may have many goals in classroom, the primary goal always is to facilitate learning. In order to do this more effectively, teachers continuously make judgments to determine and assess whether students are accurately receiving the information and whether they are reacting positively to it.

Teachers' expectations also influence their teaching. Then how are teachers' expectations formed? What role do students' communication behaviors play in how teachers perceive them and teach them? The social psychology has informed us that the role of stereotyping played in how we perceive others and the problems associated with this perception process. Some study suggests that teachers' perceptions and expectations for students are based not only on group stereotype, but also on students' achievement, performance, and level of motivation (Madon, Jussin, Keiper, Eccles, Smith & Palumbo, 1998). Another study found that teachers' behaviors are influenced more by immediate students' behaviors including students' communication rather than by students' other characteristics such as sex and age (Natriello & Dornbushch, 1983). Thus, teachers' expectations are largely related to students themselves.

Early researches have revealed that teachers respond differently to diverse students. Jackson, Silberman and Wolfson (1969) found that teachers became more personal involved with boys than with girls, and with those students who were salient rather than non-salient in the teacher's mind. Dalton (1969) noted that the teacher interacted more directly with those students rated low than with those rated high on a continuum from a typical "worst student" to "best student." Another study conducted by Ho and Mitchell (1982) indicated that students could give more direct eye gaze, more head-nods, and smiles in a "warm" condition, while students gave more backward leaning, frowns, shaking heads in a "cold" condition.

More recently, some studies testified that students' classroom behaviors can influence teachers' teaching since teachers use students' communication as information to monitor and evaluate their own teaching effectiveness. Gage and Berliner (1992) stated that teachers, like dancers, actors, and musicians, assess their performance by "reading" their audience. Clark and Peterson (1986) argued that during instruction the greatest proportion of a teacher's thoughts deals with how well instruction is being received by students. Students' response is one important source for teachers to adjust their teaching. Jenkins and Deno's (1989) research showed that teachers who received positive feedback from the student experimenters found the teaching experience more enjoyable to themselves and profitable to the students than teachers who received negative feedback. Klein's (1971) study also confirmed that students' behaviors did influence the verbal and nonverbal behaviors of the teachers and the direction of the influence was predictable. When the students behaved positively, the teachers were positive and when the students behaved negatively, the teachers were negative. What is more, students' nonverbal messages convey their emotions. As Mehrabian & Ferris (1967) stated, from students' emotions, teachers can judge their responses to teaching and learning.

6.2.1.2 The Difficulty to Interpret Student Nonverbal Behavior

In classroom, it is much easier for the teacher to consciously and unconsciously send nonverbal cues, but it is much difficult to identify and interpret these nonverbal cues from the students (Trenholm & Jensen, 2008). What is more, as Knapp and Hall (1992) noted, "people differ markedly in their skills in judging and using nonverbal cues" (476). It is entirely likely that one teacher may be more skilled or sensitive to vocalics, while another teacher is more sensitive to facial expressions. Much of the sensitivity comes from the teacher's experience and gender and cultural background.

The classroom is a very dynamic environment, so it is difficult for the teacher to track the most primary classroom activity, let alone picking up on nonverbal cues made by a single student. Often the signals that predict trouble are subtle and can be lost in the mass of nonverbal activity. Radford (1990) suggested that to truly attempt to observe and process everything that occurs in a classroom would result in the teacher being "paralyzed by continuous conscious analysis." The mental multitasking requires the teacher a sense of comfort in the classroom environment and confidence in the subject matter.

Another difficulty of identifying nonverbal cues is the awareness that students have about their own nonverbal projection. Without fully realizing it, students proactively seek to make their nonverbal cues. This is particularly true of cues that would suggest lack of understanding. Unfortunately, in many academic environments, it is considered a weakness to reveal confusion in front of one's peers. Thus, men are significantly more likely to adopt a "poker face" in classroom than their female counterparts (Helweg-Larsen et al., 2004).

Zoric et al. (2007) pointed out that nonverbal cues typically occur in clusters, which can clarify or confuse the observations. For example, a student who sits far away from the teacher, projects his/her legs to side, slouches, and crosses his/her arms over the chest should be identified as unengaged in the learning. However, a student that is seated near the front of the classroom, is seated erect, frequently yawns and glances at the clock, may be bored with the material or may actually enjoy the class, but be looking forward to his/her nap immediately after class. Knapp and Hall (1992) stated that it can be difficult for teachers to not immediately assume that they are interpreting observations correctly.

It is also difficult for teachers to judge whether all observed nonverbal cues are a reaction to the course material or teachers' performance. For example, the strained look on a student's face may be confusion, or it could also be a reaction to a bad lunch, a personal relationship issue, or the person seated next to him/her that is wearing an excessive amount of cologne/perfume. Students have lives beyond the classroom walls and those lives influence their mindset throughout the day.

Miller (2005a) claimed, "No formalized reliable means has been developed to identify and interpret all nonverbal behaviors" (74). He further noted that students' nonverbal cues are "autonomic, idiosyncratic, and ambiguous" when not considered in context. Hall (2006) and Miller (2005a) both warned that teachers should not jump to conclusions, overstereotype, or make broad generalizations, they should take the culture, gender and a student's pattern of normal behavior into consideration.

What is more, Jenkins and Deno (1989) put forward other reasons, one is that "a clear rationale for examining student effects on teachers has not been formulated;

therefore, motivation on the part of research workers for doing research on this topic is low." Another is that "making causal inferences regarding student effects on teachers' behavior requires that students' behavior be manipulated in an experimental design and students' behavior is usually not subject to appropriate control; therefore, research workers interested in causal relationships are unaware of opportunities for experimental studies in studying these effects."

6.2.2 Communicative Effectiveness

Communication effectiveness has been defined in a variety of ways. One approach to effectiveness examined in instructional context is socio-communicative style, which consists of a person's assertiveness and responsiveness. The two dimensions refer to an individual's tendency to react, associate, and adapt to another communication situation (Richmond & McCroskey, 1990; Wheeless & Reichel, 1990). Being appropriately assertive and responsive is considered to be a component of effective communication (McCroskey & Richmond, 1996, 93), however, previous research has consistently found teachers' responsiveness, and to a lesser degree to students' responsiveness. If we are to understand how communication functions in classroom, we need to understand what it means to be an effective student as well as what it means to be an effective teacher.

6.2.2.1 Teacher Effectiveness

Most researchers agree that teacher effectiveness is the central concern of most teacher-education institutions. "Effective teacher" is an important concept in teaching, but difficult to define. Mitzel (1960) provided three criteria to identify effective teachers. Of the three criteria, only one specifies that it is changes in students' behaviors that are important (product criteria). The other two criteria, process and presage, specify for the most part that what is important are the classroom practices, the personality characteristics, or the subject-matter knowledge of the teachers. Mitzel (1960) stated that "unfortunately, most studies have used process and presage criteria in identifying effective teachers, rather than determining whether a functional relationship exists between process and presage criteria as independent variables and product criteria as a dependent variable."

It is obvious that teachers do judge their effectiveness on the basis of product criteria. Hand-raising, smiling, sitting straight, etc., are commonly used as evidence to judge the success of class teaching. Mottet and Richmond (2002) pointed out that teacher who focuses on interactive and student-centered concepts has been shown to invest the large portion of their thought into evaluation of how well their teaching is received by students. When expressing the teaching content and interacting with students, they simultaneously assess their teaching effectiveness.

Some studies explored teacher effectiveness by examining the results of various feedbacks of students to teachers. Most of them involved student written feedback. Gage's (1963) investigation indicated that if teachers learned how the students wanted them to behave, they would become more like the student's ideal. Tuckman and Oliver's (1968) study found that teachers changed their behaviors positively according to suggestions received from their students. These studies seemed to indicate that certain teacher effective responses were influenced by student written feedback.

Jecker, Maccoby, Breitrose and Rose (1964) investigated how well teachers assess students' understanding of their teaching content and effectiveness based on students' visual feedback cues. They predicted that if teachers make their judgments of students' comprehension based on visual nonverbal cues, they would be more likely to make some misperceptions of students' comprehension than judgments based on verbal cues. Their findings support their prediction. When audio was absent, teachers were significantly less able to accurately assess cognitive understanding. When audio was present, regardless of video, teachers were significantly more able to accurately assess students' comprehension. This research suggests that with the number of students enlarging in one classroom in recent years, students' verbal feedback has become less likely to occur, teacher effectiveness would be benefit from learning more about students' nonverbal behaviors and how to interpret them.

Another study conducted by Jenkins and Deno (1989) examined whether or not students' nonverbal feedback has influence on teachers' evaluation of their performance in terms of effectiveness and satisfaction. The results show that teachers who received more positive nonverbal feedback, such as smiling, hand-raising, sitting straight, and behaving excitedly, thought their teaching more enjoyable to themselves and profitable to the students, and predicted that they would be more effective teachers and considered that their students learned more than teachers who received negative nonverbal feedback from their students.

6.2.2.2 Student Effectiveness

Finding positive relationships between effective student communication constructs and student outcomes (e.g., learning) is the first step in the process of understanding effective student communication in the classroom context.

Some teachers may believe that students who receive a good grade in learning are the effective students. A review of literature on study skills shows that some scholars view an effective student as someone who has learned how to learn and manage the learning environment (Nist & Simpson, 2000) and emphasize learning strategies, organizing content, and metacognitive processing (Kiewra, 2002), but they lack the emphasis on student ability to communicate effectively with the teacher. If we assume the communication apprehension is an analogue of communication effectiveness, then effective students need to be effective communicators. From above discussion, we can see that being responsive would contribute to being an effective student. Accordingly, a component of being an effective student involves being responsive.

6.2.2.3 Students' Nonverbal Responsiveness

Students' nonverbal responsiveness is an important element to increase classroom atmosphere and effective way to show their interests. Responsive students raise their hands to ask or answer questions, engage in frequent eye contact and note taking, display positive facial features, and often sit upright towards the front of the classroom.

Students' nonverbal responsiveness has a positive impact on teachers, and acts as an "important source in the formation of teachers' impressions, attitudes, beliefs, and reciprocal behavioral expressions" (Brooks & Woolfolk, 1987). Mottet (2000) examined the students' nonverbal responsiveness and found that teachers who perceived fewer students' nonverbal responsive cues, especially audible nonverbal cues such as vocal assurance and interrupters, evaluated more negatively both their students and the quality of the teacher-student relationship. He also found that if teacher's perceptions of students' nonverbal responsiveness decreased, the teacher would consider themselves to be less effective in classroom. And that teachers would likely perceive students who are responsive in classroom more positively and have more positive impressions of the students. In another study, Mottet, Beebe, Raffeld and Paulsel (2004) claimed that students' nonverbal responsiveness is positively related to teachers' self-efficacy and job satisfaction. Along a similar vein, Baringer and McCroskey's (2000) survey of college teachers found that when teachers perceived students as using immediate behaviors, they perceived students as being more attractive and reported having more affect for the students, and the teachers were more motivated to teach those students and projected greater achievement for those students. Mottet & Beebe (2006) stated that students' nonverbal responsiveness is positively related to teachers' assessments of their speech grades, indicating that student responsiveness could affect teachers' subjective evaluations of students' work. They suggested that students' responsive behaviors may function to satisfy teachers' needs for affirmation and confirmation in classroom.

6.2.3 Reciprocal Relation between Teachers and Students

One basic feature of human communication is the reciprocity, that is, we give people what we perceive they have given us. The origination of reciprocity is difficult to isolate—it is chicken-egg argument— but a participant can alter the cycle at any point. Some researchers have examined students' nonverbal communication and its influence on teachers and teaching. They claim that nonverbal communication is a transactional process in which students and teachers mutually and simultaneously influence each other's reciprocal behaviors.

6.2.3.1 Teachers' Perception of Students' Credibility

As aforementioned, most previous researches have focused on teachers' nonverbal behavior and its effects on students' perceptions of teachers and learning outcomes. Conversely, students' nonverbal immediacy can influence teachers and their perceptions of students. One early study on the impact of students' behavior on teachers by Rosoff (1978) showed that students who provided positive feedback as opposed to neutral or negative feedback, were perceived more positively by their teachers on credibility, attraction, solidarity, and potential for educational success.

Credibility is a perception of believability and is based on how competent and trustworthy we perceive others to be. For example, when we perceive others to be outgoing, warm, we may think they are socially attractive. So credibility and personal attraction are important variables that influence teacher and student relationships. As Baringer and McCroskey (2000) predicted, students' nonverbal immediacy would be positively correlated with how teachers perceive students' credibility and interpersonal attraction. That is, teachers would perceive their students as being more credible and more interpersonally attractive according to students' immediate behavior. They are more motivated to teach those immediate students and project those students would do better in the course than those who are less immediate.

Brophy and Evertson (1981) found that teachers don't like students who avoid eye contact in class. These students are perceived as being unhappy, inattentive, and/ or uncooperative. Mottet & Richmond (2002, 50) pointed out that when students' nonverbal attentive behaviors increase, teachers' perceptions of their students' competence and teachability can also increase. In contrast, when students' nonverbal attentiveness decreases, teachers' perceptions of their students' competence, teachability, and attitude can also decrease.

These studies confirm that not only a teacher's nonverbal behaviors influence positive outcomes in students, but also students' nonverbal immediacy and responsiveness get positive outcomes in teachers. That is to say, if a student perceives that a teacher is using coercive power, then he/she will respond in a negative fashion. If a student perceives that a teacher is immediate, then he/she will be more responsive to the teacher. When a student perceives that a teacher doesn't like him/her, the student most likely will learn to dislike the teacher. For example, the student who is staring out the window and has a totally bored expression on his/her face is not likely to be called on by the teacher, except as punishment. This student also is not likely to receive any preferential treatment from the teacher.

6.2.3.2 Teachers' Reciprocal Behavior

According to the interaction adaption theory (Burgoon, Stern & Dillman, 1995), communication between people is transactional. Unlike linear conceptualizations of communication where teachers' messages affect students' messages, communication as transaction means that both teachers' and students' communicative behaviors simultaneously affect the other's. This theory suggests that both parties adapt to the other's behaviors and both are responsible for relational outcomes.

The interaction adaptation theory stipulates that when people get involved in communication transactions with others, they have certain requirements, expectations, and desires. This is also true to teachers in classroom teaching. Firstly, teachers have requirements in classroom context. They have the need of safety and comfort that can influence their communication with students. Some teachers are more structured than others and have a difficulty in deviating from a prepared lesson plan, even when a teachable moment exists. The prepared structure makes them feel safe which they require in front of their students. Experimenting with a new idea or teaching technique may make them uncomfortable. But for other teachers, they may not have this kind of security needs. Secondly, teachers have various expectations in classroom. For example, they expect their students to be more responsive to their teaching and expect the students paying attention and responding accordingly to their instruction. They also expect their students to ask questions when they are confused. Finally, when teachers interact with students, they hope to achieve a desired level of behavior. They have a desire to remain on schedule and accomplish their teaching plans and make their teaching effective.

This theory implies that each communicative behavior is determined by what is needed (required), anticipated (expected), and preferred (desired) in any communication. In classroom, the communication between teachers and students is also filled with what is needed, anticipated, and preferred. Thus, the classroom interaction patterns are reciprocated back and forth from teachers to students to teachers. But if student's behavior does not match what teachers require, expect and desire, teachers have to adapt their communication to bring about their communication goals.

Mottet and Richmond (2002, 55) provided three examples to illustrate the application of this theory, assuming that the teacher has a required need for control, an expectation for students to complete the lesson and a desire to set up cooperative classroom atmosphere. (1) In the first class, students interact a way that allows the teacher to maintain control. They keep in the task and finish the lesson. The teacher is able to establish a cooperative atmosphere. Students' behaviors meet teacher's requirement, expectation and desire. In this class, the teacher adapts his/her behaviors by reciprocating students' on-task and cooperative communication behaviors. Mottet and Richmond comment this as a good lesson. (2) In the second class, students interact in the way which makes the teacher sense a lack of control. They do not keep in the task and will not finish the lesson. Students' behaviors do not meet the teacher's interaction needs. In order to reciprocate their behaviors, the teacher has to adapt his/her behaviors in a divergent manner. The teacher becomes authoritative and directive. He/She interacts with students in a firm manner to bring them in line with his/her interaction needs. Mottet and Richmond think this is not a good lesson. (3) In the third lesson, students keep in the task, cooperative. Their behaviors not only meet the teacher's interaction needs, but exceed them. In this class, the teacher adapts his/her communication behaviors by converging. That is, the teacher increases his/her level of interaction and encouragement. The teacher provides students with maximum freedom. Mottet and Richmond considered this as a very good lesson.

Comstock's (1999) study has tested the theory of interaction adaption in classroom. The author predicted that when students increase their level of nonverbal involvement in classroom, teachers would reciprocate by increasing their own involvement. On the contrary, when students decrease and maintain a lower level of nonverbal involvement in classroom, teachers would adapt their communication accordingly to bring about their communication for students' nonverbal responsiveness. The prediction was supported. The results show that even during a single, ten-minute class presentation, the teacher's role performance was directed by their students. Based on the results she concluded that "teacher-student interaction is transactional and that teacher-student relationships involve mutual influence, with each other partner partially responsible for the other's role performance and important relational outcomes" (Comstock, 1999, 22).

Cantor and Gelfand's (1974) study on the behaviors of adults and children found that adults took care more to responsive children, for instance, those who looked, smiled and reacted enthusiastically to the adults. The adults also related the children as more attractive and competent when they behaved responsively than when they were unresponsive. Accordingly, they concluded that influence is bidirectional in adult-child interactions and suggests that awkward children can be trained to promote positive reactions from adults.

Now we can conclude that not only a teacher's nonverbal behaviors can lead to positive outcomes in students, but students' nonverbal immediacy and responsiveness can also influence positive outcomes in teachers. The rule of reciprocity can explain much of the immediacy and responsiveness occurring in classroom. When teachers show nonverbal immediacy, students may also become more nonverbal responsive which can reinforce teachers' immediacy. Conversely, when students are more nonverbally immediate with teachers, teachers may become more responsive reinforcing students' immediacy.

6.2.4 Implications

Based on the researches on reciprocal nonverbal behaivors in classroom, Mottet and Richmond (2002, 56) summarized some implications in the following list:

(1) Teachers' pre-existing expectations for students influence how they teach students.

(2) Teachers' attitudes and expectations for students are based partially on how students behave in classroom, in addition to students' attributes such as sex, race, or socioeconomic status.

(3) Teachers perceive students' nonverbal behavior and these perceptions influence their attitudes and expectations for students.

(4) Students who sit closer to their teachers and engage in attentiveness behaviors are perceived more positively than students who sit far away and students who fail to make eye contact, nod their heads.

(5) Students who interrupt teachers and respond to their questions in appropriate

and timely manner are perceived more positively than students who fail to notice appropriate time for interruptions and who require additional time to respond to question.

(6) Students who remain nonverbally immediate or responsive in classroom are liked more, considered more teachable, competent, and trustworthy, and considered more interpersonally attractive by their teachers.

(7) Teachers' initial attitudes and expectations for students influence how they perceive students' nonverbal behaviors. Two students may convey the same nonverbal message, but because of the teacher's existing attitude or expectation, he/she perceives one student's nonverbal message in a positive manner and the other's in a negative manner.

(8) Teachers and students mutually influence each other's classroom interaction behaviors. Teachers who perceive students negatively, treat them less positively. Students react to these less-than-positive communication behaviors by reciprocating similar behaviors, which in turn reinforce the teacher's original attitudes and expectations for students.

(9) Teachers remain more motivated to work with nonverbally immediate or responsive students, consider their teacher-student relationship to be of higher quality, and project that these students will not only do better in their courses, but in life in general.

(10) Teachers who perceive more of their students' nonverbal responsive and attentive behaviors consider themselves to be more effective as teachers and more satisfied in their teaching profession.

6.3 The Functions of Students' Nonverbal Behavior

In classroom, students' nonverbal behavior is considered as a sign of attentiveness. A student's upright posture, leaning forward position, eye contact, head nodding, and smiling can usually be interpreted as attentive behaviors which are positively related to teachers' evaluation of the student's competence, learning, teachability, and attitude.

Students' nonverbal behavior is closely related to their confidence and emotion. As Miller (1988, 18) stated, "Body postures and movements are frequently indicators of self confidence, energy, fatigue, or status." In classroom, students who are keen to receive body messages of enthusiasm and boredom about the subject matter being taught can sense confidence or frustration from the unconscious behavior of the teachers. Observant teachers can also tell when students understand the content presented or when they have trouble in grasping the major concepts.

Students' behavior can also show their anxiety and uncertainty as some researches have claimed that a classroom is an anxiety-producing situation for many students. Some students use more adaptors in classes where they feel anxious or bored. These behaviors are often perceived as a form of misbehavior and are punished. The student who is constantly clicking his/her pen is perceived by the teacher as disruptive. Students may not realize that they are engaging in such behavior until they are reprimanded for it. Kroehnert (2006) highlighted the indication for detecting uncertainty among the students in classroom and pointed out that if we ask a question, and while the student attempts to cover his/her mouth, it may indicate the student is trying to hide what he/she is saying. Similarly, if a person rubs his/her nose while answering or talking, it can again indicate that the person is uncertain or lying about his/her response. Looking down and rubbing an eye can also indicate a lie or uncertainty. It may indicate that the student can't see, or don't want to see the point that is making. However, these behaviors are only indicators, and their interpretations should not be taken as gospel. They merely give teachers an indication that the student may not be telling the truth, or that they don't believe what the teachers are saying.

6.4 Students' Nonverbal Behavior in Classroom

There is currently very little available literature that focuses on this specific topic. This section cannot hope to present a comprehensive summary of students' nonverbal cues specific to the classroom that relate to all situations, but the following is a recommended group of common nonverbal cues that all instructors should develop a sensitivity to and an ability to interpret.

6.4.1 Appearance

Students also project their outward view of the world through their dress, hairstyle, jewelry, etc. (Thompson, 1973). Though physical appearance is not necessarily a real indication of a student's cognitive state, it does often provide context in which teachers can better situate other nonverbal cues.

Scholars have found some very interesting relationship between attractiveness and student-teacher interaction. Teachers make judgments about students based on their dress. In some teachers' minds, the student slopping dressed does not seem to take pride in his/her personal appearance, they may be perceived by teachers as lazy, slow and not very interested in learning. Teachers might negatively perceive the students who dress in an unusual or wired manner. They often punish or criticize the student who does not fit the norm of school dress, which may impair the students' learning and the communication between teacher and students. In the early sixties in America, many schools had very strict dress codes. These codes didn't allow young women to wear slacks and young men had to keep their hair short. The same situation also occurs in middle schools in China. For the middle school students, many of them have to wear the school uniform and aren't allowed to wear strange clothes on campus, and also they shouldn't dye their hairs.

Observations indicate teachers engage in less interaction with unattractive students and initiate more communication as well as response to comments from their more attractive students readily. Attractive students have actually been found to receive higher grades than their less attractive counterparts. In classroom, the unattractive students are commonly ignored by teachers, given less time to answer questions, encouraged less to talk, given less eye contact and more distance, touched less by their teachers. Not only do we see such behavior from teachers, but class peers are also less likely to communicate with the less fortunate looking classmates. Teachers' nonverbal behaviors would make these students feel that they are not good as the other students, which may eventually make them tune out of the classroom environment and learn less.

For those students who have a neat, clean, acceptable appearance are generally accepted by teachers, peers and administrators. They are often given more latitude than the sloppy and unusually dressed students. For example, students who dress as the teacher thinks are more attractive to the teacher and are likely to be helped more. The teacher will spend more time interacting with them and helping them with their assignments. What is more, the attractive students are often given better treatment than unattractive students who are discriminated against in classroom. Teachers communicate more with the attractive students and interact more positively with them.

We should point out that dress code may be culturally controlled and regulated in some cultures. It could furthermore be indicative of a particular student's socio-economic status, which could impact on social acceptability among peers and the individual's self-image that regularly are erected in social behavior and ultimately culminate in academic achievement.

6.4.2 Students' Facial Behavior

Students' facial behaviors also influence how teachers react to them. Here we mainly focus on students' facial expression, eye contact and smiling.

6.4.2.1 Facial Expression and Eye Contact

Students' facial expression is an indication of students' satisfaction with their current environment, while a frown and/or wrinkled brow is an indication of anger or confusion. The involuntary reflex of yawning is an indication of boredom or fatigue (Miller, 2005a). Eye contact and smiling are two main ways of expressing students' feeling in classroom.

It is common for teachers to witness students who avoid eye contact which is interpreted by Knapp and Hall (1992) as the students who do not know the answer to a question. Miller (2005a) pointed out that students will avoid eye contact when they simply dislike or are disinterested in the subject matter. Hartley and Karinch (2007) considered that the low self-esteem students are also likely to avoid eye contact. Breed and Colaiuta (2006) found a positive correlation between the amount of students' eye contact with an instructor and students' comprehension. Specifically, higher test scores were associated with increased time looking at the teacher during discussion and less time looking elsewhere in the room.

Students' eye movement can provide teachers with an indication of his/her mindsets and thoughts. Since images are stored in the visual cortex, which is located in the rear of the brain, when students attempt to recall an image, their eyes tend to drift upwards, and also when they recall a sound, their eyes tend to drift to the left or right and in line with the ears (Hartley & Karinch, 2007). Hartley and Karinch (2007), pointed out that thoughts associated with intense feelings and emotions can result in eyes projecting down and to the right. If the teacher observes a student's eyes repeatedly migrating towards the clock, it could be interpreted as the student bored with the current discussion or he/she is concerned about events to be occurring in the near future (Miller, 2005a). Thompson (1973) and Miller (2005a) also noted that pupil dilation is a nonvoluntary reaction to viewing something pleasing.

6.4.2.2 Smiling

The smiling expression is mostly recognized as an enjoyable facial expression, but its meaning is context-sensitive since it takes a full account of the individual's affective and personality traits during social interactions. Students' smiles can show their personal feelings and attitudes in relation to what happens when interacting with their classmates and the teacher. Their smiles tend to be an interactive result of what occurs in different class events. This is due to the fact that smiling depends on the contextual factors in which it occurs and on what social and interactional motivation it is based. According to its realization in specific contexts, smiles can have communicative, informative and interactive meanings (Freitas-Magalhães, 2006). Therefore, students' smiles indicate different interactive and informative meanings depending on the class activity they were involved in and on the interactive moments they were inserted among their classmates and with the teacher.

de Araújo Nóbrega (2012) analyzed students' spontaneous smile in an EFL classroom environment at college level and its learning implication to their speech production. The researcher found that students had different nonverbal behaviors when they interacted with their classmates and their teacher. In pair and group work activities, they seemed to be more self-confident in exchanging ideas, and their smiles appeared as pleasure and agreement. On the contrary, when they made direct contact with their teacher or in open discussion with all the students, the students' smiles tended to appear as an instrument of defense. These interactive meanings can serve as fundamental aspects for a better understanding of the learning implications in relation to their speech production.

One aspect in smile investigation is its cultural implication in classroom interaction. Bohn (2004) examined how the Japanese culture on smile influences Japanese students' oral participation in an ESL classroom. Through a questionnaire to students and classroom observations, the author found out that the smile serves as a sign of politeness or a kind of etiquette for the Japanese students, and between the students and the teacher. In addition, the smile tends to be used to protect privacy, to show interest, to seem friendly and to listen carefully. In protecting privacy, the smile is often managed as a way to prevent the personal feelings on the event itself. For example, when asked if they understand the lesson or not, Japanese students tend to smile instead of verbally expressing their sensations. The spoken discourse is replaced by the smile as a way to sign a lack of desire to orally participate in class activities.

Students' smile is also considered as a responsive mechanism of teacher's speech, and could be seen as contextualization cues (Gumperz, 1982) in teacher and students' interactions and among the students. As a contextualization cue, the student's smile is seen as a signaling mechanism of contextual inferences or presuppositions. To understand the interactive meaning behind one student's smile, we should understand under what context the smile is displayed, how semantic content is related to the smile and which sentences precede or follow the smile within the talk units.

6.4.3 Posture

Students' body posture, while seated and standing, is a clear-cut and accurate nonverbal cue. Miller (2005a) claimed that a content person tends to walk with an erect posture, while a boredom or a discouraged state is indicated by slumping or slouching when seated. According to Neill & Caswell (1993) and Miller (2005a), an attentive and engaged student will sit predominately erect and lean forward slightly towards the teacher. A student's relaxed posture when addressing is an indication of a lack of respect for the teacher who may perceive the student as bored, or arrogant. Miller (2005a) further claimed that the body alignment while seated with legs in front indicates a higher level of respect than legs turned to the side. If the students place hands on hips while standing, it may be perceived as defiance or dissention by the teacher (Hartley & Karinch, 2007). Therefore, students' posture may indicate whether he/she is attentive, he/she may be bored or daydreaming unintentionally, or he/she may be fatigue or drowsiness. It conveys different messages to the alert and sensitive teacher who is constantly on the lookout for these subtle clues and nonverbal communicative messages.

6.4.4 Gesture

Students' gestures can help express themselves and clarify verbal questions or response. According to Miller (2005a) and Thompson (1973), steepling, either the process of interlocking one's fingers or merely placing the fingertips of opposing hands together, indicates confidence, while excessive preening is an indication of stress and anxiety (Neill & Caswell, 1993). Students' attention is obtained by raising a hand in classroom, but the "frantic hand waver" is excited to offer a possible solution (Knapp & Hall, 1992). In American classes, shrugging of the shoulders is a common expression of lacking sufficient knowledge. Neill and Caswell (1993) stated that arms folded across the chest is an indication of dominance, but Miller (2005a) interpreted that gesture as a defensive cue or withdrawal from the discussion.

Stevanoni and Salmom (2005) pointed out that when students use gestures to help recall an event, they report more details about the event than students who are not instructed to gesture. Similar research has found that gestures enhance messages involving communication of complex geometric shapes (Graham & Argyle, 1975), that gestures help the sender of an elaborate message and to get the message across (Ekman & Friesen, 1972), or that there exists a positive correlation between verbal fluency and gesture use (Cohen & Harrison, 1973).

6.4.5 Proxemics

Research shows that the place where a student sits on the first day of class affects teacher's perceptions of him/her. Students who decide to sit closer to their teacher are perceived to be more attentive, likeable, initiative, and responsive than students who decide to sit farther away. Teachers perceive students who sit closer to them as being willing to participate and those who sit farther away as avoiding classroom participation. Brooks and Woolfolk (1987) stated that "if one of the first impressions is that the student is reluctant to participate, then the teacher's reaction could be either inviting or defensive. In either case, the impression affects the teacher's response, and this response in turn affects the students' impression of teachers."

The student who backs away when the teacher approaches, or will not allow a teacher to stand or sit close to him/her, will be perceived in a similar manner by the teacher. The student who withdraws from the teacher might be perceived as uninterested or hostile. However, we should know that some people simply do not like being approached by others. These people are touch-avoidance. When someone approaches them, they move away or back to avoid contact. We must be cautious to not judge the student who draws away from interaction too harshly. He/she might simply be from a touch-avoidance culture (Andersson & Leibowitz, 1978).

Studies show that personal space and arrangement of physical items in a classroom have a surprisingly significant influence on students' comfort within the learning environment. Breed and Colaiuta (2006) found that there was a positive correlation between students' seating choices and both attentiveness and academic performance. That is, students that self-selected seating in the center and forward portions of a classroom tended to be more attentive and performed better academically. Neill and Caswell (1993) stated that filtering for cultural differences, the personal distance established by a student, between the student and the teacher, is an indication of the student's confidence and comfort. The closer interaction is an indication of high confidence and comfort. Rocking, leg swinging, or tapping are indications that a student feels uncomfortable with the established personal distance (Thompson, 1973).

6.4.6 Silence

Students' silence is "the most common nonverbal expression"(Gukas, Leinster, & Walker, 2010, 7) and has been considered as a big problem in language teaching. It has been interpreted as a "challenge" to the teacher (Suinn, 2006, 407), a lack of understanding, a feeling of inferiority (Gukas, et. al., 2010), a lack of knowledge, fear of failure (Davis, 2009; McCroskey, Richmond & McCroskey, 2006). It has also been considered as a product of learning preference or cultural background and a fear of failure (McCroskey et al., 2006; Gukas et al., 2010).

6.4.6.1 Previous Research on Asian Students' Silence

It is not strange we often hear the comments about Asian students: "They are quiet and hardworking," and teachers frequently ask: "How do I get them to talk more in class?" Perceptions of Asian students as silent have been widely debated in applied linguistics and education. In many studies, examining Asian students' communicative behavior in Western education contexts has been largely concerned with the extent to which essentialized notions of Asian culture are in operation and the consequences for teaching and learning. The students' silence and the expectations of their teachers for speech have been viewed as a clash of perceptions deriving from cultural differences and widely accepted as a problem arising from the normative behavior of Asian students.

For example, the Japanese have long been described as attaching strong values to silence. As Lebra (1987) stated that "there are many indications that Japanese culture tilts toward silence." Davies and Ikeno (2002) suggested that silence is more commonly found in various social contexts in Japan than in the West, and that it has "played a very important role in creating harmony and in avoiding direct conflict" (53). When it comes to classroom interaction, some convincing discussion (Anderson, 1993; McVeigh, 2002) argued that a culture of silence prevails in the parts of students. As Nakane (2007) found, students of high schools in Japan rarely participated orally and their utterances consisted of no more than one sentence or one word. This can account for the Japanese students' behavior in Western universities.

Asian students are consistently described as reticent, quiet, silent, nonparticipatory, and passive in fields such as TESOL (Lucas, 1984), English for academic purposes (Jones, 1999), higher education (Ballard, 1996; Liu, 2000), and intercultural studies. Most of these studies examined reasons why these students are silent, or reticent and how this problem can be dealt with. Some scholars emphasize the impact of the differing sociolinguistic norms applicable to the role of classroom teacher. As Jones (1999) pointed out, the expectations on Asian students to be "respectful and silent recipient of the teacher's knowledge" may lead to this behavior in the new educational environment of Western universities. Some researchers explained that Asian students consider asking questions as time-wasting and lacking consideration for other students (Milner & Quilty, 1996, 10), as a face-threatening act for the teacher if he/she cannot answer adequately, or as a face-threatening act for themselves because questioning can be interpreted as a lack of ability or intelligence (17). Other scholars suggest that the value given to modesty and the importance of face are crucial factors in understanding the silence of Asian students from Hong Kong, China (Tsui, 1996) and Japan (e.g., Anderson, 1993; Turner & Hiraga, 2003).

However, there are some critiques of this stereotype of reticent, silent and passive Asian students in literature. Marriott (2004) discussed the impact of the stereotypes and myths about Japanese culture, and argued the need to rethink the validity of cultural labels in the light of both relations of power and of research findings. Littlewood (2000) pointed out that the findings of East Asian students' silence do not "reflect the roles they would like to adopt in class." Zhou, Knoke, and Sakamoto (2005) claimed that the "reluctance to participate" of Chinese students in classroom is due to the educational context, they highlighted the importance of recognizing the co-constructed nature of silence in the multicultural classroom. Ellwood and Nakane (2009) explored how the miscommunicated expectations about silence and speech may negatively affect teaching and learning experiences in intercultural classroom and demonstrated a commonality of teachers' and students' perceptions of what has previously been seen as a mismatch between students' and teachers' expectations in Western classroom.

6.4.6.2 Functions of Students' Silence

Many scholars have claimed that silence goes beyond the non-communicative absence of speech. It has been described as a complex linguistic item whose functioning needs a comprehensive and explanatory treatment in a plethora of frameworks as Politeness Theory, Relevance Theory, Discourse Analysis, etc. (Jaworski & Sachdev, 1998).

Silence in classroom generally has narrow and specific range of interpretation. Teachers associate articulateness and being talkative with positive qualities whereas quietness is perceived to be negative characteristic that decreases academic achievement. Generally speaking, a student's silence tends to have negative connotations as Giles et al.(1992, 219) stated, "Silence tends to be interpreted variously as lack of interest, an unwillingness to communicate, a sign of hostility, rejection or interpersonal incompatibility; anxiety or shyness; or a lack of verbal skills."

However, the functions of students' silence appear as a rich communicative resource which needs a sophisticated and interdisciplinary analysis as Saville-Troike (1985, 3-18) presented. Schultz (2009, 11) considered silence as a kind of participation in classroom. She argued that paying attention to students' silence as a form of participation can open up further possibilities for understanding individual students and classroom interactions. Based on her own teaching experience, Schultz (2009, 30-50) categorized classroom silence into five functions: as resistance, power, protection, a response to trauma, and a space for creativity and learning. She also pointed out that the functions and uses of silence are multifaceted and often appear together.

Several reasons are supported both speculatively and empirically that students fail to participate in class as follows:

Silence as Resistance

One common explanation for silence is that it means a student's resistance to learning or participating in activity. But there are many possible ways to understand silence as resistance. It might reflect a refusal to learn or to engage in the teacher's lesson for a couple of reasons. Through silence, a student can simultaneously resist on assignment and participation in classroom. Choosing not to speak can also be an act of refusal to be dominated (Duncan, 2004). As Minh-ha (1990) explained, like speech, silence operates as a discourse and as a will to "unsay" or refuse to participate in dominant discourse.

Silence as Power

Acts of silence are often closely related to the uses of power. Shultz (2003) conducted a survey in which a student named Luis used silence to enact a powerful stance in classroom. Luis, during the past several weeks, kept silent until close to the end of the semester, he uttered his first statement to the whole class. When he spoke, Luis delivered a powerful indictment of the growing consensus in the class, reminding everyone, including the teacher, of the film they had recently viewed.

His classmates listened carefully to his words and his statement changed the course of the conversation, which resumed with renewed energy and emotion. From his stance, his teacher interpreted him as the "gang-related" and wondered if he lacked the knowledge of the discussion. It is difficult to reconcile his decision to keep quiet in classroom with his clear engagement in writing outside of the classroom (Schultz, 2003). His silence can be a form of reflection and a desire to choose his words carefully and can be interpreted as a self-protective refusal to engage in complicated racial and cultural dynamics of the classroom rather than a refusal to participate in the academic acuities (Schultz, 2008). The effect of his decision was to draw his classmates' attention to his comment, which allowed him to use silence as power. In the process of teaching, teachers sometimes find there are certain students who keep silent most time in class, but once when it is his/her turn to participate, he/she always says valuable stuffs which show that he/she is pretty knowledgeable on what is discussing.

Silence as Protection

Many studies focus on the hazards of silence for students' success (e.g., Raider-Roth, 2005, Carter, 2001), while the instrumental purpose of silence as a protection is rarely acknowledged. Students are sometimes silent to protect their intelligence; they may choose to be silent as a form of camouflage. In some situation, a student may choose silence or compromise over an overt display of intelligence in order to hold onto his/her popular status (Schultz, 2003). This inevitably leads to negative consequence. In contrast to silence sometimes impedes the academic progress, Fordham (1993) described how high-achieving African American girls become successful by adopting a silent stance:

> The most salient characteristics of the academically successful females at Capital High is a deliberate silence, a controlled response to their evolving, ambiguous status as academically successful student. Consequently, silence as a strategy for academic success at Capital is largely unconscious. Developing and using the strategy at the high school level enables high-achieving African-American females to deflect the latent and not too latent hostility and anger that might be directed at them were they to be both highly visible and academically successful.

Since schools and classrooms are often filled with ridicule and rejection, some students often choose to be silent or withdraw from a situation to protect themselves from these behaviors (Bosacki, 2005, Finders, 1996). It is not simply an individual choice but one constructed in relation to their teachers, peers and the interaction of the classroom, schools and even society.

In order to encourage students to speak out, teachers can begin by establishing classroom that emphasizes relationship and trust and provide ways for students to speak through silence and to be heard in ways that appear safer to them. Reading silence as the need for protection, respecting the need to refrain from speech is equally difficult and important.

Silence as a Response to Trauma

In her research, Rogers (2006) explained that when she was 16, she stopped speaking for 5 months as a result of traumatic events in her family. Through silence, she protested engagement with others. For her, silence was both protest and protection. It protected her from the world that threatened to be unkind and misunderstood her, providing her with a place to retreat. Her silence came from an inability to find words that were adequate to convey the events that had transpired in her life (cited from Schultz, 2009, 45).

From Rogers' story, we can also predict that some silent students may also experience some trauma in their lives. For them, silence is a way of telling different stories and is often connected to painful memories and at times, holds a place for them. For example, a student may keep silence, when he/she is uninformed or not clear about what a teacher says, or he/she is unwilling to answer a question. Cha (1995) juxtaposed textual silence with more public forms of silencing in *Dictee*, illustrating how the limitations of the language available to use render some ideas "unspeakable" or incomprehensible. Some students may live under the threat of becoming invisible in classroom and schools. They made daily choices about when to speak and when to remain silence. As Campano (2007) explained, silence is a presence that shifts according to context and time.

As the result of trauma, students find themselves having no words to describe their circumstances, often falling into silence. At times, silence coincides with a need for protection, at others times, it arises from a sense that words can not adequately capture and convey an emotion, idea, or experience connected to trauma. Silence can also be a container for thoughts, memories, and events that are difficult to put into words.

Silence as a Time and Space for Creativity and Learning

Researches show that some students may participate in silence in classroom since they retreat to their imagination, or they keep silence as they need more time to think, especially for those students who have difficulty in keeping with the quick pace of teaching. For other students, they may like to try out their ideas through other ways, such as small group discussion, writing, etc. Accordingly, teachers need to learn to read students' nods and facial expressions to understand their silence as a form of participation, and to understand that silent students may be engaged in learning. On the other hand, as Schultz (2009, 51) stated, "Silence is often critical for language learning and reflection. When students learn a new language, there is often a period of silence. A person may not speak or produce the new language at first because he/she is still listening and absorbing." The space created by the silence provides students with time to develop skills and to draw on creative resources, so silence is a necessary for students to move forward.

In this section, we have mainly focused on research on students' silence in classroom context and functions of silence. Our discussion is in accordance with approaches which see classrooms as heterogeneous and recognize the complexity of students' identity. It also shows that improved communication practices between teachers and students are possible following a re-examination of the privileging of talk and deprivileging of silence in intercultural classrooms.

6.5 Investigations of Students' Nonverbal Behavior in Classroom

Based on the above discussion, this part will present two researches on Chinese students' nonverbal behaviors in classroom. The first one focuses on teachers' perceptions of students' nonverbal immediacy, and the second is related to students' explanation of silence from their own perspectives.

6.5.1 Chinese Teachers' Perception of Students' Immediacy

In Chapter Five, we have discussed that the teacher's immediacy can increase students' affinity for the teacher, students' learning, and motivation, etc. According to reciprocity theory, we can conclude that students' immediacy would certainly influence teachers' behaviors. As Mottet and Richmond (2002) indicated that students' use of space, attentiveness, and use of time can influence teachers' impressions of students. So in this section, the relationships between students' immediacy and teachers' perception on their credibility including competence, trustworthiness, and good-will are examined. The hypothesis of this survey is that students' immediacy will be positively correlated with their credibility scores.

6.5.1.1 Methodology

Participants

Participants in this study were 132 teachers across 10 departments at Linyi University. The questionnaires were distributed to these participants through QQ or email during the first semester of 2014 school year. Teachers were asked to complete the questionnaire while keeping a randomly selected student in mind. All the participants responded with completed questionnaires.

Instruments

Two instruments were used in this survey. One was the questionnaire (Appendix C) which includes two parts. Part one is about the measurement of students' immediacy. Part two is related to teachers' perception about the immediate students. Detailed discussion is shown in the following:

(1) Immediacy. 10 items, adapted from McCroskey et al.'s (1996) study, were used to assess teachers' perception of students' immediacy in classroom. It was originally designed for students to assess the teacher's nonverbal immediacy. In this survey, it was reworded to reflect the teacher's perception of the student. The coefficient Alpha for the students' immediacy scale was .77 (Table 6.1). This reliability is very similar to that finding for the original form.

(2) Credibility. 18 items, adapted from McCroskey and Teven's (1999) study, were used to assess teachers' perception of students' credibility. There are three dimensions of credibility in the scale including competence, good-will and trustworthiness. Competence items on the scale got an Alpha of 0.85 and coefficient Alphas for the good-will and trustworthiness items were 0.84 and 0.93 respectively (Table 6.1).

Table 6.1 Description of measurements used in this study

Instruments	Variables (items)	Alpha Value
Immediacy	Immediacy Items	0.7703
Credibility	Good-will	0.8424
	Trustworthiness	0.9331
	Competence	0.8525

The second instrument was the interview conducted among 6 teacher participants on the question whether they are motivated or non-motivated by those students who are immediate in classroom, and they were asked to provide some examples to illustrate their points.

6.5.1.2 Results and Discussion

Means and standard deviations were calculated for each scale and each item of the questionnaire. The hypothesis was analyzed using simple correlations to determine the magnitude of the relationships between students' immediacy and the teacher's perception measures of students' credibility. Statistical significance was tested at the 0.01 level due to the number of tests conducted.

Table 6.2 Means and standard deviations of measures employed

Variables	Average Value	Standard Deviation
Immediacy	24.5	6.2
Competence	32.2	6.3
Good-will	27.4	5.9
Trustworthiness	35.5	6.3

The correlational analyses were performed to test the hypothesis predicted that students' immediacy would be positivity correlated with teachers' perceptions of the Chinese students' credibility. The results on the three credibility dimensions were: competence, $r=0.51$, $p<0.01$; good-will, $r=0.53$, $p<0.01$; and trustworthiness, $r=0.54$, $p<0.01$. Hypothesis was supported by the all three dimensions of credibility.

Combined with the interview and these statistics, it is reasonable to conclude that students who were perceived as immediate also were perceived more positively in other ways by their teachers. The literature review has indicated that immediate teachers are perceived more positively by their students. Therefore, it is safe to say that both teachers and students influence each other through the use of nonverbal immediacy behaviors in classroom. The present survey suggests that if students wish to be perceived more positively by their teachers, they should engage in such immediate behaviors, such as sitting close to the teacher, establishing eye contact with the teacher, smiling at the teacher, leaning forward to the teacher while talking, nodding heads positively to the teacher, being vocally expressive when talking. Those immediate behaviors can influence teachers' behaviors in the following way.

Generating Teachers' Motivation

Richmond (1990) found that students' motivation levels were modified in classroom through the use of immediacy, so it is reasonable that the student may have the ability to influence teachers' motivation as well. From the interview, the researcher found that teachers were more motivated to teach those students who were immediate. As one teacher said:

> I was motivated by the students who sit close to me, and always raised their hands while answering some questions. Particularly, those students always sit in the first row of the classroom and give me quick response, and they make me feel that my teaching makes them more eager to learn. I think these are good students who are more active and more willing to learn. I like them.

Generating Teachers' Pride and Liking

Students' immediate behaviors may show that they are interested in the teaching and in what the teacher is sharing. Everyone has this feeling: we are more likely to continue and be more interested in sharing when we perceive that others are listening to what we are talking. The attentive students show great eagerness to learn and liking to the teacher. One teacher confirmed:

> I really like my students showing me immediacy in classroom since it indicates that students like me and like my teaching. I can be greatly encouraged to present the lesson more interesting and vividly with their immediate behaviors. And also I am proud of being a teacher.

Getting More Positive Outcomes for both Teacher and Student

The rule of reciprocity may account for much of the immediacy that takes place in classroom as aforementioned. When someone is immediate with us, our response often is to be immediate in return. If a student shows immediacy to a teacher, the teacher unconsciously feels obligated to reciprocate immediacy to the student. So more immediacy will take place among teachers and students. The outcome of immediacy appears to be positive not only for teachers, but students as well. So we can assume immediacy may lead to mutually positive outcomes for teachers and students. This was confirmed by one teacher's statement:

> I think the immediacy between teacher and students can help the teaching and learning achievements. I have a good relationship with my students. We often communicate with each other on QQ, Wechat. Students like to tell me their worries, their liking, etc. This makes them active in classroom and also makes me feel confident in teaching. I think that is the reason why there are more students in my class who passed the GET-4 examination this year.

From above discussion, we can see that a student's nonverbal immediacy serves as an important source in the formation of teacher's impressions, attitudes, beliefs, and reciprocal behavioral expressions. In other words, students' classroom behaviors influence teachers' expectation for them and nonverbal messages have a tendency to be more trustworthy, competent, and stimulate more emotional meanings in messages than verbal messages.

6.5.2 Chinese Students' Silence in Classroom

As aforementioned, students' silence is a common phenomenon in classroom in China, which has become a major concern for teachers since classroom discussion is a major activity. Researches have found that the influence of cultural and educational background and the lack of English communicative skills are the main reasons for students' lack of participation. However, these studies consider talk as a norm in communication, and ignore the role of silence as a means of communication. What is more, many studies have examined silence from teachers' perspectives and failed to take into account students' own perceptions. So the present study tries to explore this phenomenon from the students' perspectives.

Another motive to conduct this investigation is from the researcher's personal teaching experience. The researcher often felt uncomfortable with silent students in the class and wondered why some students behaved like this and did not use the valuable learning opportunities in class. The discomfort with attempts to challenge silent students encourages her to open a discussion with students asking them about the way they perceive their silence. This encouraged the researcher to investigate this, an area relying heavily in the practical part on teaching experience with the silent students.

The purpose of this study is to explore the role and functions of students' silence in Chinese classroom and try to get some new ways to understand silence and how silence works in classroom. Through the retrospective account of the students and observations in classroom, it aims to identify, describe, and analyze the reasons behind silence of the majority part of the silent students at university level, which is based on the following questions:

(1) What are the Chinese students' beliefs about talk and silence in classroom?

(2) How do the beliefs influence their classroom participation?

6.5.2.1 Methodology

Based on the questions, the researcher adopted a qualitative descriptive multi-case study approach. According to Merriam (2001, p.29), a case study is defined by three features: (1) being particularistic: "A case study focuses on a particular situation, event, program, or phenomenon." (2) Being descriptive: the end product of a case study is a rich, "thick" description of the case, which refers to "a complete, literal description of the incident or entity being investigated." (3) Being heuristic: "Case studies can bring about the discovery of a new meaning."

Subjects

6 non-English majors in Linyi University were chosen as the subjects in which the three of them were considered as the silent students by their teachers and classmates. They consented to take part in the study voluntarily. All of them were undergraduate students in Linyi University at the time of the data collection.

Data Collection

Data was collected at the first academic semester of 2014, consisted of verbatim transcription of formal weekly and bi-weekly interviews with the participants, extensive field notes of class sessions, transcription of a focus group interview. A variety of data sources served to ensure data triangulation.

The interview was conducted in Chinese and each lasted an average of 40 minutes. The researcher used a conversational style in which she shared her own experiences and perceptions. The interview questions focused on the reasons of classroom silence, classroom experience, and specific moments of interaction. The interviewees' interpretation helped the comparison with the observation in the class.

The classes observed for the case study were the English classes taught by two young teachers. Both classes were observed for one two hour session each week and lasted for 8 weeks through the whole semester. The researcher joined all the class sessions the participants attended and the interview was conducted after the class session. Field notes were taken during each observation, which offered invaluable insights into the general classroom atmosphere and the relationship of the participants with their teachers.

A focus group interview was conducted at the end of the observations to enable the participants to talk freely about their experiences and discuss in depth the common themes that emerged in the individual interviews.

Data Analysis Procedure

Data analysis followed the typical data analysis procedures for qualitative research, and the data were analyzed recursively throughout the project. After the transcription was confirmed by the participants, the researcher read the transcription extensively to obtain a general understanding of the participants' experiences and to identify major statements, and then converted the major statements of each case into brief phrases which were color-coded and listed. In this way, the researcher tried to look for the common issues and themes from the cases. These lists served to group the issues into large categories.

6.5.2.2 Results and Discussion

From the participants' responses, the researcher found various dimensions of silence that the students experienced and categorized them into two aspects: objective and subjective reason.

Objective Reason

One reason is the cultural traits and a heightened privilege of verbal restraint in Chinese culture as the Chinese saying says "silence is gold." And the interpretation of silence as a result of lack of competence, shy personality, or lack of commitment to learning is linked to essentialized notions of Chinese culture.

China has been under the influence of Confucian ethics for thousands of years. In the Confucian code, hierarchy and obedience are the two key concepts guiding human relationships. For many Chinese, being communicatively competent means that individuals must know their place in the social hierarchy. For example, in most Chinese families, the assignment of a seat around the dinner table can show one's status in the family hierarchy. And some parents tell the children explicitly that it is rude and disrespectful to take part in adult conversations. Therefore, the fact that students talk less in classroom is rooted in the Chinese cultural emphasis on obedience. Since kindergarten, children are expected to obey their teachers and listen to their teachers. As Tannen (1994) wrote, "Feeling you are in your rightful place in a hierarchy can feel as safe and close as being in your family— a quintessentially hierarchical institution" (215). This was proved by one interviewee's statement:

> I think talking too much is not a good way in classroom. Being silent and not speaking without being invited by the teacher is a sign of respect to the teacher. And I think that teachers may be unwilling to work with students who did not show appropriate modesty in demonstrating their academic knowledge. So if I were a teacher, I would not be interested in a student who arrogantly defends his ideas.

Class size was found to be a significant determinant of participation in classroom discussion in several studies (Howard, Short, & Clark, 1996; Crawfore & Macleod, 1990) which proved that students are willing more to participate, less anxious, and less likely to be able to "hide" in smaller classes than larger classes (Hyde & Ruth, 2002; Weaver & Qi, 2005). Howard et al. (1966) found class size is more predictive of participation. Auster and MacRone (1994) confirmed by their research that there was more participation if the number of students was smaller, such as 10 or fewer. If the number was more than 40 or more, there would be less interaction. Often, more lectures occur in larger classes, which, in turn, means fewer participatory opportunities for students (Weaver & Qi, 2005). This can be confirmed by one student's report:

> There are too many students in our class. When the teacher assigns that activity and the content is interesting and familiar to us, many students want to talk, especially those who are "talkative." So I keep silent, do not want to get myself into trouble.

Through his silence, he was able to spare himself from an unwanted situation in cases where he perceived it was unwise to talk, so the large class tends to hamper the communication.

Subjective Reason

Students' silence in classroom is due to the following subjective reasons:
(1) Silence as a Result of Being Shy
Saville-Troike (1985) stated that "an essential part of the acquisition of communicative competence is how children learn when not to talk, and what silence means in their speech community" (11). So shyness may demonstrate a culturally learned style of communication.

We often use the word "shy" to label those students who keep silent in classroom. However, shyness is a behavior that could be the result of any one or a combination of the factors including skill deficiencies, social introversion, social alienation, ethnic/cultural divergence, unfamiliarity with academic discourse, lacking confidence in subject matter, and/or communication apprehension, etc. As one shy student reported:

> I am an introvert person, and seldom speak out my thoughts. My friend said I am a shy person. But I like writing. I write what I see and what I think. Although I was silent in classroom, I am still learning by listening. Listening is also a good way of learning and thinking.

(2) Silence as a Face-Saving Strategy

Silence is used by some students to protect them from losing face when they feel that their language abilities and content knowledge are insufficient to express themselves. They are afraid of making mistakes. This anxiety is due to the traditional teaching approach in China. Since the elementary and secondary schools, students were expected to be quiet, compliant and obedient in classroom. What they had to do is to memorize what they learned. They were taught to read "model essays" and wrote like the models. Students spent most time listening, taking notes, and trying to memorize as much as they could. They seldom engaged in the exploratory talks to discuss what they know and what they do not know. The teacher did most of the talking, dominated the whole class. The teacher's role was to assess and judge students' response. When students made some mistakes, the teacher usually criticized them directly, which made them embarrassed in the presence of their classmates. Therefore, in the university, those students are still accustomed to the role they acted in classroom. Fearing of making mistakes or not providing correct answers, they have to keep silence sometimes. As one student said:

> I prefer to be silent when I feel I do not have some good ideas to share. I think that students expose their intelligence and ignorance to the teacher through their questions. This can also damage their public image. I usually talk when I think I have enough words to express.

Through the silence, the student avoided his lose of face. He also believed that speaking with limited knowledge could result in an embarrassing situation.

(3) Silence as a Means of Participation

Three participants in this study usually were described as silent students. Although they seemed to "deviate" from the standard norm of participation in the form of talk, they remained mentally active in class. They attentively listened to others' contributions and they responded to questions or comments through their gestures and body language or through taking notes. For example, one student spoke up only three times in class discussion during the researcher's observation period, but he seemed to be very cooperative in group discussion and actively contributed to the work. One participant showed her interest in and engagement with classes in an alternative way: "I don't think participation is only speaking. Email the teacher is also participation."

In statements, some participants associated their learning with listening. Especially when the course was heavy with content, they preferred to focus on listening to teachers. One participant considered this is the best way to understand the course material:

> I don't like speaking in the class. I like listening. While I am learning, I listen instead of speaking...since I will miss a lot while trying to organize my sentences. Listening can help me understand better.

In this way, the student used active listening. He thought that by listening, he could understand how people construct sentences, where they place the stress, how they open a statement so as to expand their knowledge about the subjects. Another student said she liked writing "rather than talking." When asked if she followed up on the issues raised in class discussion, she informed that she often returned to notes she had complied during class and during her reading to reconsider a question. Clearly, writing on her own allowed her a more comfortable way than talking to express her ideas and remember her thoughts. So for some students, silence is a way of doing mental work in classroom.

(4) Silence as a Reaction to Others' Contribution

Some participants reported that they felt uncomfortable when some peers provided some comments which were not relevant to the topic under discussion. In such case, they chose to keep silent as a protest against the perceived low quality of contributions:

> If I learned from what they said, if I gained something from their talk, I would not care how much they talked. But their talk is just...has no direction, no purpose... And there were too many "noises"... I feel lost and I don't want to talk.

> If what I had in mind was not really valuable, I prefer not to say that. But some classmates do not think that way and I think they are stealing class time. They deprive me from learning

opportunities.

These responses suggest that the participants felt resented to students who tended to dominate the discussion. For some students, the noise was a cause of their silence. Maybe they were so used to teacher's monologue in classroom. So it is not surprising that they believed that excessive talk in classroom is inappropriate and left fewer opportunities for them to learn. In addition, it could deprive the time of other students.

(5) Silence as the Product of Lack of Confidence

Students' silence was due to the feeling of "incapability" of their insufficient language skills and strategies of speaking, which can result in their anxiety. Studies show that high levels of anxiety associated with students' lack of confidence in classroom is likely to result in silence regardless of the cultural background of students and teaching objectives. For example, Lehtones and Sajavaara (1985) had demonstrated that the Finnish learners' increased levels of anxiety led to an increase in their reticence. This anxiety may be generated by the ambiguity in students' self-perceptions about their own levels of knowledge.

It is apparent that students may feel anxious about giving incorrect answers and making mistakes, and their anxiety contributes to their silent behavior. Their anxiety is deeply rooted in their prior school experience in China. Fear of making mistakes or not supplying the correct answers could be crippling and renders them in a linguistic exile. As one student reported:

> I do not want to make any mistake, so I need more time to think what I'm going to say, especially when the idea was vague and tentative. But when I'm thinking, someone will have the answer. And sometimes, my tongue just gets tied since I was too anxious to speak.

From this study, we can see that certain psychological and pedagogical factors are the two main sources of Chinese students' silence in classroom. Silence is not necessarily an indication of lack of knowledge or interest but may be a conscious choice for some students. The participants' illustration of their silence indicates that silence might be an alternative mode of participation in which students internalize knowledge in a low-anxiety environment.

Therefore, teachers should interpret active listening and silent reflection as effective learning methods. They should understand that for students who grew up learning how to be silent, especially for those who have developed psychological resistance to speaking up. In class discussion, simply allowing some space in which the quiet students can think their own thoughts, instead of following other people's train of thought, is a welcoming step towards helping them to reconnect their experience with consciousness.

6.6 Conclusion

The available literature focusing on nonverbal classroom communication is significantly partial towards projected cues of teachers and provides surprisingly little content specific to decoding students' generated cues. Based on the study of Chapter Five, this chapter has attempted to solve this problem with the analysis of students' nonverbal behaviors in classroom. One benefit is that the findings can help teachers find out their capability of understanding the students, their interest or participation in teaching process. As Radford (1990) argued, "Only when we can accurately perceive what is occurring can we reflect upon what the student is learning and upon what interests and feelings they bring with them to the learning situation." Accordingly, it is quite valuable for teachers who seek for appropriate information to achieve more effectiveness on their instructional communication competence.

Another benefit is that it can help teachers develop strong sensitivity and ability to interpret students' nonverbal communication. As Miller (2005a, 67) stated, "A good teacher is a good listener, not only to words being spoken, but also to silent messages that signal agreement/disagreement, attention, inattention, interest/boredom, and the desire of the student to be heard." "An observant teacher can…tell when students understand the material or if they are having trouble grasping major concepts" (Miller, 2005a, 30). Without question, it is also rewarding to identify definitive nonverbal indications that students are comfortable with the course content. As Gregersen (2005) argued, it is more critical that teachers identify anxious and confused nonverbal cues, as those are the students' need for our assistance.

We should point out that understanding nonverbal cues requires the background knowledge and teaching experience. It is easy to be misled or to misinterpret cues that are not filtered for context, gender and personal bias.

Part IV

Strategy for Improving Classroom Nonverbal X-Factor

Chapter Seven

Approaches to Developing Nonverbal Communicative Competence

7.1 Introduction

Based on the findings and discussion of previous chapters, this chapter will specifically focus on some pedagogical implications of nonverbal X-Factor in teaching, consisting of reforming the syllabus and curriculum, informing students of their nonverbal behaviors, collecting various sources to form expectation, being chary about their reciprocate nonverbal behavior, improving the interpretation of students' nonverbal communication, becoming an careful observers, using assertive and equitable behaviors, treating students' according to their personalities, combing nonverbal with verbal cues, and handling students' silence strategically. Some communicative activities related to improve students' nonverbal skills, a summary of good and bad nonverbal behaviors, and approaches to improve students' intercultural communication competence are also provided.

7.2 Pedagogical Implications

7.2.1 Reforming the Syllabus and Curriculum

As far as the present author knows, nonverbal communication has not aroused the syllabus designers' full attention although the cultural teaching has become an important aspect in language teaching in China for many years. It is advisable that nonverbal communication should be incorporated into syllabus and textbooks because students would benefit from being familiarized with a large range of nonverbal strategies with training in learning. As such, the importance of the nonverbal behavior in communication and training in effective use can be included in the FL methodology. Cohen (1998, 67) advocated that foreign language program administrators may include strategy training as part of the foreign language curriculum since the explicit training can enable students to "find their own pathways to success, and thus it provides learner autonomy and self-direction" (67).

By constructing a curriculum system of nonverbal communication, teachers can design a course of nonverbal behavior training which is culturally orientated. In the course design, teachers can use as many illustrations introducing nonverbal behavior as possible which contain nonverbal cues that can arouse students' interest in learning and train them to communicate effectively. As Wylie (1985) claimed, "Most people could learn to communicate in a foreign culture more enjoyably, more effectively, and more convincingly, if, to the degree that it is possible, their whole bodies were trained to act as a unit in adopting new patterns of behavior."

7.2.2 Informing Students of Their Nonverbal X-Factor

The majority of students have no idea about how their own behaviors influence the type and quality of instruction they receive from teachers, so teachers should inform students that how their nonverbal behaviors affect their teachers and the quality of instruction they receive and inform them that teaching and learning are a partnership and that the success of the class depends on students' classroom involvement and contributions.

Teachers should help students understand or take seriously their role in the instructional communication process and make them aware that they are responsible for their own learning and the quality of their educational experience. In this way, students can ultimately get more from the classroom experience if they engage in good student behaviors in classroom. They should know how their behaviors, good, bad, or indifferent, influence teachers' perceptions and teaching. It is their responsibility to help teachers and bring out the best in most of their teachers so as to improve their teachers' professionalism.

What is more, informing students of their nonverbal behaviors can help raise their awareness which is the first step to improve effective use of nonverbal behaviors since learners' view or attitude to nonverbal behaviors can affect their uses in communication. Teachers should make students fully understand the concept, the nature, the major types, and the functions of nonverbal communication to help them understand the importance of nonverbal communication, and keep on reminding them that improving intercultural communicative competence is the predominant project in their university career. Thus, they should learn more knowledge of nonverbal communication as much as possible.

And also teachers should make students understand that language and culture can not be separated, we must accept the cultural differences in nonverbal cues because some people are reluctant to accept the cultural differences in communication and often act on their own culture norms in interaction. The inappropriate nonverbal behavior can lead to misunderstanding between interactants and failure in communication. Therefore, as language learners, students should accept the cultural differences, which is also the basic requirement of raising their cultural awareness.

7.2.3 Collecting Multiple Sources to Form Expectation

In previous chapters, we have put forward that teachers may form expectation based on students' nonverbal behaviors. However, they should not rely on too heavily nonverbal messages instead of using more information to form an expectation since sometimes some students can not regulate or control their nonverbal behaviors. For example, they may be late for reasons beyond their control. And also, since they are required to sit in assigned seats, they can not obtain a front and center seat to present a positive impression. Or some students may not be as attentive as they would like to be due to distractions caused by less concerned students whose misbehaviors go undetected by the teacher.

Mottet and Richmond (2002, 57) provided suggestions to deal with the above situations for teachers. First, teachers should check their perceptions with students. Second, they should gather information from multiple sources and channels before solidifying expectations. They further explain, in order to check perceptions, the teacher can describe what he/she sees, and asks for clarification to insure that the perception is correct. The teacher may assume that the student appears uninterested in the class, rather than assuming they disinterest in the class, then ask for clarification and be prepared for their interactions. Students may not be interested in the content, or they may be interested, but distracted. If students lack interest, then adapt the content accordingly, and the perception checking process may allow the teacher to eliminate the distractions for the students. As for the second suggestion, they state that the teacher should increase the number of communication channels they use before solidifying perceptions of students and give students additional options for communicating in classroom. For those quiet students who are nonverbally unexpressive and don't fell comfortable when talking in class, the teacher can use email, Wechat, QQ and bulletin boards which can complement classroom interaction nicely. These instructional media give teachers additional channels from which they can receive and evaluate students' communication.

7.2.4 Being Chary about Reciprocate Nonverbal Behavior

Teachers must guard against the natural tendency to reciprocate nonverbal behavior in classroom. Some teachers have experienced that once they are confronted with lethargic and apathetic students, they would feel drained and defeated no matter how much they are energized and optimistic in teaching. For these teachers, they are more susceptible to students' nonverbal behaviors and ultimately adapt to or reciprocate similar communicative behaviors. But for the more experienced teachers, they may be not only aware of students' undesirable behaviors, but adapt their behaviors to stimulate appropriate students' communicative behaviors that is conducive to learning.

One reason for these easy-susceptible teachers is that they consider students' nonverbal behaviors as a way of confirming themselves rather than determining students' comprehension of course content. While the experienced and effective teachers attaching importance to students' nonverbal behaviors is not for self-evaluation, but for adapting their instructional communication to insure that they are meeting students' learning need, expectations, and desires.

What is more, teachers who are more vulnerable to students' nonverbal behavior may be because of their need for immediate feedback. For these teachers, they can assess their teaching effectiveness periodically by asking students for formative feedback instead of asking for summative feedback at the end of the whole semester. The periodical feedback can help teachers assess immediately how they are doing and make necessary adjustment to their teaching if necessary. This may enable teachers to focus less on students' nonverbal behaviors for self-validation and more on how well their students comprehend course content. These teachers can find simple tips on classroom assessments and ways that assess their teaching effectiveness.

7.2.5 Improving the Interpretation of Nonverbal Behavior

Teachers should be more careful in how to read students' nonverbal behavior and learn to understand whether students' behaviors are a reaction or a response to them or their teaching or other stimuli. For example, is it due to student's lack of responsiveness in classroom, a response to the teacher's instructional communication, or is it a response to their not enough sleep in the night before?

Mottet and Richmond (2002, 59) provided three ways that teachers can use to improve the interpretation of students' nonverbal behavior: placing the nonverbal behavior in its context; interpreting multiple nonverbal behaviors rather than a single behavior; and noticing whether the verbal and nonverbal dimensions of the message remain congruent or not. It is obvious that the interpretation process is a bit more complicated and confusing since teachers do not treat all nonverbal violators equally. They have a tendency to assign positive valence to individuals they like, find interpersonally attractive, and credible. On the contrary, teachers assign negative valence to those they do not like, find interpersonally unattractive, and non-credible.

Another way that may enhance how teachers interpret students' nonverbal behaviors is by understanding the role that the expectation for proper student plays in classroom. As long as the student does not violate expectation, his/her behavior will not likely get attention, but behavior that violates the expectation will get noticed. Teachers should know that their own preconceived expectation for a student or a group of students can also frame how they interpret students' nonverbal messages. For example, if a student from a basketball team is in the class and the teacher has a less than favorable preconceived expectation for this particular group. Teachers may have a tendency to evaluate his/her nonverbal behavior in a way that fits this particular expectation. Another student may show the same nonverbal behavior, but due to his/her group affiliation and the preconceived expectation for this certain group, the behavior may stimulate different meanings and reciprocal behaviors from the teacher.

7.2.6 Becoming a Careful Observer

Self-analysis and observing other people's behaviors can help us become aware of effective and ineffective nonverbal practices. People usually use some nonverbal signals consciously or unconsciously to communicate for some specific purposes. If we can observe and decode them carefully and correctly, we can communicate effectively with each other, otherwise, effective communication can not be achieved.

In classroom, nonverbal observations reveal unspoken thoughts and attitudes. Students also expect to be observed by teachers and behave in predictable ways. With a full awareness that the teacher is looking in their direction, a studious attitude may be projected, and student may appear attentive, interested to convince the teacher.

Miller (1988, 6) claimed that teachers should be aware of nonverbal behavior in classroom due to two reasons: (1) to become better receivers of students' messages and (2) to gain ability to send students positive signals that reinforce learning, and also become adept at avoiding negative signals that stifle learning. A student's nonverbal expression serves as an important source in forming a teacher's impressions, attitudes, beliefs and reciprocal behavior expressions. Being a good message receiver requires more than just listening to words. It also needs teachers to attune many of the subtle cues. Without the help of these cues, the teacher would not be able to asses the teaching methods and strategies. Observant teachers can tell when students understand the content presented or when they have trouble grasping the major concepts.

Students' comfort or distress in classroom is useful for recording a distinction. For example, comfortable silence is characterized by times of reflection, thought, or work. Distressing moments are produced by embarrassment or are tension-filled times. If students are stimulated or exhibit excitement, it means they are comfortable at that moment. If they are disorganized, or disoriented, they may feel distressed. Thus, students' nonverbal cues set the stage for either comfortable or distressful classroom occurrences.

What is more, because of different cultures we live in, we think the way we behave is normal and any other different ways of doing things are abnormal. So teachers need to be more objective about the kind of behavior that students exhibit and realize that there are many different ways of being and acting.

7.2.7 Using Assertive and Equitable Classroom Behavior

According to Emmer, Evertson and Worsham (2003), assertive behavior is "the ability to stand up for one's legitimate rights in ways that make it less likely that others will ignore or circumvent them" (146). It differs significantly from both passive behavior and aggressive behavior. Teachers can display assertive behavior by:

(1) Using assertive body language by maintaining an erect posture, facing the offending students but keeping enough distance so as to appear threatening, and matching the facial expression with the content of the message being presented to students.

(2) Using an appropriate tone of voice, speaking clearly and deliberately in a pitch that is slightly but not greatly elevated from normal classroom speech.

Some practical strategies that emphasize equitable and positive classroom interactions with all students include:

(1) Make eye contact with each student. Teachers can make eye contact by scanning the entire room as they speak and by freely moving around all sections of the room.

(2) Deliberately move towards and stand close to each student during the class period. Make sure that the seating arrangement allows the teacher and students clear and easy ways to move around the room.

(3) Attribute the ownership of ideas to the students who initiate them. For instance, in a discussion a teacher might say, "Wang Li provides a good idea of job hunting, what do you think…?"

(4) Allow and encourage all students to participate in class discussion and interactions. Make sure to call on students who do not commonly participate, not just those who respond most frequently.

(5) Provide appropriate "wait time" for all students to respond to questions, regardless of their past performance or the teacher's perception of their abilities.

7.2.8 Treating Students Differently Based on Their Personalities

R. J. Marzano & J. S. Marzano (2003) provided some effective skills in managing the classroom according to five categories of different students' need and suggested classroom strategies for each category and subcategory, which can be applied to in teaching for university students.

1. Passive Students

Definitions & Source:
Behavior that avoids the domination of others or the pain of negative experiences. The student attempts to protect self from criticism, ridicule, or rejection, possibly reacting to abuse and neglect. Can have a biochemical basis, such as anxiety.

Characteristics:
●Fear of relationships: Avoids connection with others, is shy, doesn't initiate conversations, attempts to be invisible.

●Fear of failure: Gives up easily, is convinced he/she can't succeed, is easily frustrated, uses negative self-talk.

Suggestions:

Provide safe adult and peer interactions and protection from aggressive people; provide assertiveness and positive self-talk training; reward small successes quickly; withhold criticism.

2. Aggressive Students

Definitions & Source:

Behavior that overpowers, dominates, harms, or controls others without regard for their well-being. The child has often taken aggressive people as role models; has had minimal or in-effective limits set on behavior; is possibly reacting to abuse and neglect. Condition may have a biochemical basis, such as depression.

Characteristics:

- Hostile: Rages, threatens, or intimidates others; can be verbally or physically abusive to people, animals, or objects.
- Oppositional: Does opposite of what is asked; demands that others agree or give in; resists verbally or nonverbally.
- Covert: Appears to agree but then does the opposite of what is asked; often acts innocent while setting up problems for others.

Suggestions:

Describe the student's behavior clearly; contract with the student to reward corrected behavior and set up consequences for uncorrected behavior; be consistent and provide immediate rewards and consequences; encourage and acknowledge extracurricular activities in and out of school; give student responsibilities to help teacher or other students to foster successful experiences.

3. Attention Problem

Definitions & Source:

Behavior that demonstrates either motor or attentional difficulties resulting from a neurological disorder. The child's symptoms may be exacerbated by family or social stressors or biochemical conditions, such as anxiety, depression, or bipolar disorders.

Characteristics:

- Hyperactive: Has difficulty with motor control, both physically and verbally; fidgets, leaves seat frequently, interrupts, talks excessively.
- Inattentive: Has difficulty staying focused and following through on projects;

has difficulty with listening, remembering, and organizing.

Suggestions:

Contract with the student to manage behaviors; teach basic concentration, study, and thinking skills; separate the student in a quiet work area; help the student list each step of a task; reward successes; assign a peer tutor.

---

4. Perfectionist

Definitions & Source:

Behavior that is geared towards avoiding the embarrassment and assumed shame of making mistakes. The child fears what will happen if errors are discovered; has unrealistically high expectations of self; has possibly received criticism or lack of acceptance while making mistakes during the process of learning.

Characteristics:

Tends to focus too much on the small details of projects; will avoid projects if unsure of outcome; focuses on results and not relationships; is self-critical.

Suggestions:

Ask the student to make mistakes on purpose, then show acceptance; have the student tutor other students.

---

5. Socially Inept

Definitions & Source:

Behavior that is based on the misinterpretation of nonverbal signals of others. The student misunderstands facial expressions and body language; hasn't received adequate training in these areas and has poor role modeling.

Characteristics:

Attempts to make friends but is inept and unsuccessful; is forced to be alone; is often teased for unusual behavior, appearance, or lack of social skills.

Suggestions:

Teach the student to keep the appropriate physical distance from others; teach the meaning of facial expressions, such as anger and hurt; make suggestions regarding hygiene, dress, mannerisms, and posture.

(Adapted from Marzano, 2003, 104-105)

R. J. Marzano & J. S. Marzano (2003) further illustrated the implications of the five types of strategies in managing the classroom based on different characteristics of students.

They defined the passive students as those who fear relationships and who fear failure and suggested that teachers can build strong relationships with these students by refraining from criticism, rewarding them with small successes, and creating a lively classroom atmosphere in which students feel safe from aggressive people.

Three subcategories of aggressive students include hostile, oppositional, and covert. Hostile students often can't control their anger, and have low capacity for empathy and are not able to see the consequences of their actions. Oppositional students show milder forms of behavior problems, but they consistently resist following rules, argue with adults, use harsh language, and tend to annoy others. The covert students may be quite pleasant at times, but they are often nearby when trouble starts and they never quite do what authority figures ask of them. R. J. Marzano & J. S. Marzano (2003) suggested that teachers should help to create behavior contracts and provide immediate rewards and consequences. Most important of all, teachers must know that aggressive students, although they may appear highly resistant to behavior change, are still children who are experiencing a significant amount of fear and pain.

Students with attention problems include those who are hyperactive and inattentive. These students may respond well when teachers contract with them to manage behaviors; teach them basic concentration, study, and thinking skills; help them divide tasks into manageable parts; reward their successes; and assign them a peer tutor.

Students who are perfectionists are driven to succeed at unattainable levels. They are self-critical, have low self-esteem, and feel inferior. Teachers can help these students by encouraging them to develop more realistic standards, accept mistakes, and giving them opportunities to tutor other students.

Socially inept students have difficulty making and keeping friends. They may stand too close and touch others in annoying ways, talk too much, and misread others' comments. Teachers can help these students by counseling them about social behaviors.

7.2.9 Combining Nonverbal with Verbal Cues

Verbal and nonverbal behaviors are considered as indispensable components of human communication, so they become inseparable from the teaching of foreign languages. In classroom, whether teachers' influence is direct or indirect, it is the unique combination of verbal and nonverbal information that influences meaning.

Effective nonverbal behavior can be a great asset to a teacher in managing classroom interaction. Many teachers apparently accept students' feelings, offer praise or encouragement, or criticize students by means of either simple or elaborate patterns of nonverbal cues and verbal language which are closely related, and the meaning of the words depends on how they are said. Nonverbal cues reinforce the verbal message, otherwise it may be ambiguous. Teacher's praise and encouragement are stimulating behaviors, but incongruity may occur when praise is given perfunctorily. When the teacher asks a personalized question, he/she should have a sense of nearness and proximity, while impersonal question-asking means detachment, aloofness, and a sense of distance. When the student is talking, the teacher's behaviors can be receptive or inattentive. The receptive behaviors reflect attitudes of listening and interest and the inattentive behaviors usually involve a lack of eye contact and extraneous movements.

The congruity of the teacher's verbal and nonverbal behaviors has been examined. Houser and Frymier (2009) testified that the teacher's response to a student will be reflected through both verbal and nonverbal communication. If the teacher's nonverbal communication patterns are congruent and reinforcing, it will be able to provide students with a clear sense of confidence in their actions, otherwise, challenges will arise and create a high degree of uncertainty for the students. This can impact the student's confidence level and reduce the overall sense of accomplishment which is established through verbal communication tactics. This research not only demonstrates the importance of nonverbal communication in students' development, but also reinforces the need for congruity between verbal and nonverbal cues provided by the teacher.

7.2.10 Dealing with Silent Students Strategically

The reasons that some students don't speak out in classroom discussion are complicated, ranging from personality and mood to confusion about the course material. Teachers should interpret silence from wide perspectives. For example, some students keep quiet perhaps because of insufficient preparation for class, or simple, he/she has a shy personality, or his/her irritation and impatience with the inconclusive nature of personal interpretation. As different as each student is, so too are their reasons of silence in classroom. Schultz (2009, 11-12) stated that teacher should have a few conceptual tools for understanding students who remain silent in classroom discussion. The following questions should be observed carefully:

(1) Are the students who choose not to speak aloud simply shy?

(2) Do they lack the knowledge or facility of English to participate in group conversation?

(3) Are they following cultural practices that guide them to speak only when they are asked?

(4) Do students who enact silence act out of conscious resistance or are they simply daydreaming?

In terms of helping all students be ready and willing to speak out their ideas in classroom discussion, we provides the following ways:

(1) Encourage students to generate questions and bring them to class for discussion.

(2) Allow five to ten minutes at the beginning of class for students to collect their thought so to skim the assignment.

(3) Before discussion, have students written their own reaction to their reading and, after the discussion ask them to assess the influence of the class talk on their thinking.

(4) Organize small group or paired talk to generate discussion questions—open ended questions that invite multiple perspectives about a reading.

(5) Occasionally, plan five to ten minutes to write individual responses to the questions under discussion.

(6) Allow time and demand that everyone explains their responses with reference to the text under discussion.

(7) Give students a chance to rehearse their thinking by talking with a congenial partner.

(8) Plan a series of opportunities for students to write about their developing thinking.

Teachers must find ways to encourage all students to reflect on issues and deliberatively explore multiple perspectives. Even when their voices are silent, discussion gives all students, including quiet and talkative alike opportunities to form their thinking and stretch their understanding.

7.2.11 Training Activity of Nonlinguistic Strategies

An effective approach to help students understand the importance of nonverbal communication is to discuss with them what are "good" or "bad" nonverbal behaviors by analyzing their performance in the communicative activities. The discussion makes

Haastrup (1991) believed that "conscious-raising based on learners' own performance and experience is a fruitful way of developing procedural knowledge" (131). By offering the activities involving nonverbal behaviors and subsequently discussing their values in communication may help students find out that nonverbal communication can help them success in communication, and provide opportunities for students to use various nonverbal behaviors in communication. Here is a list of a few training activities.

Activity 1: Watching Video Clips

Watching video clips or TV programs is a very useful and effective way to help students observe nonverbal behaviors in the target culture and compare them with those of the native culture. First, the teacher tells students to watch a segment of a video with the sound turned off. Students watch the video paying attention to the nonverbal cues. Then the teacher plays the video with the sound on, and students examine how the gestures help the speaker convey his/her ideas.

After watching video clips or TV programs, teachers require students to make lectures or discussion about the impressions of the speakers and how the impression takes place and make them believe that the X-Factor operates important roles in the impressions. At the same time, the teacher asks students to discuss the cultural differences or similarities between the target culture and native culture. This activity can tell students how important the nonlinguistic strategies are and help them understand how nonverbal cues work in communication and how they are different from culture to culture. It can also be done in ordinary lessons, and will not take too much time.

Activity 2: Acting as a Speechless Tourist

This is a pair work. In each pair, one student plays the role of a Chinese tourist shopping in an American store, and the other student plays the role of a store clerk. The tourist tries to express some meanings through nonlinguistic strategies, and the store clerk tries to guess what the tourist is saying.

Procedures:

(1) The teacher prepares some sentences to be guessed.

The sentences are written on different cards. Each sentence includes some words or phrases that must be used by nonverbal behaviors.

(2) The teacher prepares some handouts. (See Appendix D)

The teacher prepares two sets of handouts, and each student in the same pair receives a different handout.

(3) The teacher provides models.

The teacher plays the role of a tourist, and students guess the meaning.

(4) Practice

Volunteer student A plays the role of a tourist, and the other students try to guess the meaning. Two or three volunteer students come to the front of the class in turn. Each volunteer student receives a card from the teacher and tries to convey the meaning of the sentence written on the card.

(5) Pair work

The teacher divides students into pairs and distributes two sets of handouts and makes sure each pair gets different handouts. In each pair, one student acts as the tourist, and the other guesses the meaning. When the correct answer is found, they switch the roles. Each pair tries to find as many answers as possible within a limited time.

Activity 3: Breaking Students' Silence

Hu and Fell-Eisenkraft (2003) presented a way—Jigsaw Discussion, to deal with the silent, shy immigrant students, which is useful to handle the silent students in classroom.

This is an effective way to empower students making them engage in peer-led small group work to insure that students feel that they have power over what they say. This activity involves breaking a text into the same number of students in each group. Once the students individually read their sections thoroughly and take notes, they first meet with all of the other students who read the same section. They use this time to agree on the main points, clarify anything they find confusing. Once everyone is ready, they reconfigure so that each small group is comprised of people who have all read different sections. Together, the group represents the entire text—each student is a piece of the "jigsawed" text. The groups start at the beginning, and each member of the group is responsible for presenting the material from his/her section.

The most meaningful jigsaw takes place when students interact with one another by asking for clarification, bringing up relevant questions, and drawing connections between the sections. It is especially helpful to students who claim to be shy. In grouping students, Teacher should make sure that students have a lot of support in the initial groups, as they check their understanding of the same text against one another. Another benefit of this activity is to train students' teamwork. Everyone plays a key role in their peers' complete understanding of the text. This means that students who do not usually elect to speak during whole class discussion must participate within the small group.

To sum up, teachers should remember that the meanings of nonverbal cues need to be taught in the same way as the meaning of essential classroom language and provide a wide range of communicative channels, such as discussion, debate, analysis, brainstorming, group work, pair work, etc. in teaching. These communicative channels are established on such a psycholinguistic assumption that effective language teaching and efficient language learning only occur in a positive class climate, which involves three essentials—easy atmosphere, motivating environment and active participation (Littlewood, 1984, 70). So, the training is fruitful in language teaching and also beneficial to incorporate the training in a communicative syllabus, especially in English speaking course.

7.3 Summary of Good and Bad Classroom Nonverbal X-Factor

Based on the findings and strategies discussed above, we can summarize the good and poor nonverbal communication elements that higher education teachers need to be mindful of.

Generally speaking, the characteristics of effective teachers in classroom include:
① not positioned behind podium;
② move around the classroom;
③ use hand gestures frequently;
④ frequent voice fluctuation;
⑤ make eye contact with all students;
⑥ vary facial expressions.

While the non-effective teachers' nonverbal communication include:
① positioned behind podium for a majority of the time;
② do not move around the classroom;
③ do not use hand gestures frequently;
④ do not utilize voice fluctuation;
⑤ do not make eye contact with all students;
⑥ do not vary facial expressions.

Besides, there are some errors in nonverbal communication:
① poor personal habits;
② always stiff;

③ over-exaggerated hand gestures;

④ tapping or shaking legs and hands (Kroehnert, 2006, 151-153).

In order to succeed in communication, we should provide honest nonverbal skills, such as:

① Smile genuinely. A fake smile is obvious because the timing isn't right and the wrinkles don't follow.

② Keep an appropriate distance between you and others, and use touch only when appropriate.

③ Respect students with eye contact.

④ Adopt a handshake that matches personality and intention (Bovee et al., 2003).

All in all, it is not only what the teachers say in classroom that is important, but it's how they say it that can make the difference to students. Teachers should develop individual nonverbal repertoires, and the systems for instruction, correction and management which well-trained students respond to immediately. A system of nonverbal behaviors can help teachers to be efficient in teaching, managing classroom. We should point out that few nonverbal behaviors convey meaning isolated, they have to be interpreted in clusters, and be used to reinforce the words.

7.4 Developing Intercultural Communication Competence

So far we have provided various strategies to improve nonverbal communicative ability, but that is far from enough. In a world of increasing internationalization, learning a foreign language does not simply mean grasping nonverbal skills. According to Koester and Olebe (1988), to be competent in intercultural communication, we must understand the social customs and social systems of the host culture, and understand how people think and behave in communication. To achieve the intercultural communication competence, both teachers and students should command the following requirements which are important components of ICC (Du Ruiqing, etc., 2004, 432).

Display of Respects

The need to display respect for others is a culture-general concept, but within every culture there are specific ways to show respect and there are specific expectations about those to whom respect should be shown. What stands for respect in one culture will not necessarily be so regarded in another culture.

Respect is shown through both verbal and nonverbal symbols. Language that can be interpreted as expressing concern, interest, and an understanding of others will often convey respect, as will formality do in language, including the use of titles, the absence of jargon, and an increased attention to politeness rituals. Nonverbal displays of respect include showing attentiveness through the position of the body, facial expressions, and the use of eye contact in prescribed ways. A tone of voice that conveys interest in the other person is another vehicle by which respect is shown. The action of displaying respect increases the likelihood of a judgment of competence.

Orientation to Knowledge

Orientation to knowledge refers to the terms people use to explain themselves and the world around them. A competent orientation to knowledge occurs when people's actions demonstrate that experiences and interpretation are individual and personal rather than universally shared by others.

In learning a culture, people develop belief about the "rightness" of a particular way of seeing events, behaviors, and people. It is actually very natural to think, and then to behave, as if personal knowledge and experiences are universal. Intercultural competence, however, requires an ability to move beyond the perspective of our cultural framework.

Empathy

Empathy is the ability of people to see others from their points of view. It is an ability to communicate with an awareness of another person's thoughts, feelings, and experiences. Those who lack empathy, and who therefore indicate little or no awareness of even the most obvious feelings and thoughts of others will not be perceived as competent. Empathetic behaviors include verbal statements that identify the experiences of others and nonverbal codes that are complementary to the moods and thoughts of others.

It is necessary to point out that empathy doesn't mean "putting yourself in the shoes of others." It is both physically and psychologically impossible to do so. But it is possible for people to be sufficiently interested in and aware of others' shoes. The skill we are describing here is the capacity to behave as if one understands the world as others do.

Interaction Management

Some individuals are skilled at starting and ending interactions among participants and at taking turns and maintaining a discussion. These management skills are important because through them all participants are able to speak and contribute. In contrast, dominating a conversation or being non-responsive to the interaction is detrimental to competence. The interaction management skills require knowing how to indicate turn-taking both verbally and nonverbally. We should develop our ability to initiate, take turns in, and terminate a conversation in the process of intercultural interaction. These interaction management skills are of great significance because we know how to provide equal opportunity for conversation to all participants if we acquire high interaction management skills.

Relational Role Behavior

Relational role behaviors concern efforts to build or maintain personal relationships with group members. These behaviors may include verbal and nonverbal messages that demonstrate support for others and that help to solidify feelings of participation. Examples of competent relational role behaviors include harmonizing and mediating conflicts between group members, encouraging participation from others, general displays of interest, and a willingness to compromise one's position for the sake of others.

Tolerance of Ambiguity

Tolerance of ambiguity concerns a person's responses to new, uncertain, and unpredictable intercultural encounters. Some people react to new situations with greater comfort than others. Others are extremely nervous, highly frustrated, or even hostile towards the new situations and those who may be present in them. Those who don't tolerate ambiguity well may respond to new and unpredictable situations with hostility, anger, shouting, sarcasm, withdrawal, or abruptness.

Others view new situations as a challenge and they seem to do well whenever the unexpected or unpredictable occurs, and they quickly adapt to the demands of changing environments. Competent intercultural communicators are able to cope with the nervousness and frustrations that accompany new or, unclear situations, and they are able to adapt quickly to changing demands.

Interaction Posture

Although the specific verbal and nonverbal messages that express judgments and evaluations can vary from culture to culture, the importance of selecting messages that do not convey evaluative judgments does not vary. Statements based on clear judgments of rights and wrongs indicate a closed or predetermined framework of attitudes, beliefs, and values, and they are used by evaluative, and less competent, intercultural communicators. Non-evaluative and non-judgmental actions are characterized by verbal and nonverbal messages based on descriptions rather than interpretations or evaluations.

To sum up, in order to be effective in intercultural communication we must learn the preferences of the host culture for supporting arguments and determining knowledge. Only with the mastery of intercultural communication competence can persons from different cultures communicate effectively and appropriately.

7.5 Conclusion

Nonverbal communication is a universal and well-defined form of interaction. This chapter has provided some strategies to improve both teachers' and students' classroom communication X-Factor. The benefits for teachers to develop strong sensitivity and ability to interpret students' nonverbal communication should be self-evident. However, understanding nonverbal cues requires background knowledge and teaching experience. We should know that the same nonverbal communication may be interpreted differently by people from different cultures. And different nonverbal communication may also be used to convey the same idea or emotion. Thus, it is easy to be misled or to result in misinterpreting cues that are not filtered for context, culture, gender, and personal bias. Without the fully comprehension of nonverbal communication, the achievement of intercultural communicative competence can not be fulfilled.

Chapter Eight

Conclusion

8.1 Introduction

This chapter will summarize the main findings of this study, and provide some suggestions for future research in the field of nonverbal communication.

8.2 Major Findings and Implications

This book has established a broader understanding of how nonverbal behaviors relate to teacher effectiveness and student effectiveness within the university classroom. The major findings of the study include:

(1) The investigation of teachers' appearance from students' perspective found that teachers' appearance is related to their teaching performance. Students perceive that a teacher's knowledge of subject matter, concern for students and ability to communicate effectively could be displayed by their appearance. Teachers' appearance shows his/her enthusiasm for teaching, and level of expertise. The male respondents were significantly more likely to attribute teachers' ability to communicate in the classroom setting effectively and overall performance with their appearance. The female students were less likely to view teachers' ability to communicate in classroom effectively and overall performance by their appearance.

(2) Findings in the research on teachers' body language from students' perceptive showed that all students liked and motivated by the teacher's smile, especially female students when they encountered difficulty in learning. The majority of students tended to avoid eye contact with the teacher when they didn't know the answer, but the number of female students was bigger, and they thought that the teacher had more eye contact with talented students. Most students, especially female students, become

motivated when the teacher appreciated their involvement through facial expressions. Students thought that the teacher's eye contact and facial expression can provide source of motivation, concentration and improve classroom atmosphere, and can reflect the teacher's mood and confidence.

As for the teacher's gesture, students reported that it could provide them a source of motivation, enthusiasm and confidence to learning, and a means of maintaining attention, creating live atmosphere, and helping them understand topic better. Most students were encouraged by the teacher's nod, while the motivation of male students by teachers' head nodding was greater than the females.

In terms of punctuality, most students did not take class seriously if the teacher was unpunctual. A lot of students felt impatient if the teacher took over time in class, especially male students.

Female students were likely to sit close to the teacher than male students. And students did not like teachers' monotonous tone in teaching which could make them feel bored and thought the teacher was incapable of teaching. All the students agreed that teachers' movement in classroom could keep them active.

(3) The study on students' immediacy from teachers' perspective found that students' immediacy was positively correlated with teachers' perceptions of their credibility including three dimensions: competence, good-will, and trustworthiness. That is, the teacher perceived immediate students were more competent and bright, concerned and cared the teacher, and honest and trustworthy. Students' immediacy could generate teachers' motivation in teaching, making the teacher proud, and getting more positive outcomes both for teaching and learning.

(4) The study on students' silence in classroom showed that students' silence in classroom resulted from some objective and subjective reasons. The objective reasons were due to the cultural traits and a heightened privilege of verbal restraint in Chinese culture, and the class size in which students found difficult to take part in the conversation in classroom discussion. The subjective reasons were due to their shyness, lack of confidence, reactions to other's contribution, and some students thought their silence was a face-saving strategy and a means of participation.

Based on the data interpreted, findings, and conclusions of the study, some recommendations are made:

(1) Nonverbal communication is a skill, which should be utilized by teachers and students at all levels of education.

(2) Teachers should be given an orientation in nonverbal communication and the acquired skills should be used in their teaching methodologies so as to enhance

students' interest and make them attentive in class.

(3) Teachers' appearance can positively or negatively impact teacher-student relationship in classroom, so it suggests that the teacher may dress formally for a week or two until credibility is established and then dress more casually to project the image that one is open to students' interaction.

(4) Facial expressions and eye contact are the primary types of nonverbal communication which can enhance understanding of the concepts taught in classroom, thus, teachers should use them widely for transmitting the messages in order to improve the teaching and learning process.

(5) Proper distance between the teacher and students in classroom is very sensitive. The teacher's body movements can create interest and attentiveness of students and activate the classroom atmosphere, so teachers should purposefully use their body movements in teaching. But they should be aware of the fact that too excessive use of body movements can spoil the purpose of its utilization.

(6) Intonation plays a very essential role. Teachers should vary their tone in the teaching to create interest among the students. Rise and fall in the voice can help students understand the theme, setting, and beauty of the language.

Now we can summarize the benefit of appropriate nonverbal cues, which can ① reduce teachers' unnecessary talking time; ② increase learners' participation; ③ build confidence; ④ reduce fear of silence; ⑤ give clear instructions; ⑥ manage classroom efficiently; ⑦ activate classroom atmosphere; ⑧ improve listening skills; ⑨ improve performance in pair and group activities; ⑩ help self and peer correction; ⑪ avoid misunderstandings; ⑫ improve teacher-student relationship; ⑬ improve intercultural communicative competence.

8.3 Suggestions for Future Research

Results of the present study indicate the important role nonverbal behaviors playing in judgments of teacher and student effectiveness. Nonverbal behaviors can be taught and learned. Through instruction and practice, teachers and students can employ nonverbal cues to facilitate positive classroom interactions. Indeed, if teachers and students are knowledgeable of the specific nonverbal behaviors associated with effective teaching and learning, they may be more reflective of their own expressive behaviors in classroom.

The following recommendations are made for the improvement of the state of affairs and future researchers.

(1) Future researchers may wish to examine teachers' use of nonverbal behaviors during sequential patterns of instruction and in various pedagogical approaches commonly used in classroom. An understanding of the relationship between nonverbal behaviors and various aspects of effective teaching may increase the likelihood that teachers will exhibit those behaviors conducive to students' learning.

(2) It is recommended that curriculum planners and policy makers should also recognize the importance of nonverbal communication and makes it a part of teachers' education program, especially in the FL methodological course for prospective teachers which they are trained the important technology. As Ambady and Rosenthal (1993) confirmed that teachers "should be made aware of the possible impact of their nonverbal behaviors and perhaps even trained in nonverbal skills" (440).

(3) All the textbooks should incorporate the skill of nonverbal communication in the supplementary material for the effective use of teachers.

(4) This study has opened avenues for other researchers to study the importance and use of nonverbal communication skills on the same lines in other subjects of the curricula taught at different levels of education.

8.4 Conclusion

With the globalization of the world, it is generally acknowledged that the ultimate goal of language teaching is to improve learners' intercultural communication competence. Under the current situation of China, improving learners' ICC becomes an urgent project for language teachers, especially with the carrying out of the new policy— "Tne Belt and Road" recently. As one basic component of intercultural communication, nonverbal behavior is of great importance in keeping communication going on and effectively. However, the study on nonverbal communication in China is far more enough, particularly in the field of education. Based on these, this book provides a comprehensive introduction of nonverbal communication theories and the experimental researches on teachers' and students' nonverbal behaviors in English classroom.

Nowadays, the importance of nonverbal communication in language teaching and learning has accelerated with increasing diversity within today's classroom. EFL classroom interaction is meant to be the result of the teacher and students' joint efforts for accomplishing an effective learning and teaching environment for students' foreign language production. Through our experience in language teaching in China, classes with low percentage of using nonverbal cues have difficulty in communication and thus have unsuccessful outcomes. Both teachers and students should know about the importance of nonverbal X-Factor and how it affects communication. If teachers and students become aware of their nonverbal behaviors, it certainly helps them to become more proficient at receiving messages as well as more proficient at sending accurate messages.

It is hoped that this research can serve as a brick to attract jade, and stimulate further studies of nonverbal communication in China.

Appendix A

This questionnaire is used to elicit information leading to completion of an important academic study. Your cooperation and support would be highly appreciated. The information would be kept confidential and use only for this research. Please answer the questions to the best of your knowledge.

Personal Information

Please provide the following information.

1. Gender: male_____ female_____
2. Your Majors: _____

Below is the 5-point Likert scale. Please indicate the degree to which you agree or disagree to the given statements.

① Strongly Agree (SA)
② Agree (A)
③ Neutral
④ Disagree (DA)
⑤ Strongly Disagree (SD)

Do you think teacher's dress or attire can influence his/her:

① Preparation for class
② Enthusiasm for teaching
③ Knowledge of the subject matter
④ Concern for students
⑤ Ability to prepare students for a successful career
⑥ Professionalism
⑦ Credibility
⑧ Level of expertise
⑨ Ability to communicate in the classroom setting effectively
⑩ Overall performance

Appendix B

Name (optional): _____ Name of the College (optional): _____

In the following statements you will have to tell us about your feelings regarding the nonverbal messages of your language teachers as you observe them in classroom. Below is the 5-point Likert scale. Please indicate the degree to which you agree or disagree to the given statements.

① Strongly Agree (SA)
② Agree (A)
③ Neutral
④ Disagree (DA)
⑤ Strongly Disagree (SD)

1. Smiling teachers teach more effectively than those who are always serious.
2. It is easy to speak in front of those teachers who encourage students by nodding their heads.
3. I feel nervous when the teacher indicates a particular student with their raised finger while asking questions.
4. It is hard to speak in front of those teachers who stare at their students coldly.
5. I avoid eye contact when I do not know the answer of the question asked.
6. I pay more attention when the teacher makes eye contact with me in class.
7. Teachers make eye contact only with the talented students.
8. I become motivated when teacher appreciates my involvement through his/her facial expressions in classroom.
9. I never take those classes seriously whose teachers are unpunctual.
10. I see my wrist watch when the teacher takes over time in class.
11. Sitting close to the teacher in the front row helps me understand the lecture more.
12. I feel bore in those classes where the teacher teaches in a monotonous tone.
13. Poor teachers make meaningless sounds again and again in explanation.
14. Teachers' movements in the classroom keep students active.

Appendix C

Part One: Perceived Nonverbal Immediacy Behavior Scale

Direction: Below are a series of description of things some teachers have been observed doing in some classes. Please respond to the statements in terms of how often they are applied to your students. Please use the following scale to respond to each of the statement.

Never= 0   Rarely= 1   Occasionally= 2   Often= 3   Very Often= 4

1. Gestures while talking in the class. (   )
2. Uses monotone/dull voice while speaking. (   )
3. Looks at the class while talking. (   )
4. Smiles and nods in class while talking. (   )
5. Has a very tense body position while talking to the class. (   )
6. Sit close to the teacher or in the front rows of the classroom. (   )
7. Always respond actively to the teacher's questions. (   )
8. Has a very relaxed body position while talking in the class. (   )
9. Avoid eye contact with others while talking. (   )
10. Uses a variety of vocal expressions when talking to the teacher. (   )

Part Two: Measure of Credibility

Direction: Please indicate your impression of the students who are considered to be more immediacy in classroom by circling the proper number between the pairs of adjectives below. The closer the number is to an adjective, the more certain you are of your students.

Competence	Intelligent 1 2 3 4 5 6 7 Unintelligent	
	Untrained 1 2 3 4 5 6 7 Trained	
	Inexpert 1 2 3 4 5 6 7 Expert	
	Informed 1 2 3 4 5 6 7 Uninformed	
	Incompetent 1 2 3 4 5 6 7 Competent	
	Bright 1 2 3 4 5 6 7 Stupid	
Good-will	Cares about me 1 2 3 4 5 6 7 Doesn't care about me	
	Has my interests at heart 1 2 3 4 5 6 7 Doesn't have my interests at heart	
	Self-centered 1 2 3 4 5 6 7 Not self-centered	
	Concerned with me 1 2 3 4 5 6 7 Unconcerned with me	
	Insensitive 1 2 3 4 5 6 7 Sensitive	
	Not understanding 1 2 3 4 5 6 7 Understanding	
Trustworthiness	Honest 1 2 3 4 5 6 7 Dishonest	
	Untrustworthy 1 2 3 4 5 6 7 Trustworthy	
	Honorable 1 2 3 4 5 6 7 Dishonorable	
	Moral 1 2 3 4 5 6 7 Immoral	
	Unethical 1 2 3 4 5 6 7 Ethical	
	Phoney 1 2 3 4 5 6 7 Genuine	

Part Three: Interview Questions

Are you motivated or not by students' immediacy in classroom? Please use examples to illustrate your points.

Appendix D

The Speechless Tourist

Handout A

1. You are shopping in a department store in America.

Tell the clerk (your partner) what you want in English.

You can't use the words in brackets. Try to use gestures or explain in other words.

(A) I'd like some (cigarettes).

(B) I'd like some (watches).

(C) I want to buy some (cosmetics)

(D) I want to buy some (red wine).

2. Now you are a clerk. A Chinese tourist (your partner) visits your department store and tells you what he or she wants. Guess what he or she is trying to say.

Example:

A: I'd like some… (gesture).

B: You want some medicine?

A: Yes. For… (gesture).

B: For a stomachache? You'd like some medicine for your stomachache?

A: Yes. Thank you!

Handout B

1. You are a store clerk working in an American department store. A Chinese tourist (your partner) visits your store and wants to buy something, and you respond to him/her.

Example:

A: I'd like… (gesture).

B: You'd like some medicine?

2. Now you are a Chinese tourist shopping at an American department store. Tell the clerk (your partner) what you want in English.

(A) I'd like some (ice cream).

(B) I'd like some (face cream).

(C) I want to buy some (T-shirts).

(D) I want to buy some toys for my (nephew).

References

Abercrombie, D. (1968). Paralanguage. *International Journal of Language & Communication Disorders*, 3(1), 55-59.

Aghayeva, K. (2011). Intercultural Nonverbal Communication. Paper presented on the 6 Silk Road International Conference "Globalization and Security in Black and Caspian Seas Regions".

Al-Halawachy, H. (2008). A Synthetic Approach to the Study of Avoidance in Language Production. Unpublished PhD Dissertation: University of Mosul.

Al-Halawachy, H. (2014). EFL Learner's Silence at University Level: Where to? *Journal of Education and Practice*, 5(12), 90-119.

Al-Humaidi, M. (2008). The Silent Way. Retrieved November 11, 2013, from http://ksu.edu.sa/pdf/O_marketing/101_Ws_security/55astronomy.pdf.

Allen, L. Q. (2000). Nonverbal Accommodations in Foreign Language Teacher Talk. *Applied Language Learning*, 11, 155-176.

Allen, L. O. (1999). Functions of Nonverbal Communication in Teaching and Learning a Foreign Language. *The French Review*, 72(3), 469-480.

Allen, E. D & Valette, R.M. (1994). *Classroom Techniques: Foreign Languages and English as a Second Language*. Prospect Heights, IL: Waveland Press.

Allen, M., Witt, P. L. & Wheeless, L. R. (2006). The Role of Teacher Immediacy as a Motivational Factor in Student Learning: Using Meta-analysis to Test a Causal Model. *Communication Education*, 55(1), 21-31.

Ali, M., & Ali, S. (2011). The Use of Nonverbal Communication in the Classroom. Papers presented on 1st International Conference on Foreign Language Teaching and Applied Linguistics May 5-7, 2011 Sarajevo. Retrieved December 12, 2014, from http://www.gfsoso.com/scholar?cluster=16279396176133846671&hl=zh-CN&as_sdt=0,5.

Ambady, N. & Rosenthal, R. (1993). Half a Minute: Predicting Teacher Evaluations from Thin Slices of Nonverbal Behavior and Physical Attractiveness. *Journal of Personality and Social Psychology*, 64(3), 431-441.

Amulya, J. (2004). Guide to Integrating Reflection into Field-Based Courses. *Center for Reflective Community Practice*. Retrieved May 20, 2014, from http://crcp.mit.

edu.

Andersen, P.A. (1999). *Nonverbal Communication: Forms and Functions.* Mountain View, CA: Mayfield Publishing Co.

Anderson, P. A. & Leibowitz, K. (1978). The Development and Nature of the Construct Touch Avoidance. *Environmental Psychology and Nonverbal Behavior*, 3, 89-106.

Anderson, F. E. (1993). The Enigma of the College Classroom: Nails That Don't Stick Up. In P. Wadden (ed.), *A Handbook for Teaching English at Japanese Colleges and Universities*. Oxford: Oxford University Press.

Andersen, J. (1979). Teacher Immediacy as a Predictor of Teaching Effectiveness. In D. Nimmo (ed.), *Communication Yearbook* 3. New Brunswick, NJ: Transaction Books.

Andersen, J. F. (1986). Instructor Nonverbal Communication: Listening to Our Silent Messages. *New Directions for Teaching and Learning*, (26), 41-49.

Anderson, J. W. (1994). A Comparison of Arab and American Conceptions of "Effective" Persuasion. In L. Samovar & R. Porter (eds.), *Intercultural communication: A reader* (7th, ed.). Belmont, CA: Wadsworth.

Angelo, T. A. & Cross, K. P. (1993). *Classroom Assessment Techniques: a Handbook for College Teachers* (2nd, ed.). San Francisco: Jossey-Bass Publishers.

Argyle, M. (1986). *Bodily Communication*. London: Routledge.

Argyle. M. (1988). Social Cognition and Social Interaction. *The Psychologist,* (1), 177-183.

Argyle, M. (1982). Intercultural Communication. In Bochner, S. (ed.), *Cultures in Contact: Studies in Cross-Cultural Interaction*. New York: Pergamon Press.

Arasaratnam, L. A. & Banerjee, S. C. (2007). Ethnocentrism and Sensation Seeking as Variables That Influence Intercultural Contact-Seeking Behavior: A Path Analysis. *Communication Research Reports*, 24(4), 303-310.

Armstrong, P. (2007). Cultures of Silence: Giving Voice to Marginalized Communities. Paper presented in 37th Annual SCUTREA Conference. Belfast, Northern Ireland. Retrieved January 12, 2013, from http://www.leads.ac.uk/documents/163812.htm.

Asher, J. J. (1981). Comprehension Training: The Evidence from Laboratory and Classroom Studies. In Winitz (ed.), *The Comprehension Approach to FL Instruction*. Rowley: Newbury.

Asher, J. J., Kusudo, J. A. & R. de la Torre. (1974). Learning a Second Language through Commands: The Second Field Test. *Modern Language Journal,* 58, 24-32.

Auster, C. J. & MacRone, M. (1994). The Classroom as a Negotiated Social Setting:

An Empirical Study of the Effects of Faculty Members' Behavior on Students' Participation. *Teaching Sociology*, 22, 289-300.

Bachman, L. (1990). *Fundamental Consideration in Language Testing*. Oxford: Oxford University Press.

Bachman, L. & Palmer, A. (1996). *Language Testing in Practice*. Oxford: Oxford University Press.

Ballard, B. (1996). Through Language to Learning: Preparing Overseas Students for Study in Western Universities. In H. Coleman (ed.), *Society and the Language Classroom*. Cambridge: Cambridge University Press.

Baringer, D. K. & McCroskey, J. C. (2000). Immediacy in the Classroom: Student Immediacy. *Communication Education*, 49(2), 178-189.

Barrera, I. & Kramer, L. (1997). From Monologues to Skilled Dialogues—Teaching the Process of Crafting Culturally Competent Early Childhood Environments. In Winton, P.J., McCullum, J. A. & Catlett, C. (eds.), *Reforming Personnel Preparation in Early Intervention: Issues, Models, and Practical Strategies*. Baltimore, MD: Paul H. Brookes.

Barnlund, D. (1968). *Interpersonal Communication: Survey and Studies*. Boston: Houghton Mifflin.

Bassett, R. (1979). Effects of Source Attire on Judgments of Credibility. *Central States Speech Journal*, 30, 282-285.

Beebe, S.A., Beebe, S.J. & Redmond, M. V. (1999). *Interpersonal Communication*. Boston: Allyn & Bacon.

Benson, P. G. (1978). Measuring Cross-Cultural Adjustment: The Problem of Criteria. *International Journal of Intercultural Relations*, 2, 21-37.

Bettinghaus, E. P. (1968). *Persuasive Communication*. New York, NY: Holt, Rinehart & Winston.

Bertsch, K. M., Houlihan, D., Lenz, M. A. & Patte, C. A. (2009). Teachers' Commands and Their Role in Preschool Classrooms. *Electronic Journal of Research in Educational Psychology*, 7(1), 133-162.

Birdwhistell, R. L. (1952). *Introduction to Kinesics*. Kentucky: University of Louisville.

Birdwhistell, R, L. (1970). *Kinesics and Context*. Philadelphia: University of Pennsylvania Press.

Birjandi, P. & M, Nushi. (2010). Non-verbal Communication in Models of Communicative Competence and L2 Teachers' Rating. *Journal of English Studies*, 1(1), 3-22.

Bissa, G. & A. Sharma. (2009). Teaching Learning Process: A Study with Special

Reference Nonverbal Communication. *International Research Journal,* 1(6), 57-61.

Bilmes, J. (1994). Constituting Silence: Life in the World of Total Meaning. *Semiotica,* 98(1-2), 73-88.

Blanck, P.D., Rosenthal, R., Snodgrasss, S., DePaulo, B. & Zuckerman, M. (1981). Sex Differences in Eavesdropping on Nonverbal Cues: Developmental Changes. *Journal of Personality and Social Psychology,* 41, 391-396.

Bloom, B. S. (1969). *Taxonomy of Educational Objectives: The Classification of Educational Goals.* London: Longman.

Bochner, A.P. & Kelly, C. W. (1974). Interpersonal Competence: Rationale, Philosophy, and Implementation of a Conceptual Framework. *Speech Teachers,* 23, 279-301.

Bohn, M. T. (2004). Japanese Classroom Behavior: A Micro-analysis of Self-reports vs. Classroom Observations—with Implications for Language Teachers. *Applied Language Learning,* 14(1), 1-35.

Borg, J. (2008). *Body Language.* London: Pearson.

Bosacki, S. L. (2005). *The Culture of Classroom Silence.* New York: Peter Lang.

Botas, P. C. P. (2006). Students' Perceptions of Teachers' Pedagogical Styles in Higher Education. *Educate,* 4(1), 16-30. Retrieved February 23, 2014, from http://www.educatejournal.org/index.php/educate/article/viewFile/77/74.

Bovee, L. C., Thill, V. J. & Barbara. (2003). *Business Communication Today* (7th, ed.). New Jersey, USA: Prentice Hall.

Boys, C. (1995). National Vocational Qualifications: The Outcomes-Plus Model of Assessment. In A. Edwards & P. Knight, (eds.), *Assessing Competence in Higher Education.* London: Kogan Page.

Boyd, F.D. (2000). Nonverbal Behavior of Effective Teachers of at-Risk African American Male Middle School Students. Unpublished PhD Dissertation, Faculty of the Virginia Polytechnic Institute and State University, Blacksburg, Virginia.

Bowden, J. & Marton, F. (1998). *The University of Learning: Beyond Quality and Competence in Higher Education.* London, United Kingdom: Rogan Page.

Bradford, L., Allen, M. & Beisser, K. R. (2000). Meta-analysis of Intercultural Communication Competence Research. *World Communication,* 29, 28-51.

Breed, G. & Colaiuta, V. (2006). Looking, Blinking, and Sitting: Nonverbal Dynamics in the Classroom. *Journal of Communication,* 24(2), 75-81.

Breed, G. (1971). *Nonverbal Behavior and Teaching Effectiveness: Final Report.* Vermilion, SD: South Dakota University.

Brislin, R. (1993). *Understanding Culture's Influence on Behavior.* Fort Worth, TX:

Harcourt Brace Jovanovich College Polishers.

Brophy, J. & Evertson, C. (1981). *Students Characteristics and Teaching*. New York: Longman.

Bruneau, T. J. (1973). Communicative Silences: Forms and Functions. *The Journal of Communication*, 23, 17-46.

Brooks, D. M. & Woolfolk, A. E. (1987). The Effects of Students' Nonverbal Behavior on Teachers. *Elementary School Journal,* 88, 50-63.

Brown, H. D. (1987). *Principles of Language Learning and Teaching*(2nd, ed.). New Jersey; Prentice-Hall.

Brown, H. D. (1980). The Optimal Distance Model of Second Language Acquisition. *Tesol Quarterly*, 157-164.

Burgoon, J. K., Stern, L. A. & Dillman, L. (1995). *Interpersonal Adaptation: Dyadic Interaction Patterns.* New York: Cambridge University Press.

Byram, M. (1997). *Teaching and Assessing Intercultural Communicative Competence.* Clevedon: Multilingual Matters.

Calero, Henry, H. (2005). *The Power of Nonverbal Communication: How You Act is More Important than What You Say.* Los Angeles: Silver Lake Publishing.

Campano, G. (2007). *Immigrant Students and Literacy: Reading, Writing, and Remembering.* New York, NY: Teachers College Press.

Canale, M. (1983a). From Communicative Competence to Communicative Language Pedagogy. In Jack C. Richards & Richard W. Schmidt(eds.), *Language and Communication*. London: Longman.

Canale, M. (1983b). On Some Dimensions of Language Proficiency. In J. Oller (ed.), *Issues in Language Testing Research*. Rowley: Newbury.

Canale, M. & Swain, M. (1980). Theoretical Bases of Communicative Approaches to Second Language Teaching and Testing. *Applied Linguistics,* (1), 1-47.

Cantor, N. L. & Gelfand, D. M. (1974). Effects of Responsiveness and Sex of Children on Adult's Behavior. *Child Development,* 48, 232-238.

Capretz, P. J., Abetti, B. & Marie-Odile G. (1987). *French in Action.* New Haven: Yale University Press.

Carter, S. P. (2001). The Possibilities of Silence: African-American Female Cultural Identity and Secondary English Classroom. Unpublished PhD Dissertation, Vanderbilt University, Nashville.

Carr, D., Davies, T. & Lavin, A. (2009). The Effect of Business Faculty Attire on Student Perceptions of the Quality of Instruction and Program Quality. *College Student Journal*, 43(1), 45.

Cardon, P. W. & Okoro, E. A. (2009). Professional Characteristics Communicated by Formal versus Casual Workplace Attire. *Business Communication Quarterly*, 72(3), 355-360.

Cegala, D. J. (1984). Affective and Cognitive Manifestations of Interaction Involvement during Unstructured and Competitive Interactions. *Communication Monographs*, 51(4), 320-338.

Cha, T. H. K. (1993). *Dictee*. Berkeley, CA: Third Woman Press.

Chen, G. M. & Starosta, W. J. (2007). *Foundations of Intercultural Communication*. Shanghai: Shanghai Foreign Language Education Press.

Chen, G. M. & Starosta, W. J. (1999). A Review of the Concept of Intercultural Awareness. *Human Communication*, 2, 27-54.

Chen, G. M. & Starosta, W. J. (1996). Intercultural Communication Competence: A Synthesis. In S. Deetz (ed.), *Communication Yearbook* 19. Thousand Oaks, CA: Sage.

Chomsky, N. (1965). *Aspects of the Theory of Syntax*. Cambridge, Massachusetts: MIT Press.

Christopher, E. (2002). Gender Differences in Non-verbal Behavior. Retrieved January 23, 2014, from http://www.qnselm.edu/internet/psych/theses/seniors2002/christopher/webpage.html.

Church, R., Ayman-Nolley, S. & Mahootian, S. (2004). The Role of Gesture in Bilingual Education: Does Gesture Enhance Learning? *International Journal of Bilingual Education and Bilingualism*, 7, 303-319.

Clark, C. & Peterson, P. (1986). Teachers' Thought Processes. In M. Wittrock (ed.), *Handbook of Research on Teaching* (3rd, ed.). New York: Macmillan.

Cohen, A. (1998). *Strategies in Learning and Using a Second Language*. Essex, England: Longman.

Cohen, A. A. & Harrison, R. P. (1973). Intentionality in the Use of Hand Illustrators in Face-to-Face Communication Situations. *Journal of Personality and Social Psychology*, 28(2), 276.

Cohen, D. (2007). *Body Language, What You Need to Know*. London: Sheldon Press.

Collier, M. J. (1989). Cultural and Intercultural Communication Competence: Current Approaches and Directions for Future Research. *International Journal of Intercultural Relations*, 13, 287-302.

Collier, M. J. & Thomas, M. (1988). Cultural Identity: An Interpretive Perspective. In Y. Y. Kim & W. B. Gudykunst (eds.), *Theories in Intercultural Communication (International and Intercultural Communication Annual*, Vol. 12). Newbury Park,

CA: Sage.

Comadena, M. E., Hunt, S. K. & Simonds, C. J. (2007). The Effects of Teacher Clarity, Nonverbal Immediacy, and Caring on Student Motivation, Effective and Cognitive Learning. *Communication Research Reports*, 24(3), 241-248.

Comstock, J. (1999). Mutual Influence in Teacher–Student Relationships: Applying IAT to Access Teacher Adaptation to Student Classroom Involvement. Paper presented at the annual meeting of the National Communication Association, Chicago, IL.

Condon, J. C. & Yousef, F. S. (1975). *An Introduction to Intercultural Communication*. Indianapolis & New York: Bobbs-Morrill Company, Inc.

Cooper, C. C. (1988). Implications of the Absence of Black Teachers/Administrators on Black Youth. *Journal of Negro Education*, 57(2), 123-124.

Crawford, M. & MacLeod, Moo (1990). Gender in the College Classroom: An Assessment of the "Chilly Climate" for Women. *Sex Roles*, 23, 101-122.

Creswell, J. W. (2003) *Research Design: Qualitative, Quantitative and Mixed Methods Approaches*. London: Sage.

Cruickshank, D. R., Jenkins, D. B. & Metcalf, K. K. (2005). *The Act of Teaching*. New York: McGraw-Hill Companies.

Dalton, W. B. (1969). The Relations between Classroom Interaction and Teacher Ratings of Pupils: An Exploration of One Means by Which a Teacher May Communicate Her Expectancies. Paper presented at the annual meeting of the Southeastern Psychological Association, New Orleans.

Davies, R. J. & Ikeno (2002). *The Japanese Mind*. Boston: Turtle Publishing.

Davis, B. G. (2009). *Tools for Teaching* (2nd, ed.). San Francisco, CA: Jossey-Bass.

de Araújo Nóbrega, D. G. (2012). Students' Spontaneous Smile in the EFL Classroom. *Acta Scientiarum. Language and Culture*, 34(2), 233-240. Retrieved May 2, 2015 from http://www.redalyc.org/articulo.oa?id=307426652011.

Diekman, A.B. & Goodfriend, W. (2006). Rolling with the Changes: A Role Congruity Perspective on Gender Norms. *Psychology of Women Quarterly*, 30, 369-383.

Deutsch, F.M., LeBaron, D. & Fryer, M.M. (1987). What Is in a Smile? *Psychology of Women Quarterly*, 11, 341-352.

Duchenne de Boulogne, G. B. (1990). *The Mechanism of Human Facial Expression*. R. A. Cuthbertson (ed.). Cambridge: Cambridge University Press.

Duncan, P. (2004). Learning English and How to Be Silent: Students in Sioux and Cherokee Classroom. In C. Cazden, V. P. Johns & D. Hymes (eds.), *Functions of Language in the Classroom*. Prospect Heights, IL: Waveland Press.

Dodd, C. H. (1989). *Dynamics of Intercultural Communication*. Dubuques, IA: Wm. C. Brown Publishers.

Dörnyei, Z. & Scott, M. (1997). Review Article: Communication Strategies in a Second Language: Definition and Taxonomies. *Language Learning* 47(1):173-210.

Doucas, E. K. (1996). Using Attitude Scales to Investigate Teachers' Attitudes to the Communicative Approach. *ELT Journal*, 50(3), 187-198.

Driscoll, J. (1969). The Effects of a Teacher's Eye Contact, Gestures and Voice Intonation on Student Retention of Factual Material. Unpublished PhD Dissertation, University of Southern Mississippi.

Edwards, V. & Redfern, A. (1992). *The World in a Classroom: Language in Education*. Clevedon: Multilingual Matters.

Edwards, A. & Knight, P. (eds.) (1995). *Assessing Competence in Higher Education*. London: Kogan Page.

Edwards, V. & Redfern, A. (1992). *The World in a Classroom: Language in Education in Britain and Canada* (Vol. 87). Clevedon: Multilingual Matters.

Ehrman, M. E.& Dörnyei, Z. (1998). *Interpersonal Dynamics in Second Language Education: The Visible and Invisible Classroom*. Thousand Oaks, CA: Sage.

Ekman, P. & Friesen, W. V. (1969). The Repertoire of Nonverbal Behavior: Categories, Origins, Usage, and Coding. *Semiotica*, 1(1), 49-98.

Ekman, P. & Friesen, W. V. (1967). Origin, Usage and Coding: The Basis for Five Categories of Nonverbal Behavior. Paper presented in Symposium on Communication Theory and Linguistic Models in the Social Sciences, Buenos Aires, Argentina.

Ekman, P. & Friesen, W. V. (1976). Measuring Facial Movement. *Environmental Psychology and Nonverbal Behavior*, 1(1), 56-75.

Ekman, P. & Friesen, W. V. (1978a). *Investigator's Guide to the Facial Action Coding System* (Part ②). Palo Alto, Calif.: Consulting Psychologists Press.

Ekman, P. & Friesen, W. V. (1978b). *Manual for the Facial Action Coding System*. Palo Alto, Calif.: Consulting Psychologists Press.

Ekman, P., Friesen, W. V. & Ellsworth, P. (1972). *Emotion in the Human Face: Guide-Lines for Research and an Integration of Findings*. New York: Pergamon Press.

Ekman, P. (2003). *Emotions Revealed: Recognizing Faces and Feelings to Improve Communication and Emotional life* (2nd, ed). New York: A Holt Paperback.

Ekman, P. (ed.) (1973). *Darwin and Facial Expression: A Century of Research in Review*. New York: Academic Press.

Ellwood, C. & Nakane, I. (2009). Privileging of Speech in EAP and Mainstream

University Classrooms: A Critical Evaluation of Participation. *TESOL Quarterly*, 43, (2), 203-230.

Ellyson, S. L. & Dovidio, J. F. (1985). Power, Dominance, and Nonverbal Behavior: Basic Concepts and Issues. In Ellyson, S. L. & Dovidio, J. F. (eds.), *Power, Dominance, and Nonverbal Behavior*. New York: Springer-Verlag Inc.

Emmer, E.T., Evertson, C. M. & Worsham, M. E. (2003). *Classroom Management for Secondary Teachers*(6th, ed.). Boston: Allyn and Bacon.

Ephratt, M. (2008). The Functions of Silence. *Journals of Pragmatics*, 40, 1909-1938.

Fantini, A. E., Arias-Galicia, F. & Guay, D. (2001). Globalization and 21st Century Competencies: Challenges for North American Higher Education. Working Paper #11 (Publication Number 2A343). Western Interstate Commission for Higher Education.

Fantini, A. E. (1997). A Survey of Intercultural Communication Courses. *International Journal of Intercultural Relations*, 21(1), 125-148.

Fantini, A. E. (2000). A Central Concern: Developing Intercultural Competence. In *SIT Occasional Papers Series: About Our Institution*. Brattleboro, Vermont, USA, School for International Training. Retrieved January, 12, 2015, from http://citeseerx.ist.psu.edu/viewdoc/download?doi=10.1.1.117.8512&rep=rep1&type=pdf#page=33.

Fast, J. (1971). *Body Language*. New York: Simon and Schuster.

Feyereisen, P. & de Lannoy, J. D. (1991). *Gestures and Speech: Psychological Investigations*. Cambridge: Cambridge University Press.

Feldman, R.S. (1990). *The Social Psychology of Education: Current Research and Theory*. Cambridge: Cambridge University Press.

Fiksdal, S. (1990). *The Right Time and Pace: A Microanalysis of Crosscultural Gatekeeping Interviews.* Norwood, NJ: Ablex.

Finders, M. J. (1996). Queens and Teen Zines: Early Adolescent Females Reading Their Way toward Adulthood. *Anthropology and Education*, 64(2), 157-174.

Freitas-Magalhães, A. (2006). *The Psychology of Human Smile*. Porto, Portugal: Fernando Pessoa University Editions.

Fordham, S. (1993). Those Loud Black Girls: (Black) Women, Silence, and Gender "Passing" in the Academy. *Anthropology and Education Quarterly*, 24(1), 3-32.

Forgas, J. (1988). Episode Representations in Intercultural Communication. In Y. Y. Kim & W. B. Gudykunst (eds.), *Theories in Intercultural Communication*. Newbury Park, CA: Sage.

Gage, N. L. (1963). A Method for Improving Teacher Behavior. *Journal of Teacher*

Education, 14, 261-266.

Gage, N. L. & Berliner, D.C. (1992). *Educational Psychology*. Boston: Houghton Mifflin.

Gardiner, J. C. (1969). The Effects of Perceived Audience Response on Speaker Attitudes. PhD Dissertation, Michigan State University.

Gattegno, C. (1972). *Teaching Foreign Languages in Schools: The Silent Way*. New York: Educational Solutions Worldwide Inc.

Gee, J. P. (1993). *An Introduction to Human Language—Fundamental Concepts in Linguistics*. New Jersey: Prentice Hall.

Gilmore, P. (1985). Silence and Sulking: Emotional Displays in the Classroom. In D. Tannern & M. Saville-Troike (eds.), *Perspectives on Silence*. Norwood, NJ: Ablex.

Giles, H., Coupland, N. & Wiemann, J. M. (1992). "Talk is Cheap" but "My Word is My Bond": Beliefs about Talk. In K. Bolton and H. Kwok (eds.), *Sociolinguistics Today: Eastern and Western Perspectives*. London: Routledge.

Givens, D.B. (2000). The Nonverbal Dictionary of Gestures, Signs, and Body Language. Center for Nonverbal Studies. Retrieved October 26, 2008, from http://members.aol.com/ nonverbal2/ diction. Html.

Goldin-Meadow, S. (2004). Gesture's Role in the Learning Process. *Theory into Practice*, 43, 314-321.

Gower, R. and Walters, S. (1983). *Teaching Practice Handbook.* Oxford: Heinemann.

Grant, B. M. & Hennings, D. G. (1971). *The Teacher Moves: An Analysis of Non-Verbal Activity*. New York: Teachers College Press.

Graham, J. A. & Argyle, M. (1975). A Cross-Cultural Study of the Communication of Extra-Verbal Meaning by Gestures. *International Journal of Psychology*, 10(1), 57-67.

Green, J. W. (1982) *Cultural Awareness in the Human Services*. Englewood Cliffs, NJ: Prentice Hall.

Gregersen, T. S. (2005). Nonverbal Cues: Clues to the Detection of Foreign Language Anxiety. *Foreign Language Annals*, 38(3), 388-400.

Gukas, I. D., Leinster, S. J. & Walker, R. (2010). Verbal and Nonverbal Indices of Learning during Problem Based Learning (PBL) among First Year Medical Students and the Threshold for Tutor Intervention. *Medical Teacher,* 32, e5-e11. Retrieved July 15, 2010, from http://informahealthcare.com/doi/abs/10.3109/01421590903398232.

Gullberg, M. (2006). Some Reasons for Studying Gesture and Second Language Acquisition. *International Review of Applied Linguistics in Language Teaching*, 42(2), 103-124.

Gumperz, J. J. (1982). *Studies in Interactional Sociolinguistics* 1. Cambridge: Cambridge University Press.

Gudykunst, W. B. (2003). Intercultural Communication Theories. In W. B. Gudykunst (ed.), *Cross-Cultural and Intercultural Communication*. Thousand Oaks: Sage.

Gudykunst, W. B. (1992). Being Perceived as a Competent Communicator. In Gudykunst, W. B. & Kim, Y. Y. (eds.), *Readings on Communicating with Strangers*. New York: McGraw-Hill College.

Haastrup, K. (1991). Developing Learners' Procedural Knowledge in Comprehension. In Phillipson, R., Kellerman, E. et al. (eds.), *Foreign/Second Language Pedagogy Research*. Clevedon: Multilingual Matters.

Hall, E. T. (1959). *Silent Language*. New York: Fawcett.

Hall, E. T. (1966). *The Hidden Dimension*. New York: Anchor Books.

Hadley, A. C. O. (1993). *Teaching Language in Context* (2nd, ed.). Boston: Heinle and Heinle.

Hall, J. (1978). Gender Effects in Decoding Nonverbal Cues. *Psychological Bulletin*, 68, 845-857.

Hall, J. A. & Halberstadt, A.G. (1986). Smiling and Gazing. In J. S. Hyde & M. C. Linn (eds.), *The Psychology of Gender: Advances through Meta-analysis*. Baltimore, MD: Johns Hopkins University Press.

Hall, J. A. (2006). Women's and Men's Nonverbal Communication: Similarities, Differences, Sterotypes, and Origins. In V. L. Manusov & M. L. Patterson (eds.), *The SAGE Handbook of Nonverbal Communication*. Thousand Oaks, Calif.: Sage.

Hammer, M. R. (1987). Behavioral Dimensions of Intercultural Effectiveness: A Replication and Extension. *International Journal of Intercultural Relations*, 11, 65-88.

Hartley, G. & Karinch, M. (2007). *I Can Read You Like a Book: How to Spot the Messages and Emotions People Are Really Sending with Their Body Language*. Franklin Lakes, NJ: Career Press.

Harris, M., James, J. Chavez, J., Ftiller, M., Kent, S. Massanari, C. & Wash, F (1983). Clothing: Communication, Compliance, and Choice. *Journal of Applied Psychology*, 13, 88-97.

Hassan, M.M.T. (2007). Non-Verbal Communication: The Language of Motivation for Pakistani Students. *Journal of Language in India,* 7, Aug. 2007.

Hatch, E. (1983). Simplified Input and Second Language Acquisition. In Roger W. Andersen (ed.), *Pidginization and Creolization as Language Acquisition*. Rowley: Newbury.

Havelock, P., Hasler, J., Flew, R., McIntyre, D., Schofield, T. & Toby, J. (1995). *Professional Eeducation for General Practice*. Oxford: Oxford University Press.

Hecht, M. A. & Ambady, N. (1999). Nonverbal Communication and Psychology: Past and Future. *Atlantic Journal of Communication*, 7(2), 156-170.

Henley, N. M. (1977). *Body Politics: Power, Sex, and Nonverbal Communication*. Englewood Cliffs, NJ: Prentice Hall.

Helmer, S.& Eddy, C. (2003). *Look at Me When I Talk to You: ESL Learners in Non-ESL Classrooms*. Tonawanda, NY: Pippin.

Helweg-Larsen, M., Cunningham, J. A. Carrico, A. & Pergram, M.A. (2004). To Nod or Not to Nod: An Observational Study of Nonverbal Communication and Status in Female and Male College Students. *Psychology of Women Quarterly*, 28, 358-361.

Hildson, J. (1996). Silence in the Classroom: Issues of Control, Facilitation and Empowerment. Unpublished Manuscript. University of Wales, Cardiff.

Ho, R. & Mitchell, S. (1982). Students' Nonverbal Reaction to Tutor's Warm/Cold Nonverbal Behavior. *The Journal of Social Psychology*, 118, 121-130.

Hogan, K. & Stubbs, R. (2003). *Can't Get through 8 Barriers to Communication*. Grenta, LA: Pelican Publishing Company.

Hopkins, W. D. (2004). Laterality in Maternal Cradling and Infant Positional Basis: Implications for the Development and Evolution of Hand Preferences in Nonhuman Primates. *International Journal of Primatology*, 25,1243-1265.

Hostetter, A. B. (2011). When Do Gestures Communicate? A Meta-analysis. *Psychological Bulletin*, 137(2), 297-315.

Houser, M. L. & Frymier, A.B. (2009). The Role of Student Characteristics and Teachers Behaviors in Students' Learner Empowerment. *Communication in Education*, 58(1), 35-53.

Houston, J. E. (1984). *Thesaurus of ERIC Descriptors* (10th, ed.). Phoenix: Oryx Press.

Howard, J. R. & Henney, A. L. (1998). Student Participation and Instructor Gender in the Mixed-Age College Classroom. *Journal of Higher Education*, 69(4), 384-405.

Howard, J. R., Short, L. B. & Clark, S. M. (1996). Student Participation in the Mixed-Age College Classroom. *Teaching Sociology*, 24, 8-24.

Hu, Y. & Fell-Eisenkraft, S. (2003). Immigrant Chinese Students' Use of Silence in the Language Arts Classroom: Perceptions, Reflections, and Actions. *Teaching and Learning-Grand Forks*, 17, 55-65.

Hymes, P. (1972). On Communicative Competence. In J. Pride and J. Holmes (eds.), *Sociolinguistic*. Harmondsworth: Penguin.

Hyde, C. A. & Ruth, B. J. (2002). Multicultural Content and Class Participation: Do Students Self-censor? *Journal of Social Work Education*, 38(2), 241-256.

Jackson, P. W., Silberman, M. L. & Wolfson, B, J. (1969). Signs of Personal Involvement in Teachers' Descriptions of Their Students. *Journal of Educational Psychology*, 60, 22-27.

Jaworski, A. (1993). *The Power of Silence*. California: Sage.

Jaworski, A. (1997). *Silence-Interdisciplinary Perspectives*. Berlin: Mouton de Gruyter, Inc.

Jaworski, A. & Sachdev, I. (1998). Beliefs about Silence in the Classroom. *Language and Education,* 12(4), 273-292.

Jecker, J., Maccoby, N., Breitrose, H. S. & Rose, E. D. (1964). Teacher Accuracy in Assessing Cognitive Visual Feedback from Students. *Journal of Applied Psychological*, 48, 393-442.

Jenkins, J. R. & Deno, S. L. (1989). Influence of Student Behavior on Teacher's Self-Evaluation. *Journal of Educational Psychology,* 60, 489-442.

Jensen, V. J. (1973). Communicative Functions of Silence. *ETC: A Review of General Semantics*, 30, 249-257.

Jensen, J. V. (1970). Perspectives on Nonverbal Intercultural Communication. In L.A. Somovar & R. E. Porter (eds.), *Intercultural Communication: A Reader*. Belmont, CA: Wadsworth.

Johnson, K. (1979). Communicative Approach and Communicative Processes. In C.J. Brumfit & K. Johnson (eds.), *The Communicative Approach to Language Teaching*. Oxford: Oxford University Press.

Jones, J. F. (1999). From Silence to Talk: Cross-Cultural Ideas on Students' Participation in Academic Group Discussion. *English for Specific Purposes*, 18, 243-259.

Kealey, D. J. (1990). *Cross-Cultural Effectiveness: A Study of Canadian Technical Advisors Overseas*. Hull, Quebec: Canadian International Development Agency.

Keith, L. T., Tornatzky, L. G. & Pettigrew, L. E. (1974). An Analysis of Verbal and Nonverbal Classroom Teaching Behaviors. *The Journal of Experimental Education,* 42(4), 30-38.

Kendon, A. (2004). *Gesture: Visible Action as Utterance*. Cambridge: Cambridge University Press.

Kelly, S. D. & Goldsmith, L. H. (2004). Gesture and Right Hemisphere Involvement in Evaluating Lecture Material. *Gesture*, 4(1), 25-42.

Kiewra, K. A. (2002). How Classroom Teachers can Help Students Learn and Teach Them How to Learn. *Theory into Practice,* 41, 71-80.

Kirch, M. S. (1979). Non-Verbal Communication across Cultures. *Modern Language Journal*, 63: 416-23.

King, P. & Witt, P. (2009). Teacher Immediacy, Confidence Testing, and the Measurement of Cognitive Learning. *Communication Education*, 58(1), 110-123.

Kim, Y. Y. (1992). Intercultural Communication Competence: A Systems-Thinking View. In W.B. Gudykunst & Y.Y. Kim (eds.), *Readings on Communicating with Strangers: An Approach to Intercultural Communication*. New York: McGraw-Hill.

Kim, Y.Y. & Ruben, B. D. (1992). Intercultural Transformation. In W.B. Gudykunst & Y.Y. Kim (eds.), *Readings on Communicating with Strangers: An Approach to Intercultural Communication*. New York: McGraw-Hill.

Kim, M. S. (1993). Cultrual-Based Interactive Constraints in Explaining Intercultural Strategic Competence. In R. L. Wiseman & J. Koester (eds.), *Intercultural Communication Competence*. Newbury Park, CA: Sage.

Klemp, G. O., Jr. (1979). Identifying, Measuring and Integrating Competence. In P.S. Pottinger & J. Goldsmith (eds.), *Defining and Measuring Competence*. San Francisco: Jossey-Bass.

Klinzing, H. G. & Gerada-Aloisio, B. (2004). Intensity, Variety, and Accuracy in Nonverbal Cues and De-/Encoding: Two Experimental Investigations. Paper present at the annual meeting of the American Educational Research Association, San Diego, CA, April.

Klein, S. S. (1971). Student Influence on Teacher Behavior. *American Educational Research Journal*, 403-421.

Kluckhohn, F. R. & Strodtbeck, F. L. (1961). *Variations in Value Orientations.* Evanston, IL: Row, Peterson.

Knapp, M. L., Hall, J. A. & T G. Horgan. (2012). *Nonverbal Communication in Human Interaction* (8th, ed.). TX: Wadsworth Gengage Learning.

Knapp, M. L. (1997). *The Role of Nonverbal Communication in the Classroom.* Toronto: Holt, Rinehart and Winston.

Knapp, M. L. (1980). *Essentials of Nonverbal Communication*. New York: Holt, Rinehart and Winston.

Knapp, M. L. & Hall, J. A. (1992). *Nonverbal Communication in Human Interaction* (3rd, ed.). Fort Worth: Holt Rinehart and Winston

Kaufman, P. (2008). Gaining Voice through Silence. *Feminist Teacher*. 18(2), 175-177. Retrieved December 31, 2013, from http://muse.jhu.edu/journals/feminist_teacher/VO18)18.2kaufman.pdf.

Kohls, L. R. (1979). *Survival Kit for Overseas Living.* Chicago: Intercultural Network/

SYSTRAN Publications.

Koester, J. & Olebe, M. (1988). The Behavioral Assessment Scale for Intercultural Communication Effectiveness. *International Journal of Intercultural Relations*, 12, 233-246.

Krashen, S. D. (1981). *Second Language Acquisition and Second Language Learning*. Oxford: Pergamon.

Kroehnert, G. (2006). *Basic Training for Trainers* (3rd, ed.). New Delhi, India: McGraw-Hill.

Kaufman, P. (2008). Gaining Voice through Silence. *Feminist Teacher*, 18(2), 175-177. Retrieved December 31, 2013, from http://muse.jhu.edu/journals/feminist_teacher/VO18)18.2kaufman.pdf.

Kvale, S. (1996). *Interviews: An Introduction to Qualitative Research Interviewing*. Thousand Oaks: Sage.

La Forge, P. (1975). *Research Profiles with Community Language Learning*. Apple River, Illinois: Apple River Press.

La Forge, P. (1977). Uses of Social Silence in Interpersonal Dynamics of Community Language Learning. *TESOL Quarterly,* 11(4), 373-382.

Lafayette, R. (1988). Integrating the Teaching of Culture into the Foreign Language Classroom. In Alan J. (ed.), *Toward a New Integration of Language and Culture. Reports of the Northeast Conference on the Teaching of Foreign Languages.* Singerman. Middlebury: Northeast Conference.

Lazaraton, A. (2004). Gesture and Speech in the Vocabulary Explanations of one ESL Teacher: A Micro-analytic Inquiry. *Language Learning,* 54, 79-117.

Lebra, T. (1987). The Cultural Significance of Silence in Japanese Communication. *Multilingua,* 6, 343-357.

LeBaron, M. (2003). Cross-Cultural Communication. Beyond Intractability. In G. Burgess & H. Burgess (eds.), *Conflict Research Consortium*. University of Colorado, Boulder. Retrieved August 1, 2006, from http://www.beyondintractability.org/essay/cross-cultural_communication.

Lee, Y. (2006). Towards Re-specification of Communicative Competence: Condition of L2 Instruction or Its Objective. *Applied Linguistics,* 27(3), 349-376.

Leeds-Hurwitz, W. (1990). Notes in the History of Intercultural Communication: The Foreign Service Institute and the Mandate for Intercultural Training. *Quarterly Journal of Speech*, 76(3), 262-281.

Ledbury, R., White, I. & Darn, S. (2004). The Importance of Eye Contact in the Classroom. *The Internet TESL Journal*, 10(8). Retrieved December 12, 2014, from http://iteslj.org.

Lederer, W. J. & Burdick, E. (1958). *The Ugly American.* London: WW Norton & Company.

Lesikar, R. V. & Flatley, M. E. (2005). *Basic Business Communication: Skill for Empowering the Internet Generation* (10th, ed.). New York: McGraw-Hill.

Lehtonen, J. and K. Sajavaara. (1985). The Silent Finn. In D. Tannen & M. Saville-Troike(eds.), *Perspectives on Silence.* Norwood, NJ: Ablex.

Le Roux, J. (2002). Effective Educators Are Culturally Competent Communicators. *Intercultural Education*, 13(1), 37-48.

Li, H. Z. (1999). Grounding and Information Communication in Intercultural and Intracultural Dyadic Discourse. *Discourse Processes.* 28, 195-215.

Lindon, J. & Lindon, L. (2007). *Mastering Counseling Skills.* London: Palgrave Macmillan.

Liu, J. (2000). Understanding Asian Students' Oral Participation Modes in American Classrooms. *Journal of Asian Pacific Communication,* 10, 155-189.

Liu, J. (2001). *Asian Students' Classroom Communication Patterns in US Universities: An Emic Perspective.* Westport, CT: Greenwood Publishing.

Littlewood, W. (2000). Do Asian Students Really Want to Listen and Obey? *ELT Journal,* 54, 31-35.

Littlewood, W. (1984). *Foreign and Second Language Learning: Language Acquisition Research and Its Implications for the Classroom.* Cambridge: Cambridge University Press.

Lörscher, W. (2003). Nonverbal Aspects of Teacher-Pupil Communication in the Foreign Language Classroom. Retrieved Dec. 5, 2009 from: <http://www.ec.hku.hk/kd2proc/proceedings/fullpaper/.../LorscherWolfgang.pdf.

Locker, K. O. (2004). *Business and Administrative Communication* (7th, ed.). New York: McGraw-Hill.

Lustig, M. W. & Koester, J. (2003). *Intercultural Competence: Interpersonal Communication across Cultures* (4th, ed.). Boston: Allyn & Bacon.

Lustig, M. W. & Koester, J. (1993). Methodological Issues in the Study of Intercultural Communication Competence. In R.W. Wiseman & J. Koester (eds.), *Intercultural Communication Competence.* Newbury Park, CA: Sage.

Lucas, J. (1984). Communication Apprehension in the ESL Classroom: Getting Our Students to Talk. *Foreign Language Annual,* 17, 593-598.

Lynch, E.W. (1999). Developing Cross-Cultural Competence. In Lynch, E.W. & Hanson, M. J. (eds.), *Developing Cross-Cultural Competence. A Guide for Working with*

Children and Their Families (2nd, ed.). Baltimore, MD/London: Paul H. Brookes.

Lynch, E. W. & Hanson, M.J. (1999). Steps in the Right Direction. Implications for Interventionists. In Lynch, E. W. & Hanson, M. J. (eds.) *Developing Cross-Cultural Competence. A Guide for Working with Children and Their Families* (2nd, ed.). Baltimore, MD/London: Paul H. Brookes.

Lyle, J. (1990). *Body Language*. London: Reed.

Mackay, J. (2006). *Coat of Many Pockets: Managing Classroom Interactions*. Australia: Australian Council for Educational Research.

Madon, S., Jussin, L., Keiper, S., Eccles, J., Smith, A. & Palumbo, P. (1998). The Accuracy and Power of Sex, Social Class, and Ethnic Stereotypes: A Naturalistic Study in Person Perception. *Personality and Social Psychology Bulletin*, 24, 1304-1318.

Manusov, V. & Patterson, M. L. (2006). *The Sage Handbook of Nonverbal Communication*. Thousand Oaks, Calif.: Sage.

Malandro, L., Barker, L. L. & Barker, D. A. (1989). *Nonverbal Communication* (2nd, ed.). New York: Newbery Award Records.

Marriott, H. (2004). A Programmatic Exploration of Issues in the Academic Interaction of Japanese Students Overseas. *Journal of Asian Pacific Communication*, 14, 33-54.

Maricchiolo, F., Gnisci, A., Bonaiuto, M. & Ficca, G. (2009). Effects of Different Types of Hand Gestures in Persuasive Speech on Receivers' Evaluations. *Language and Cognitive Processes,* 24(2), 239-266.

Marzano, R.J. & Marzano, J. S. (2003). The Key to Classroom Management. *Educational Leadership,* 61(1), 6-13. Retrieved January 13, 2015, from http://educationalleader.com/subtopicintro/read/ASCD/ASCD_296_2.pdf.

Maslow, A. H. (1970). *Motivation and Personality* (2nd, ed.). New York: Harper & Row.

Matsumoto, D. (2006). Culture and Nonverbal Behavior. In V. L. Manusov & M. L. Patterson (eds.), *The SAGE Handbook of Nonverbal Communication*. Thousand Oaks, Calif.: Sage.

Mayberry, R. I. & Nicoladis, E. (2000). Gesture Reflects Language Development: Evidence from Bilingual Children. *Current Directions in Psychological Science*, 9, 192-196.

McCroskey, J., Richmond, V. & McCroskey, L. (2006). Nonverbal Communication in Instructional Contexts. In Manusov, V. L. & Patterson, M. L. (eds.), *The SAGE handbook of Nonverbal Communication*. Thousand Oaks, Calif.: Sage.

McCroskey, J. C. & Richmond, V. P. (1992). Increasing Teacher Influence through

Immediacy. In V. P. Richard & J. C. McCroskey (eds.), *Power in the Classroom: Communication, Control, and Concern*. Hillsdale, NJ: Lawrence Erlbaum.

McCroskey, J. C. & Richmond, V. P. (1996). *Fundamentals of Human Communication: An Interpersonal Perspective*. Prospect Heights, IL: Waveland Press.

McCroskey, J. C. & Teven, J. J. (1999). Goodwill: A Reexamination of the Construct and Its Measurement. *Communications Monographs*, 66(1), 90-103.

McNeill, D. (1992). *Hand and Mind: What the Hands Reveal about Thought*. Chicago: University of Chicago Press.

McNamara, T. F. (1996). *Measuring Second Language Performance*. London: Longman.

McVeigh, B. (2002). *Japanese Higher Education as Myth*. New York & London: Sharpe.

Mehrabian, A. (1977). *Nonverbal Communication*. New Jersey: Transaction Publishers.

Mehrahian, A. (1971). Nonverbal Betrayal of Feelings. *Journal of Experimental Research in Personality*, 5, 64-73.

Mehrahian, A. (1981). *Silent Language: Implicit Communication of Emotions and Attitudes*(2nd, ed.). Belmont, CA: Wadsworth.

Mehrabian, A. & Ferris, S. R. (1967). Inference of Attitudes from Nonverbal Communication in Two Channels. *Journal of Consulting Psychology*, 31, 248-252.

Merriam, S. B. (2001). *Qualitative Research and Case Study Applications in Education* (2nd, ed.). San Francisco: Jossey-Bass.

Merritt, Deborah J. (2008), Bias, the Brain, and Student Evaluations of Teaching, *St. John's Law Review*, 82 (1), 235-287.

Miles, M. B. & Huberman, A. M. (1994). *Qualitative Data Analysis*. Thousand Oaks, CA: Sage.

Miller, P. W. (1988). *Nonverbal Communication. What Research Says to the Teacher* (3rd, ed.). A National Education Association Publication. Retrieved February 12, 2014, from http://files.eric.ed.gov/fulltext/ED293190.pdf.

Miller, P. W. (2005a). *Body Language: An Illustrated Introduction for Teachers*. Evansville, IN: Miller and Associates.

Miller, P. W. (2005b). Body Language in the Classroom. *Techniques*, 80(8), 28-30.

Milner, A. & Quilty, M. (1996). *Australia in Asia: Communities of Thought*. Melbourne: Oxford University Press.

Minh-ha, T. T. (1990). Not You/Like You: Post-colonial Women and the Interlocking Questions of Identity and Difference. In G. Anzaldua (ed.), *Making Face, Making Soul/Hacienda Caras: Creative and Critical Perspectives by Women of Color*. San Francisco: Aunt Lute Books.

Mitzel, H. E. (1960). Teacher Effectiveness. *Encyclopedia of Educational Research*, 3(1), 1481-1486.

Mohan, B. & Helmer, S. (1988). Context and Second Language Development: Preschoolers' Comprehension of Gestures. *Applied Linguistics*, 9, 275-292.

Mohatt, G. & Erickson, F. (1981). Cultural Differences in Teaching Styles in an Odwa School: A Sociolinguistic Approach. In Traeba H., Guthrie G. and Au K. (eds.), *Culture and the Bilingual Classroom*. Rowley: Newbury.

Molloy, J. (1975). *Dress for Success*. New York: Wamer Books.

Mottet, T. P. & Beebe, S. A. (2006). The Relationships between Student Responsive Behaviors, Student Socio-communicative Style, and Instructors' Subjective and Objective Assessment of Student Work. *Communication Education*, 55, 295-312.

Mottet, T. P., Beebe, S. A., Raffeld, P. C. & Medlock, A. L. (2004). The Effects of Student Verbal and Nonverbal Responsiveness on Teacher Self-efficacy and Job Satisfaction. *Communication Education*, 53, 150-163.

Mottet, T. P. (2000). Interactive Television Instructors' Perceptions of Students' Nonverbal Responsiveness and Their Influence on Distance Teaching. *Communication Education*, 49, 146-164.

Mottet, T. P. & Richmond, V. P. (2002). Student Nonverbal Communication and Its Influence on Teachers and Teaching. *Communication for Teachers*, 47-61.

Nakane, I. (2007). *Silence in Intercultural Communication: Perceptions and Performance*. Amsterdam: John Benjamins.

Natriello, G. & Dornbusch, S. M. (1983). Bringing Behavior Back in: The Effects of Student Characteristics and Behavior on the Classroom Behavior of Teachers. *American Educational Research Journal*, 20, 29-43.

Neu, J. (1990). Assessing the Role of Nonverbal Communication in the Acquisition of Communicative Competence in L2. In R. Scarcella, E. S. Andersen & S. D. Krashen (eds.), *Developing Communicative Competence in a Second Language*. New York: Newbury House Publishers.

Neil, S. (1989). The Effects of Facial Expression and Posture on Children's Reported Responses to Teacher Nonverbal Communication. *British Educational Research Journal*, 15, 195-204.

Neill, S. (1991). *Classroom Nonverbal Communication*. London: Routledge.

Neill, S. R. & Caswell, C. (1993). *Body Language for Competent Teachers.* London; New York: Routledge.

Nist, S. L. & Simpson, M. L. (2000). College Studying. In M. L. Kamil, P. B. Mosenthal, P. D. Pearson & R. Barr (eds.), *Handbook of Reading Research* (Vol. ▢). Mahwah, NJ:

Lawrence Erlbaum.

Nuessel, F. (1985). Teaching Kinesics through Literature. *Canadian Modern Language Review,* 41, 1014-1019.

Nussbaum, J.E. (1992). Effective Teacher Behaviors. *Communication Education*, 41, 167-180.

Nwoye, G. O. (1985). Eloquent Silence among the Igbo of Nigeria. In D. Tannen & M. Saville-Troike (eds.), *Perspectives on Silence*. Norwood, NJ: Ablex.

Okon, J. J. (2011). Role of Non-verbal Communication in Education. *Mediterranean Journal of Social Sciences*, 2 (5), 35-40.

Oliver, R. T. (1962). *Culture and Communication*. Springfield, IL: Thomas.

Paivio, A. (1991). Dual Coding Theory: Retrospect and Current Status. *Canadian Journal of Psychology/Revue Canadienne de Psychologie,* 45(3), 255-287.

Parker, R. (2006). Classroom Management. *Tesol Course Articles.* Retrieved February 23, 2014, from http://www.tesolcourse.com.

Patton, M. Q. (2002). *Qualitative Research and Evaluation Methods.* London: Sage.

Pease, A. & Pease, B. (2004). *The Definite Book of Body Language.* Buderim, Australia: Pease International. Retrieved May 26, 2013, from http:/www.4shared.com/network/searches.

Pease, A. (2006). *Body Language.* Athens: Esoptron.

Pennycook, A. (1985). Actions Speak Louder than Words: Paralanguage, Communication and Education. *TESOL Quarterly,* 19(2), 259-282.

Perry, M., Berch, D. & Singleton, J. (1995). Constructing Shared Understanding: The Role of Nonverbal Input in Learning Contexts. *Journal of Contemporary Legal Issues,* 213-235.

Pike, K. (1967). *Language in Relation to a Unified Theory of the Structure of Human Behavior.* Hague: Mouton.

Plax, T. G, Kearney, P., McCroskey, J. C. & Richmond, V. P. (1986). Power in the Classroom ▢: Verbal Control Strategies, Nonverbal Immediacy and Affective Learning. *Communication Education,* 35, 43-55.

Powell, R. G. & Harville, B. (1990). The Effects of Teacher Immediacy and Clarity on Instructional Outcomes: An Intercultural Assessment. *Communication Education,* 39(4), 369-379.

Pollitt, L. (2006). Classroom Management. *Tesol Course Articles.* http://www.tesolcourse.com.

Poyatos, F. (2002). *Nonverbal Communication across Disciplines*. Philadelphia: John Benjamins.

Pottinger, P. S. & J. Goldsmith (eds.). (1979). *Defining and Measuring Competence.* San Francisco: Jossey-Bass.

Radford, K. W. (1990). Observing the Class. *Education Canada*, 30, 36-39.

Raider-Roth, M. B. (2005). *Trusting What You Know: The High Stakes of Classroom Relationships.* San Francisco: Jossey Bass.

Richards, J. and Rodgers, T. (1986). *Approaches and Methods in Language Teaching.* Cambridge: Cambridge University Press.

Richardson, J. P. (1979). Nonverbal Communication in the Teaching of Foreign Languages. *Babel, Journal of the Australian Federation of Modern Language Teachers' Association*, 15, 23-32.

Richmond, V. P., Gorham, J. S. & McCroskey, J. C. (1987). The Relationship between Selected Immediacy Behaviors and Cognitive Learning. In M. A. McLaughlin (ed.), *Communication Yearbook* 10. Newbury Park, CA: Sage.

Richmond, V. P. & McCroskey, J. C. (1990). Reliability and Separation of Factors on the Assertiveness/Responsiveness Measure. *Psychological Reports,* 67, 449-450.

Richmond, V. P. (2002). Teacher Nonverbal Immediacy. In Chesebro, J. L. & McCroskey, J. C. (eds.), *Communication for Teachers.* New Jersey: Prentice Hall.

Richmond, V.P. & McCroskey, J.C. (2000). *Nonverbal Behavior in Interpersonal Relations.* New York: Allyn & Bacon.

Richmond, V. P. (1990). Communication in the Classroom: Power and Motivation. *Communication Education*, 39,181-195.

Rogers, A. G. (2006). *The Unsayable: The Hidden Language of Trauma.* New York: Random House.

Rogers, E. M., Hart, W. B. & M., Yoshitaka. (2002). Edward T. Hall and the History of Intercultural Communication: The United States and Japan. *Keio Communication Review,* 24, 3-26. Retrieved January 12, 2014, from http://www.mediacom.keio.ac.jp/publication/pdf2002/review24/2.pdf.

Rosenshine, B. (1970). Enthusiastic Teaching: A Research Review. *School Review,* 78, 499-514.

Rosoff, J. M. (1978). The Effect of Positive Feedback on Teachers Perception of Students. Unpublished Master's Thesis. West Virginia University, Morgantown, WV.

Rosa (2004). What Did You Say? Using NVC to Improve Teacher Effectiveness. Retrieved August 1, 2009, from http://www.responsiveclassroom.org/PDF_files/feature_33.pdf.

Rossman, R. L. (1989). *Tips: Discipline in the Music Classroom.* Reston, VA: MENC.

Rowe, M. (1974). Pausing Phenomena: Influence on the Quality of Instruction. *Journal of Psycholinguistic Research*, 3(3), 203-224.

Ruben, B. D. (1976). Assessing Communication Competency for Intercultural Adaptation. *Group and Organization Studies*, 2, 470-479.

Ruesch, J. & Kees, W. (1956). *Nonverbal Communication: Notes on the Visual Perception of Human Relations*. LA: University of California Press.

Sanders, J. A., Wiseman, R. L. & Matz, S. I. (1991). Uncertainty Reduction in Acquaintance Relationships in Ghana and the United States. In S. Ting-Toomey & F. Korzenny (eds.), *Cross-cultural Perspective on Interpersonal Communication*. Newbury Park, CA: Sage.

Samovar, L.A. & Porter, R.E. 1995: *Communication between Cultures* (2nd, edition). Belmont, CA: Wadsworth Publishing Company.

Samovar, L. A., Porter, R. E. & Jain, N. C. (1981). *Understanding Intercultural Communication*. CA: Wadsworth Publishing Company.

Samovar, L.A., Porter, R. and McDaniel, E. (1999). *Intercultural Communication: A Reader*. CA: Wadsworth Publishing Company.

Samovar, L. A, Porter, R. E. & Stefani, L. A. (2006). *Communication between Cultures*. Beijing: Foreign Language Teaching and Research Press.

Sanders, J. A. & Wiseman, R. L. (1990). The Effects of Verbal and Nonverbal Teacher Immediacy on Perceived Cognitive, Affective, and Behavioral Learning in the Multicultural Classroom. *Communication Education*, 39(4), 341-353.

Savignon, S. J. (1983). *Communicative Competence: Theory and Classroom Practice, Reading*. MA: Addison-Wesley Publishing Company.

Saville-Troike, M. (1985). The Place of Silence in an Integrated Theory of Communication. In D. Tannen & M. Saville-Troike (eds.), *Perspectives on Silence*. Norwood, NJ: Ablex.

Saville-Troike, M. (1994). Silence. In Asher, R. E., Simpson, J.M.Y. (eds.), *The Encyclopedia of Language and Linguistics*. Oxford: Pergamon Press.

Schachter, J. (1981).The Hand Signal System. *TESOL Quarterly*, 15, 125-38.

Schratz, M. & Mehan, H. (1993). Gulliver Travels into a Math Class. In Search of Alternative Discourse in Teaching and Learning. *International Journal of Educational Research*, 19, 247-247.

Schultz, K. (2009). *Rethinking Classroom Participation: Listening to Silent Voices*. New York: Teachers College Press.

Schultz, K. (2003). *Listening: A Framework for Teaching across Difference.* New York: Teachers College Press.

Schultz, K. (2008). Interrogating Students' Silences. In Mica Pollock (ed.), *Everyday Antiracism: Concrete Ways to Successfully Navigate the Relevance of Race in School*. New York: The New Press.

Schegloff, E. A. (1984). On Some Gestures' Relation to Talk. In J. M. Atkinson & J. Heritage (eds.), *Structures of Social Action: Studies in Conversation Analysis*. Cambridge: Cambridge University Press.

Sime, D. (2006). What Do Learners Make of Teacher's Gestures in the Language Classroom? *International Review of Applied Linguistics in Language*, 44(2), 211-230.

Sime, D. (2008). "Because of Her Gesture, It's Very Easy to Understand" —Learners' Perceptions of Teachers' Gestures in the Foreign Language Class. In McCafferty, S. & Stam, G. (eds.), *Gesture: Second Language Acquisition and Classroom Research*. New York/London: Routledge.

Snyder, D. (1998). Classroom Management for Student Teachers. *Music Educators Journals*, 84, 37-40.

Spitzberg, B.H. & Cupach, W.R. (1984). *Interpersonal Communication Competence*. London: Sage.

Spitzberg, B. H. (2000). A Model of Intercultural Communication Competence. *Intercultural Communication: A Reader*, 9, 375-387.

Spitzberg, B. H. (1989). Issues in the Development of a Theory of Interpersonal Competence in the Intercultural Context. *International Journal of Intercultural Relations*, 13(3), 241-268.

Stam, G. (2006). Thinking for Speaking about Motion: L1 and L2 Speech and Gesture. *International Review of Applied Linguistics in Language Teaching*, 44(2), 145-171.

Stanton, N. (2009). *Mastering Communication* (5th, ed.). UK: Palgrave Macmillan.

Stevick, E.W. (1982). *Teaching and Learning Languages*. Cambridge: Cambridge University Press.

Stevick, E.W. (1996). *Memory, Meaning and Method: A View of Language Teaching* (2nd, ed.). Rowley: Newbury.

Stamatis, P. J. (2012). The Introduction of Non-verbal Communication in Greek Education: A Literature Review. *Electronic Journal of Research in Educational Psychology*, 10(3), 1463-1476.

Stevanoni, E. & Salmom, K. (2005). Giving Memory a Hand: Instructing Children to Gesture Enhances Their Event Recall. *Journal of Nonverbal Behavior*, 29, 217-233.

Stewart, E. (1972). *American Cultural Patterns*. Boston: Nicholas Brealey Publishing.

Sueyoshi, A. & Hardison, M. (2005). The Role of Gestures and Facial Cues in Second Language Listening Comprehension. *Language Learning,* 55(4),661-699.

Suinn, R. M. (2006). Teaching Culturally Diverse Students. In W. J. McKeachie, M. D. Svinicki & B. K. Hofer (eds.), *McKeachie's Teaching Tips: Strategies, Research, and Theory for College and University Teachers* (12th, ed.). Boston: Houghton Mifflin.

Tannen, D. (1985). Silence: Anything but. In D. Tannen & M. Saville-Troike(eds.), *Perspectives on Silence* . Norwood, NJ: Ablex.

Tannen, D. (1994). *Talking from Nine to Five: Women and Men in the Workplace: Language, Sex and Power.* New York: William Morrow and Company.

Tarone, E. (1981). Some Thoughts on the Notion of Communication Strategy. *TESOL Quarterly,* (15), 285-295.

Terrell, T. D. (1986). Acquisition in the Natural Approach: The Binding/Access Framework. *Modern Language Journal,* 70, 213-27.

Thomas, L. & Tchudi, S. (1999). *The English Language: An Owner's Manual*. Boston: Allyn and Bacon.

Thompson, J. J. (1973). *Beyond Words: Nonverbal Communication in the Classroom*. New York: Citation Press.

Thourlby, W. (1978). *You Are What You Wear: The Key to Business Success*. New York: New American Library.

Ting-Toomey, S. (1994). Managing Conflict in Intimate Intercultural Relationships. In D. Cahn (ed.), *Intimate Conflict in Personal Relationships*. Hillsdale, NJ: Lawrence Erlbaum.

Titsworth, B.S. (2001). The Effects of Teacher Immediacy, Use of Organizational Lecture Cues, and Students' Note Taking on Cognitive Learning. *Communication Education,* 50, 283-97.

Trager, G. L. (1958). Paralanguage: A first Approximation. *Studies in Linguistics* (13),1-12. Reprinted in D. Hymes (ed.), *Language in Culture and Society*. New York: Harper & Row.

Trenholm, S. & Jensen, A. (2008). *Interpersonal Communication* (6th, ed.). New York: Oxford University Press.

Tsui, A. B. M. (1996). Reticence and Anxiety in Second Language Learning. In K. Bailey & D. Nunan (eds.), *Voices from the Language Classroom*. Cambridge: Cambridge University Press.

Turk, C. (2003). *Effective Speaking: Communicating in Speech*. London, England: Spon

Press.

Tuckman, B. W. & Oliver, W. F. (1968). Effectiveness of Feedback to Teacher as a Function of Source. *Journal of Educational Psychology*, 59, 297-301.

Turner, J. & Hiraga, M. (2003). Misunderstanding Teaching and Learning. In J. House, G. Kasper & S. Ross (eds.), *Misunderstanding in Social Life: Discourse Approaches to Problematic Talk*. London: Pearson Education.

Tylor, E. B. (1967). *The Origin of Culture*. New York: Harper and Row.

Wainwright, R. G. (2003). *Teach Yourself, Body Language*. London: Hodder Headline.

Wardaugh, R. (1985). *How Conversation Works*. Oxford: Blackwell.

Ward, L. & von Raffler-Engel, W. (1980). The Impact of Nonverbal Behavior on FL Teaching. In Walburga von Raffler-Engel (ed.), *Aspects of Non-verbal Behavior*. Lisse: Swets and Zeitlinger.

Ware, J. & Williams, R. (1975). The Dr. Fox Effect: A Study of Lecturer Effectiveness and Ratings of Instruction. *Journal of Medical Education*, 50,149-156.

Ware, J. & Williams, R. (1977). An Extended Visit with Dr. Fox: Validity of Student Satisfaction with Instruction Rating after Repeated Exposures to a Lecture. *American Educational Research Journal*, 14, 449-457.

Wasley, P. (2007). Indiana's Tri-State University Drops Draconian Dress Code and Mohawks Are Back. *Chronicle of Higher Education*, 54(9), 431-441.

Weaver, R. & Qi, J. (2005). Classroom Organization and Participation: College Students' Perceptions. *Journal of Higher Education*, 76(5), 570-601.

Weare, K. (2004). *Developing the Emotionally Literate School*. London: Paul Chapman Publishing.

Webb, J. M., Diana, E. M., Luft, P., Brooks, E. W. & Brennan, E. L. (1997). Influence of Pedagogical Expertise and Feedback on Assessing Student Comprehension from Nonverbal Behavior. *Journal of Educational Research*, 91(2), 89-97.

Wellman, H.M., Phillips, A.T. & Rodriguez, T. (2000). Young Children Understanding of Perception, Desire and Emotion. *Child Development*, 71(4), 153-168.

Wheeless, V. E. & Reichel, L. S. (1990). A Reinforcement Model of the Relationships of Supervisors' General Communication Styles and Conflict Management Styles to Task Attraction. *Communication Quarterly*, 38, 373-387.

White, J. & Gardner, J. (2012). *The Classroom X-Factor: The Power of Body Language and Nonverbal Communication in Teaching*. London/New York: Routledge.

Winitz, H. (1981). The Comprehension Approach: An Introduction. In Harris Winitz (ed.), *The Comprehension Approach to FL Acquisition*. Rowley: Newbury.

Wiemann, M. O. & Wiemann, J. M. (1975). *Nonverbal Communication in the*

Elementary Classroom. Washington, D.C.: National Inst. of Education (DHEW). Retrieved May 20, 2015 from http://files.eric.ed.gov/fulltext/ED113771.pdf.

Wiemann, J. M. (1977). Explication and Test of a Model of Communicative Competence. *Human Communication Research,* 3, 195-213.

Wiseman, R. L. & Koester, J. (eds). (1993). *Intercultural Communication Competence.* Newbury Park, CA: Sage.

Wiseman, R. L. (2003). Intercultural Communication Competence. In B. W. Gudykunst (ed.), *Cross-cultural and Intercultural Communication.* Thousand Oaks: Sage.

Wiseman, R. L. (2001). Intercultural Communication Competence. Retrieved December 11, 2001, from http://commfaculty.cullerton.edu/rwiseman/ICCCpaper.htm.

Woolfolk, A. E. & Brooks, D. M. (1985). The Influence of Teachers' Nonverbal Behaviors on Students' Perceptions and Performance. *The Elementary School Journal,* (4), 513-528.

Wood, B. S. (1976). *Children and Communication: Verbal and Nonverbal Language Development.* New Jersey: Prentice Hall.

Wylie, L. (1985). Language Learning and Communication. *French Review,* 58, 777-785.

Yoshioka, K. & Kellerman, E. (2006). Gestural Introduction of Ground Reference in L2 Narrative Discourse. *International Review of Applied Linguistics in Language Teaching,* 44(2), 173-195.

Zeki, P. C. (2009). The Importance of Nonverbal Communication in Classroom Management. *Procedia Social and Behavioral Sciences,* 1, 1443-1449.

Zhou, Y. R., Knoke, D. & Sakamoto, I. (2005). Rethinking Silence in the Classroom: Chinese Students' Experiences of Sharing Indigenous Knowledge. *International Journal of Inclusive Education,* 9, 287-311.

Zitzen, M. & Stein, D. (2004). Chat and Conversation: A Case of Transmedial Stability? *Linguistics,* 42(5), 983-1022.

Zoric, G, Smid, K. & Pandzic, I. S. (2007). Facial Gestures: Taxonomy and Application of Nonverbal, Nonemotional Facial Displays for Embodied Conversational Agents. In Toyoaki Nishida (ed.), *Conversational Informatics—An Engineering Approach.* Retrieved July 12, 2014, from http://www.ieee.hr/images/50009014/ch907.pdf.

Zweifel, T. D. (2003). *Culture Clash: Managing the Global High-Performance Team.* New York, NY: Swiss Consulting Group, Inc.

Zwozdiak-Myers, P. & Capel, S. (2005).Communicating with Pupils Nonverbally. In Capel, S. Leaskand, M. & Turner, T. (eds.), *Learning to Teach in the Secondary School: A Companion to School Experience.* London: Routledge.

References

毕继万. (1999). 跨文化非语言交际. 北京：外语教学与研究出版社.

毕继万（译）. (1991). Brosnahan, L.（著）(*Chinese and English Gestures: Contrastive Communication*). 中国和英语国家非语言交际对比. 北京：北京语言学院出版社.

毕继万. (1998). 跨文化交际与第二语言教学. 北京：北京语言大学出版社.

毕继万. (1993). 跨文化非语言交际研究及其与外语教学之间关系. 汉语学习，(3), 7-43.

邓炎昌、刘润清. (1989). 语言与文化. 北京：外语教学与研究出版社.

窦卫霖. (2011). 跨文化商务交际. 北京：北京对外经贸大学出版社.

杜瑞清、田德新、李本观. (2004). 跨文化交际学宣读. 西安：西安交通大学出版社.

胡文仲. (1994). 文化与交际. 北京：外语教学与研究出版社.

胡文仲. (1988). 跨文化交际与应用学习. 上海：上海译文出版社.

胡文仲. (2002). 超跨越文化的屏障. 北京：外语教学与研究出版社.

耿二岭. (1988). 体态语概说. 北京：北京语言学院出版社.

何道宽. (1988). 非语言交际. 上海：上海译文出版社.

李杰群. (2002). 非语言交际概论. 北京：北京大学出版社.

刘乃美. (2005). 交际策略研究对我国外语教学的启示. 外语界，(3), 55-60.

刘乃美. (2007). 交际策略研究三十年回顾与展望. 中国外语，(5), 81-87.

刘乃美. (2013). EFL 学习者交际策略的研究与培训. 上海：上海译文出版社.

孟小平（译）. (1988). Fast, J.（著）(*Body Language*). 体态与交际. 北京：外语教学与研究出版社.

孟小平等（译）. (1991). Malandro, L., Barker, L. L. & Barker, D. A.（著）(*Nonverbal Communication*). 非语言交际. 北京：北京语言学院出版社.

汪福祥、吴汉樱. (1994). 文化与语言（论文集）. 北京：外语教学与研究出版社.

文秋芳. (1999). 英语口语测试和教学. 上海：上海外语教学与研究出版社.

王建. (2007). 体态语——蕴含丰富而变化万千的非语言交际. 西安外国语大学学报，(3), 31-33.

杨平. (1994). 非语言交际述评. 外语教学与研究，(3), 1-6.

许名央. (2015). 非言语性反馈：话轮转换中的"非语言交际". 外语学刊，(2), 61-64.

图书在版编目(CIP)数据

跨文化交际课堂中无声语言的研究/刘乃美著. —厦门:厦门大学出版社,2015.11
ISBN 978-7-5615-5739-6

Ⅰ.①跨… Ⅱ.①刘… Ⅲ.①英语-课堂教学-教学研究-高等学校 Ⅳ.①H319.3

中国版本图书馆 CIP 数据核字(2015)第 221951 号

官方合作网络销售商:

厦门大学出版社出版发行

(地址:厦门市软件园二期望海路 39 号 邮编:361008)
总编办电话:0592-2182177 传真:0592-2181406
营销中心电话:0592-2184458 传真:0592-2181365
网址:http://www.xmupress.com
邮箱:xmup @ xmupress.com

厦门市万美兴印刷设计有限公司印刷

2015 年 11 月第 1 版 2015 年 11 月第 1 次印刷
开本:720×1000 1/16 印张:16.5 插页:2
字数:350 千字
定价:48.00 元
本书如有印装质量问题请直接寄承印厂调换